The organization and structure of autobiographical memory

The organization
and structure of
autobiographical memory

Edited by

JOHN H. MACE

Eastern Illinois University

OXFORD

UNIVERSITY PRESS

UNIVERSITY PRESS

Great Clarendon Street, Oxford, OX2 6DP,
United Kingdom

Oxford University Press is a department of the University of Oxford.
It furthers the University's objective of excellence in research, scholarship,
and education by publishing worldwide. Oxford is a registered trade mark of
Oxford University Press in the UK and in certain other countries

First Edition Published in 2019

Impression: 1

Published in the United States of America by Oxford University Press
198 Madison Avenue, New York, NY 10016, United States of America

British Library Cataloguing in Publication Data

Data available

Library of Congress Control Number: 2019946638

ISBN 978–0–19–878484–5

Printed and bound by
CPI Group (UK) Ltd, Croydon, CR0 4YY

Contents

Contributors

Nicole Alea
University of the West Indies at St Augustine,
Trinidad & Tobago

Dorthe Berntsen
Center on Autobiographical Memory
Research, Department of Psychology and
Behavioural Sciences Aarhus University,
Denmark

Susan Bluck
Department of Psychology, University of
Florida, USA

Amanda M. Clevinger
Department of Psychology, Eastern Illinois
University, USA

Martin A. Conway
Department of Psychology, City, University of
London, UK

Arnaud D'Argembeau
University of Liège, Belgium

Alexandra Ernst
Laboratory of Psychology and
NeuroCognition, University of
Grenoble-Alpes, France

Robyn Fivush
Department of Psychology, Emory
University, USA

Heather Iriye
Department of Neuroscience,
Karolinska Institute, Sweden

Lucy V. Justice
Department of Psychology, Nottingham Trent
University, UK

Jonathan Koppel
Department of Psychology, University of
Portsmouth, UK

John H. Mace
Department of Psychology, Eastern Illinois
University, USA

Emily L. Mroz
Department of Psychology, University of
Florida, USA

Clare J. Rathbone
Department of Psychology, Social Work and
Public Health, Oxford Brookes University, UK

David C. Rubin
Department of Psychology & Neuroscience,
Duke University, USA

Peggy L. St. Jacques
Department of Psychology, University of
Alberta, Canada

Qi Wang
Department of Human Development, Cornell
University, USA

Theodore E. A. Waters
New York University, Abu Dhabi, United
Arab Emirates

1

Introduction and Overview

John H. Mace

Introduction

Since Rubin's (1986) pioneering and seminal work, *Autobiographical memory*, there have been quite a number of volumes devoted to autobiographical memory, ranging in coverage from the somewhat narrowly focused (e.g., false memories: Conway, 1997; involuntary autobiographical memory: Berntsen, 2009; Mace, 2007; autobiographical remembering, or retrieval: Mace, 2010) to the broadly focused (e.g., Berntsen & Rubin, 2012; Rubin, 1996). The theme of the current volume, the organization and structure of autobiographical memory, is not only a topic of broad focus, but a fundamental question that it is pivotal to understanding the nature of autobiographical memory. Whereas it certainly can be said that such a question is important for any area of memory, it is, perhaps, particularly true for autobiographical memory, given the relative complexity of this topic. For example, questions concerning future thought, development, or function are either irrelevant in other areas (e.g., implicit memory), or they are relatively less dicey problems to solve (e.g., the question of function in semantic memory versus function in autobiographical memory).

In this introductory chapter, I sketch out some of the broad themes laid out in the individual chapters of this text. I present a very brief overview of the chapters, without any real commentary, or at least that is my impression. Readers who are intimately familiar with the topic, or those who normally like to skip overview chapters, can abandon ship now and go straight to the chapters. The chapters are written in a self-contained fashion, so one could easily move around the book without losing a particular thread or line of thought.

Summary of chapters

What is autobiographical memory? The simplest conception of autobiographical memory is to view it as synonymous with episodic memory (Tulving, 1972). For example, Squire (2004) views autobiographical memory as the event memory branch of the declarative memory system. There is considerable merit to such a view, but it runs into trouble when one considers that autobiographical memories are not just episodic memories, they are also abstract (and quasi abstract) knowledge structures pertaining to the past (e.g., that one used to live in New York City, the name of the street that one grew up on) or the self (e.g., that one is a generous person, likes classical music). To account for this complexity, Baddeley (2012) views autobiographical memory as relying on both the episodic and the semantic memory systems, where memories for specific past experiences are mediated by the episodic system, and the more abstract knowledge about the past or one's self are mediated by a personal branch of the semantic system. More complex (and holistic) views on the structure of autobiographical memory can be found in Conway's (1996, 2005) self-memory system (SMS) and Rubin's (2005, 2006, 2012) basic systems model. In the early chapters of this volume, each of these views is reviewed, updated, and extended.

In chapter 2, Rubin extends the basic systems model by adding a further dimensional account, beginning initially with three continuous dimensions (explicit, event, and self-reference). These added components extend the explanatory power of Rubin's initial view, giving it enormous explanatory power and potential both within and outside of autobiographical memory. In chapter 3, Conway, Justice, and D'Argembeau reprise, review, and extend the enormously popular SMS view. The model is updated with the incorporation of autobiographical future thought into the framework of the SMS. Given the central role of the self in the SMS approach, the model is well-suited to account for the burgeoning area of autobiographical future cognition, and, with this new addition, the SMS model increases its explanatory power and range.

The development of autobiographical memory is also a complex and rich question, perhaps more so than any other area of memory. Here, one must go beyond mere neural and cognitive development, as one considers how autobiographical memory develops within a sociocultural context (Nelson & Fivush, 2004). Whereas autobiographical memories have clear adaptive functions, they also play important roles in the social milieu and in the development and maintenance of the self (Fivush, 2013), and it is here that the familial and social structures of the individual have pivotal roles. At a broader level of developmental considerations, culture also appears to play an important role in how autobiographical memory takes shape (Wang, 2013). Whereas cognitive psychology, in general, has not placed much emphasis on culture in the development of cognitive processes, autobiographical memory is (and should be) one exception.

In chapter 4, Fivush and Waters present a sociocultural account of autobiographical memory development across the lifespan. They argue that through the processes of language and sharing, coherent and detailed narratives form around personal experiences such that they are embedded in larger life narratives that encompass the lifespan. A key function of this organization is to define the self and its relations with other selves. In chapter 5, Wang considers the larger impact of culture on the development of autobiographical memory. Wang presents her cultural dynamic theory, which argues that autobiographical memory is an "open system" that emerges, shapes (and re-shapes) under the influence of a multitude of cultural factors. The theory contains three major pillars: autobiographical memory is a dynamic process situated within active individuals and their changing environment; autobiographical memory is continuously changing in time and space as a result of cultural conditioning; and autobiographical memory develops as individuals acquire cultural knowledge about the self and the purpose of the past.

The functional approach in the study of autobiographical memory has had considerable success (Baddeley, 1988; Bluck, 2003, 2009). In chapter 6, Bluck, Alea, and Mroz review the functional perspective in the study of autobiographical memory. They take the position that *form follows function*, and that one needs to keep this notion in central focus when considering how autobiographical memory is organized. In advocating their view, they remind us of the pitfalls of relying on approaches to the study of autobiographical memory organization, and of remembering, that rely solely on mechanistic and reductionistic approaches. The authors review the three classic functions (directive, social, and self, Baddeley), and ask whether additional, as yet unnamed, functions are needed to properly frame the question of organization.

Chapters 7 and 8 focus on the key role of the self in autobiographical memory. In chapter 7, Iriye and St. Jacques review and use data from various brain imaging approaches (principally, functional magnetic resonance imaging) to argue for a central place for the self in the organization of autobiographical memory. The authors trace the neural basis of the self in autobiographical memory, focusing on egocentric perspective in memory, and on autonoetic consciousness (Tulving, 1985), among other important topics. In chapter 8, Ernst and Rathbone also examine the role of the self in the organization of autobiographical memory. They examine how the self organizes how one's thinking about the past and projects oneself into the future. In addition to focusing on the role of the self in remembering the past and imagining future events, they also examine self and memory processes in various clinical populations.

The reminiscence bump (i.e., the tendency for older adults to favor the retrieval of memories from roughly 15–25 years of age: Rubin et al., 1986), although not exclusively about episodic memories, has its roots in the observation of episodic memories. In chapter 9, Koppel and Berntsen review and examine the reminiscence bump. They review the phenomenon in autobiographical memories, as well as memories for public events, arguing for a retrieval account of the phenomenon in place of the more traditional encoding accounts.

Autobiographical memory is a complex topic in various ways: with respect to the different memories that comprise (or do not comprise) autobiographical memory, nomenclature, its juxtaposition to episodic memory, just to name a few issues. Nevertheless, it is fair to say that most autobiographical memory research has focused on those brief snippets of time (seconds to minutes) that most call episodic memories, or the mental re-experience of brief, past conscious states. Whether the topic is involuntary autobiographical memories (Berntsen, 2009; Mace, 2007), reminiscence phenomena (e.g., Rubin et al., 1986), or autobiographical memory priming (Ball & Hennessey, 2009; Mace, 2005; Ball & Hennessey, 2009; Mace, 2005; Mace & Clevinger, 2013), episodic memories are generally the central focus.

Finally, in chapter 10, Mace and Clevinger focus on episodic memories. They examine the associative nature of episodic memories, arguing that whereas some associative forms can be found among episodic memories (i.e., temporal and conceptual forms), the conceptual form dominates, and it represents the overarching, default structure that episodic memories naturally or ultimately coalesce into. Like Tulving (1972, 2002), they argue that episodic memory has features in common with semantic memory.

Concluding comments

Whether the topic is the organization of autobiographical memory or an autobiographical memory phenomenon, the chapters in this book make it clear that the study of autobiographical memory has come a long way after more than three decades of intensive study. They also keenly show how complex a phenomenon autobiographical memory is. Whether we have made a complex problem even more complex with our theories, or whether these theories have accurately captured the complex nature of this phenomenon, may be up to a future generation of memory researchers to decide. One can only hope that the current collection of essays will help bring us a few steps closer to a firm answer.

References

Baddeley, A. (1988). But what the hell is it for? In M. M. Gruneberg, P. E. Morris, & R. N. Skyes (eds.), *Practical aspect of memory: Current research and issues* (pp. 3–18). Chichester, UK: Wiley.

Baddeley, A. (2012). Reflections on autobiographical memory. In D. Berntsen & D. C. Rubin (eds.), *Understanding autobiographical memory: Theories and approaches* (pp. 70–87). Cambridge: Cambridge University Press.

Ball, C. T. & Hennessey, J. (2009). Subliminal priming of autobiographical memories. *Memory, 17*, 311–322.

Berntsen, D. (2009). *Involuntary autobiographical memories. An introduction to the unbidden past.* Cambridge: Cambridge University Press.

Berntsen, D. & Rubin, D. C. (eds.) (2012). *Understanding autobiographical memory: Theories and approaches.* Cambridge: Cambridge University Press.

Bluck, S. (2003). Autobiographical memory: Exploring its functions in everyday life. *Memory, 11*, 113–123.

Bluck, S. (2009). Baddeley revisited: The functional approach to autobiographical memory. *Applied Cognitive Psychology, 23*, 1050–1058.

Conway, M. A. (1996). Autobiographical knowledge and autobiographical memories. In: D. C. Rubin (ed.), *Remembering our past: Studies in autobiographical memory* (pp. 67–93). New York: Cambridge University Press.

Conway, M. A. (2005). Memory and the self. *Journal of Memory and Language, 53*, 594–628.

Fivush, R. (2013). Maternal reminiscing style: The sociocultural construction of autobiographical memory across childhood and adolescence. In P. J. Bauer & R. Fivush (eds.), *Handbook of the development of children's memory.* NY: Wiley–Blackwell.

Mace, J. H. (2005). Priming involuntary autobiographical memories. *Memory, 13*, 874–884.

Mace, J. H. (ed.) (2007). *Involuntary memory.* Malden, MA: Blackwell.

Mace, J. H. (ed.) (2010). *The act of remembering: Toward an understanding of how we recall the past.* Malden, MA: Wiley–Blackwell.

Mace, J. H. & Clevinger, A. M. (2013). Priming voluntary autobiographical memories: Implications for the organization of autobiographical memory and voluntary recall processes. *Memory, 21,* 524–536.

Nelson, K. & Fivush, R. (2004). The emergence of autobiographical memory: A social cultural developmental model. *Psychological Review, 111,* 486–511

Rubin, D. C. (ed.) (1986). *Autobiographical memory.* New York: Cambridge University Press.

Rubin, D. C. (ed.) (1996). *Remembering our past: Studies in autobiographical memory.* New York: Cambridge University Press.

Rubin, D. C. (2005). A basic-systems approach to autobiographical memory. *Current Directions in Psychological Science, 14,* 79–83.

Rubin, D. C. (2006). The basic-systems model of episodic memory. *Perspectives on Psychological Science, 1,* 277–311.

Rubin, D. C. (2012). The basic system model of autobiographical memory. In D. Berntsen & D. C. Rubin (eds.), *Understanding autobiographical memory: Theories and approaches* (pp. 11–32). Cambridge: Cambridge University Press.

Rubin, D. C., Wetzler, S. E., & Nebes, R. D. (1986). Autobiographical memory across the lifespan. In D. C. Rubin (ed.), Autobiographical memory (pp. 202–221). New York: Cambridge University Press.

Squire, L. R. (2004). Memory systems of the brain: A brief history and current perspective. *Neurobiology of Learning and Memory, 82,* 171–177.

Tulving, E. (1972). Episodic and semantic memory. In E. Tulving & W. Donaldson (eds.), *Organization of memory* (pp. 381–402). New York: Academic Press.

Tulving, E. (1985). Memory and consciousness. *Canadian Psychology, 26,* 1–12.

Tulving, E. (2002). Episodic memory: From mind to brain. *Annual Review of Psychology, 53,* 1–25.

Wang, Q. (2013). *The autobiographical self in time and culture.* New York: Oxford University Press.

2

Placing Autobiographical Memory in a General Memory Organization

David C. Rubin

Introduction

This chapter introduces a new organization that includes the processes needed to define autobiographical memory and indicate its relation to other kinds of memories. By using processes that apply to memory in general, the organization notes what is different about autobiographical memory in an evidence-based systematic fashion. The approach is highly constructive in the tradition of Bartlett (1932) and Neisser (1967, 1976); autobiographical memories are produced at recall, not stored and retrieved. Autobiographical memory is considered to be a form of explicit memory that involves both a constructed scene and self-reference rather than a form of episodic memory (Tulving, 1983). This is because episodic memory is a complex amalgam of behavioral, neural, and theoretical processes that is better understood in terms of its component processes, as discussed in detail in this chapter's section titled "Autobiographical memory as explicit self-reference event memory". Autobiographical memories are created as scenes during recall (Rubin & Umanath, 2015) using the basic processes of cognition (Rubin, 2006). This approach leads to new insights about autobiographical memory and its place in the organization of memory in general.

The added contribution of scene construction

I have argued earlier that autobiographical memories are constructed using basic processes (Rubin, 1988, 1998) including the individual senses, emotion, and language (Rubin, 2005, 2006; Rubin et al., 2003, 2008, 2011). However, recent research from neuropsychological damage cases, neuroimaging, and research with animals has made the role of recalling a scene clearer as summarized by the theory of event memory (Rubin & Umanath, 2015). For autobiographical memory, the theory provides a frame for spatially organizing the contents of a memory and for providing the basis for a sense of reliving, vividness, and belief in the accuracy and occurrence of the memory that is based on its recall.

According to the theory of event memory, mentally constructed remembered scene differs from an abstract idea and from a collection of objects and actions that could populate a scene but that have no clear location relative to each other or to the person remembering them. The remembered scene, like a picture of a scene, need not involve the person recalling it; here this is described by a separate self-reference dimension. The remembered scene, like a picture, is a single event, even if it represents multiple encodings. The remembered scene, like a picture, can occur without any specific phenomenological state. The remembered scene, like a picture, locates the person relative to the scene; it creates a locus in space and time for the person recalling the memory and thus helps support self-reference when it exists (Neisser, 1988).

I changed the basic systems model to one more heavily dependent on the concept of a mentally constructed scene because of evidence from studies of human neuropsychological damage. The loss of scene construction, such as the inability to imagine a prototypical beach on a sunny day, and the loss of autobiographical memory occur together in hippocampal amnesia (Hassabis et al., 2007; Maguire & Mullally, 2013; Tulving, 2002). Moreover, people with damage earlier in the visual ventral stream, which is needed to construct scenes, have a rarer form of amnesia: visual-memory-deficit amnesia (Greenberg et al., 2005; Greenberg & Rubin, 2003; Rubin & Greenberg, 1998). Visual-memory-deficit amnesia provides strong independent support for the role of scene construction because the damage often spares the hippocampi, which, although necessary, are much less specific to scene construction. For either type of damage, the inability to construct a scene and amnesia co-occur. A similar claim about autobiographical memory cannot be made for any other property of memory (Rubin & Umanath, 2015).

Functional magnetic resonance imaging (fMRI) studies of vision and memory support the neuropsychological findings that the visual ventral stream is centrally involved in both scene construction and autobiographical memory (e.g., Baldassano et al., 2016; Cabeza et al., 2004; Daselaar et al., 2008; Kanwisher & Dilks, 2014; see Rubin & Umanath, 2015 for a review). For instance, the parahippocampal place area is activated more by scenes than by objects, and for indoor scenes, its activation remains even if objects are removed, leaving just the walls and floor (Epstein & Kanwisher, 1998). The parahippocampal cortex is active for objects that evoke a strong sense of the surrounding space compared to ones that do not (Mullally & Maguire, 2011, 2013). Thus, the importance of event memory to autobiographical memory and its neural basis has strong converging evidence both from neuropsychological damage cases and from studies that measure activation when intact individuals are performing tasks.

A general memory organization more suitable for autobiographical memory

The chapter first presents theoretical reasons for using a dimensional, rather than a hierarchical, organization for memory in general and autobiographical memory in particular. It then describes the three dimensions used for this organization and the benefits of using them. Next, additional dimensions that were not needed to classify the types of memories, but that are useful to account for phenomena in autobiographical memory, are considered. Earlier research on the basic processes of autobiographical and episodic memory is then integrated into the dimensional model to create a more complete account of autobiographical memory.

Dimensions versus hierarchies

Hierarchies and dimensions are two classic organizational systems in science. Unlike dimensions, in hierarchies the properties specified in one category do not have to extend to other categories. The extension of properties across categories, however, creates and makes predictions about new categories, including categories that may contain no known exemplars. Thus, the hierarchy of the biological taxonomy works to classify life forms, but unlike the dimensional structure of the periodic table of elements in chemistry, it did not predict specific categories for which life forms have not yet been observed. In contrast, the dimensions of the periodic table not only predicted categories for which elements had yet been observed, but because the dimensions had properties, they also predicted what properties those elements would have and under what conditions those elements would be observed. As observation and theory advanced together, more elements were predicted to fill missing categories in the table, and more were found.

Squire's hierarchy (1987) is the most widely used organization for human memory. Figure 2.1 is my synthesis of Squire (1987) with minor additions from Squire (2004). As illustrated in figure 2.2, instead of a hierarchy I propose a set of three dimensions, each based on a process that is conceptually independent of the others and that covers the range of categories in Squire's taxonomy. They are

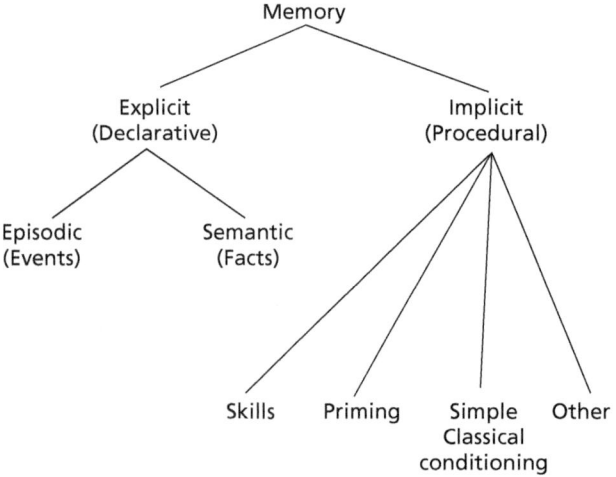

Figure 2.1 A hierarchical organization of categories of memory.
Based on Squire (1987, 2004).

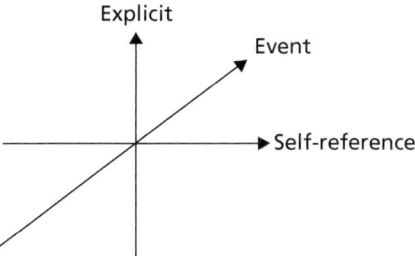

Figure 2.2 A continuous dimensional organization of memory.

self-reference, event memory, and explicit processes. Although the dimensions are continuous, language and the existing literature are based on categories. Thus, using the extremes of the continuous dimensions to denote categories allows contact with the existing research literature. Viewed as dichotomies, the three dimensions combine to form eight categories in a non-hierarchical organization, as illustrated in figure 2.3. This alternative representation generates interesting, novel, and tractable theoretical propositions and points to gaps in the literature that are basic to understanding memory.

All the dimensions are continua, as shown in figure 2.2. Individual memories vary in a continuous fashion on the extent to which they display the property of dimensions at both the behavioral and neural level. For instance, people and objects vary on the dimension of self-reference; some people and objects can be placed in the middle range of a continuum away from those at the extremes. Similarly, although most memories may be considered explicit or implicit, many are not at the extremes and seem to drift across the boundary of being in and out of consciousness (Mandler, 1994; Singer, 1966). Thus, the change to dimensions allows for the possibility of formal, quantitative models based on continuous variables that hierarchies do not have. However, using the extremes of those continua as labels for categories simplifies communication and is necessary to maintain contact with the literature.

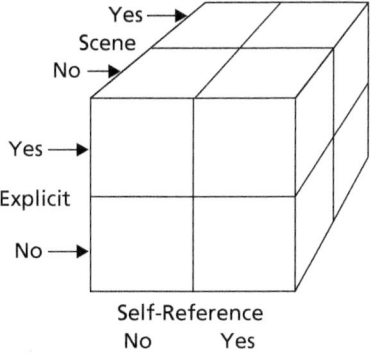

Figure 2.3 A dimensional organization of memory in which each cell is a category.

Selection criteria for the dimensions

The selection of dimensions follows directly from Squire's hierarchy and from what is now known about memory from studies of behavior, neural processes in intact organisms, and neuropsychological damage. Squire's two main divisions are explicit versus implicit memory and episodic versus semantic memory. The three dimensions shown in figures 2.2 and 2.3 are needed to account for episodic memory while replacing it with scientifically more useful concepts that are consistent with current knowledge of memory processes. One could argue that for many laboratory memory experiments, the dimensions of self-reference and event memory were of little use and not examined empirically because recall was tested for non-self-reference words or syllables shown in the same color, font, and location, on the same memory drum or computer screen in the same room. Nonetheless, from its earliest introduction to its most recent review paper, Tulving held that episodic memory was for events that happened to the person recalling them, at one time and location and thus by definition must contain at least a minimal event memory and self-reference (Tulving, 1972, 2002). Moreover, at its core, episodic memory was contrasted to semantic memory, which was free of the particular occasion of learning and had information that was generally true for all individuals; that is, they were event and self-reference free. In accounting for episodic memory, the dimensions also account for the explicit versus implicit division.

The three dimensions

Self-reference

The self-reference dimension, like the other two dimensions that follow, has a deceptively simple definition. Self-reference defines memories that are related to the person recalling them. Self-reference not only provides the processes for one of the three dimensions but is also part of nearly every definition of autobiographical memory, providing the "self" or "auto" prefix of autobiographical memory. Some memories may be higher in self-reference, such as those for events a person considers central to their identity and life story (Berntsen & Rubin, 2006), whereas others, such as memories of objects occasionally used, might be lower in self-reference. The judgment of self-reference can be made by the person recalling the memory or an observer. The concept of self-reference, and related topics dealing with the self, has a large and growing literature that integrates traditional laboratory memory research with clinical, social, and other areas in psychology and neuroscience.

The self has long played a central role in psychology (Leary & Tangney, 2012). To avoid the complexity of the concept of the self, psychology uses hyphenated selves (Allport, 1955). In these hyphenated terms, the *self* usually can be viewed as no more than a locus in space and time, which refers reflexively to the same person, possible at an earlier or future place and time. For instance, for the terms *self-concept* or *self-knowledge*, people have a concept or knowledge of themselves in much the way they might have a concept or knowledge of an apple. The needed details of the *self* are particular to the theory describing *self-concept* or *self-knowledge* (e.g., Campbell et al., 2003; Hoyle, 2006). The same lack of details holds for the *self* of *self-reference* used here, and its inclusion as a dimension is an opportunity to explore its specific meaning within autobiographical memory research.

Neuroimaging studies of self-reference provide reasonably consistent findings. The most common areas to emerge in a variety of tasks in fMRI studies of self-reference are the medial prefrontal cortex and the posterior cingulate cortex (Denny et al., 2012; Kim & Johnson, 2012; Moran et al., 2009; Morel et al., 2014). Consistent with this pattern of activity, damage to the medial prefrontal cortex removes self-reference effects (Philippi et al., 2012; also see, Rubin et al., 2017). Thus, a plausible underlying neural basis for this dimension exists.

Event memory

The second dimension is defined by the theory of event memory (Rubin & Umanath, 2015). Event memory stresses an ecological approach to memory that psychology minimized as it established itself as a science. In simplifying stimuli in order to understand complex problems of perception, memory, and neuroscience, researchers focused on isolated objects, considering the event, or scene, as a form of general context. However, for the intact, mobile organism, scenes are an important level of analysis on their own. Experiencing an event is generally talked about as a dichotomy, but the degree to which a scene is formed is a continuum. For the dimensional model and for autobiographical memory, the scene provides an organization for many of the other properties and contents of the memory.

The terms scene and scene construction are used in a variety of ways in the literature, where it can include measures as diverse as boundary extension, navigation, recall of isolated visual elements, and event segmentation. However, in this chapter, I restrict the terms to the concept described in Rubin and Umanath (2015) and summarized in this paragraph. A scene is, as in colloquial speech, a place where a real or fictitious event occurs. A scene must have contents organized in space relative to the viewer. As an example, consider the contents of a meeting you often attend (e.g., a faculty meeting): what were the main points, what was discussed and by whom (i.e., what you need in order to say you *know* what happened). Next, consider the scene: where were people sitting as seen from the location from which you recall the scene (i.e., your experience of the imagining the meeting without which you would be unlikely to say you *remember* it as an autobiographical memory). As would be the case with drawing a scene, a mentally constructed scene must be remembered from a single location. The act of mental scene construction thereby locates the person recalling it in relation to the rest of the event (Berntsen & Rubin, 2006; Butler et al., 2016; McIsaac & Eich, 2002; Nigro & Neisser, 1983; Rice & Rubin, 2011). In doing this, the act of constructing a scene forces a person to imagine him- or herself in one particular location. The theory of event memory holds that this sense of being located relative to the event during recall is needed to report experiencing an autobiographical memory with a sense of reliving and the vividness of the event, and it provides evidence that the event was witnessed and therefore should be believed (Rubin & Umanath, 2015). We have long known that visual imagery is central to autobiographical memory (Brewer, 1986; Rubin, 2006; Rubin et al., 2003); the crucial novel claim is that this is due to the spatial layout and not just the contents of the autobiographical memory.

Event memory is a general category of constructed scenes that includes autobiographical memories. Event memories can include actual witnessed events but also events about others and imagined events in the past and future. Such events all use similar processes, but vary on their degree of self-reference, effort needed for construction, and other factors (Rubin & Umanath, 2015). In addition, event memories need not be for a single occurrence; event memories can be intended as a summary or prototype (e.g., Posner & Keele, 1970) of a series of repeated events that can be constructed as the same basic scene (e.g., a generic, or future, faculty meeting you might attend).

Although the degree to which a memory has a well-developed scene is a dimension, for autobiographical memory having at least a minimal scene is a necessity. Memories of events need a "stage on which the remembered event is played or the "where" for the "what" to occur in" (Hassabis & Maguire, 2007, p. 304); they must have spatial organization (e.g., Burgess et al., 2001). Without spatial organization, the contents of an autobiographical memory lack their most basic context and therefore will be judged as knowledge (i.e., semantic memory). The scene allows the contents to be organized. "Space provides a critical contextual background for encoding and retrieving episodic memories" (Eichenbaum et al., 1999, p. 223). Judgments of field versus observer in memory (i.e., first versus third person perspective) depend on viewing a scene. Judgments of reliving, which help motivate the distinction between autobiographical memory and knowledge as different ontological categories, depend on having a scene. At the extreme of reliving in flashbulb memories and flashbacks, scenes are a key property (see Rubin & Umanath, 2015 for a review). Moreover, in autobiographical memory, reliving judgments depends on visual areas, especially in the ventral stream (Daselaar et al., 2008).

Explicit processes

The third dimension is explicit versus implicit processes. It is the main dimension of the standard hierarchy shown in figure 2.1. The idea that some knowledge is available to conscious introspection, whereas other knowledge can only be demonstrated in a procedural manner, predated the experimental study of memory. Moreover, from the earliest experimental studies, explicit and implicit processes have been intertwined. Ebbinghaus (1885) choose an implicit measure based on trials saved in relearning lists to measure gains in explicit recall.

In the modern memory literature, this dimension is generally talked about as a dichotomy. However, a continuous dimension is supported by concepts of consciousness in which memories can slowly develop and become fully conscious as a result of a strategic search or can remain below the level of consciousness and drift into conscious recollection in times of boredom, daydreaming, or mind-wandering (Mandler, 1994; Singer, 1966; for a review see Berntsen, 2009). Consistent with this continuity, the judgment of explicit content often can be made on information that was initially recalled implicitly but that later reached the level of consciousness.

For the dimensional model, memories range from explicit to implicit, but for autobiographical memory, most definitions include only explicit memories. This is one reason to focus on the declarative—procedural (Squire, 1987), declarative—nondeclarative (Squire, 2004, p. 173), or available-to-conscious-recollection (Squire, 2004, p. 171) aspects of the explicit versus implicit distinction.

The distinction between explicit and implicit memory, though nearly universally accepted, is, as Squire appreciated, complex. For instance, Squire (1987, pp. 167–169) lists many divisions of memory closely related to the explicit versus implicit memory distinction that have developed in different theoretical frameworks. He also argued that it is hard to imagine a total separation of the neural systems for this distinction, because the later-evolving explicit memory processes depend in part on earlier-evolving implicit memory neural regions. Moreover, individual implicit categories in his hierarchy can sometimes be explicit. For instance, skills are often learned as explicit memories and become implicit with practice, and priming can have an explicit component.

Squire noted specific neural regions that were relevant to the implicit tasks he included. Squire's hierarchy (2004, p. 173) (figure 2.1) includes procedural skills and habits with a neural basis in the striatum; priming and perceptual learning with a neural basis in neocortex; simple classical conditioning of emotional responses with a neural basis in the amygdala; and simple classical conditioning of skeletal responses with a neural basis in the cerebellum. However, in a review of the "porous boundaries" between explicit and implicit memory, Dew and Cabeza (2011) conclude that the constructs used in the literature to distinguish between explicit and implicit memory have not yielded data consistent with the dichotomy. They conclude, "Simple dichotomies between explicit and implicit memory are inadequate given the current state of the memory literature" (Dew & Cabeza, 2011, p. 185). This only adds to the difficulty Squire (1987) noted in uncovering a single neural basis for implicit memory.

For current purposes, this implies that unlike the self-reference and event memory there is no empirical support for a plausible neural basis for an explicit–implicit dimension in the dimensional model. Rather, new constructs will be needed, or more likely, consistent with Dew and Cabeza (2011), a collection of processes that function to different extents in different situations. A well-developed account of the neural basis of consciousness or of short-term or working memory that indicates the areas responsible for a memory being in the conscious now would therefore clarify the implicit–explicit dimension. However, it does not exist.

Squire's placement of "simple classical conditioning" under implicit memory has also been contentious. On one hand, classical conditioning, with the possible addition of operant conditioning, can be viewed as a basic process involved in all memory. Squire (1994) viewed classical conditioning occurring both with and without awareness of the contingencies and provided evidence with control subjects, as well as amnesics to support this view (Clark & Squire, 1998, 1999). However, an opposing view was that "there is no convincing evidence for conditioning in human subjects without awareness of the contingencies" (Boakes, 1989, p. 389; Brewer, 1974). Lovibond and Shanks (2002) reanalyzed data provided by Clark and Squire and agreed with Boake's and Brewer's strong claim. This suggests that memories of conditioning should not routinely be classified as implicit, but as implicit or explicit depending on their recall, similar to skills that are performed implicitly after being learned explicitly.

Three novel categories of memory

If the dimensional model as shown in figure 2.2 has each dimension divided into a dichotomy to provide the eight categories of figure 2.3, five of these eight categories do not fit easily into Squire's hierarchy and have tended to be overlooked as aspects of a general organization of memory. Labeling each of the categories by its coordinates on the three dimensions, they are: the two adjacent self-reference and non-self-reference implicit event memory, the two adjacent event and non-event implicit self-reference memory, and explicit non-self-reference event memory. They are not, by most definitions and theories, part of autobiographical memory, but they are related to autobiographical memory and help set the boundaries that distinguish autobiographical memory from other commonly studied real-world memory topics such as the effect of personality on memory, déjà vu, and memory for real and fictional events that happen to other people.

Self-reference and non-self-reference implicit event memory

Implicit event memory includes effects in perception and action that are affected by their particular event-based context. Examples include recognizing people in, but not out, of their usual physical context (e.g., Mandler's 1980 example of not recognizing the butcher on the bus); knowing and adapting to what is coming next when walking a familiar route; or knowing where to reach for things without looking while attention is on a higher-level task. The dimensional model categorizes these examples as implicit event memory and places them within an organization of memory that allows them to be compared to other phenomena in terms of well-studied dimensions.

Déjà vu also appears to be implicit event memory. Consistent with the dependence of familiarity and reliving on event memory in explicit memory, in déjà vu there is a sense of familiarity and reliving without any explicit memory of a previous

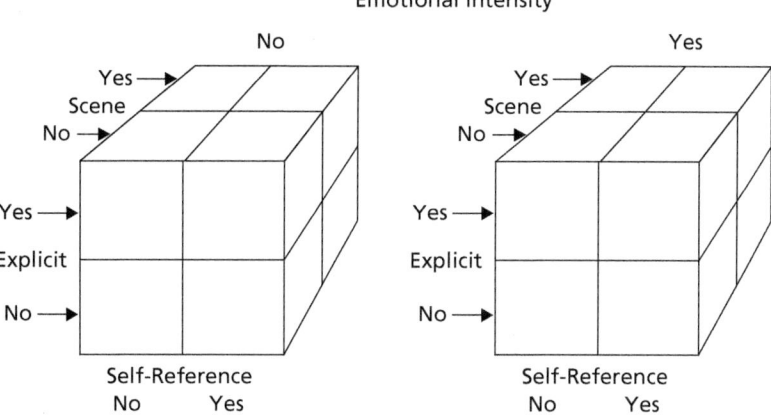

Figure 2.4 Emotional intensity.

experience (Rubin & Umanath, 2015). Brown (2003, 2004) reports several studies, based on self-reports and on analyses of participants' descriptions, in which the most common trigger of a déjà-vu state is the similarity with an earlier scene. In a direct test of the claim that déjà vu depends on a similarity in scenes that is not explicitly noted, Cleary et al. (2009) matched the configural layout, but not the contents, of two scenes. One member of the pair was presented; the other was not. Only pairs involving presented scenes that were not recalled (i.e., were not brought into explicit memory) were examined further. The non-presented scenes of these pairs had an increased probability of déjà vu states when compared to control scenes, and, when these déjà vu states occurred, the familiarity of these non-presented scenes were rated higher.

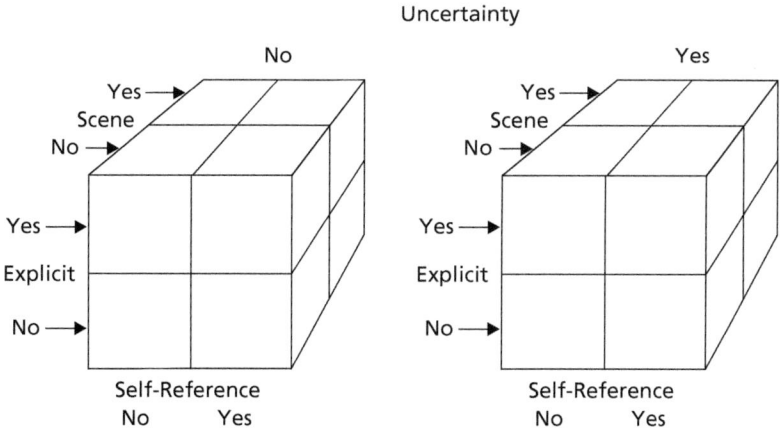

Figure 2.5 Processes for the construction of uncertain events.

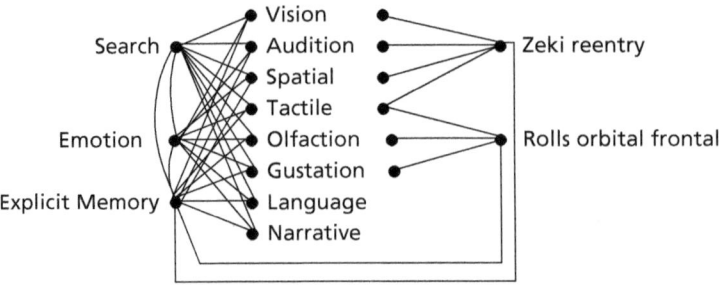

Figure 2.6 Basic systems of cognition involved in memory.
Based on Rubin (2006).

Event and non-event implicit self-reference memory

Implicit and explicit non-self-reference memories and explicit self-reference memories already have major literatures. Implicit self-reference memories do not. Whether all implicit self-reference memories differ from implicit non-self-reference memories in interesting ways is an open question, but at first glance, some implicit self-reference memories look like major components of personality and other habitual ways of acting. Considering them this way would help to integrate the individual differences variables, such as personality, into an organizational scheme for memory, providing a framework to examine their contributions. In terms of clinical phenomena, implicit self-reference memories might be considered as underlying aspects of anxiety disorders when they produce negative emotions. This could occur for complete events including posttraumatic stress disorder (PTSD) symptoms related to traumatic events and worry related to possible future events, and for non-event isolated objects in phobias.

Explicit non-self-reference event memory

The theory of event memory imposes no restrictions on an event having self-reference or not (Rubin & Umanath, 2015). The dimensional organization therefore allows real and fictional events that are not autobiographical to be considered as their own non-self-reference explicit event category, something that is missing from the current episodic versus semantic conception of memory in which episodic memories must have self-reference (Larsen, 1988; Pillemer et al., 2015; Rubin, 1995). Larsen writes that Tulving's definition of episodic memory left such non-self-reference memories, including memories for events that were reported to the person recalling them, "in no-man's land, outside the taxonomy that came to guide memory research" (Larsen, 1988, p. 331). Moreover, people often have a sense of reliving for characters in an event with whom they identify or empathize. People can even remember another person's autobiographical memory as their own (Sheen et al., 2001). Much of social communication, literature, and cinema depends upon such abilities to assimilate explicit non-self-reference event memories.

Autobiographical memory as explicit self-reference event memory

Autobiographical memories are explicit self-reference event memories. Thus, they have a category of their own. Their relationships to each of the other seven categories of figure 2.3 are thus defined in terms of differing on one, two, or three dimensions, each defined by a process. If we want to add other dimensions to the model, we could divide this category further, a possibility that is considered 'in the section titled 'Additional dimensions for understanding autobiographical memory'. If we want to add other restrictions to the definition of autobiographical memory then they would be only part of the category, which is what happens to episodic memory.

In Tulving's episodic versus semantic memory distinction, episodic memories must be recalled explicitly by the person who experienced them. They also must be for an event remembered at a specific place and time; memories about objects free of their spatial and temporal context are semantic memories. Thus, in the dimensional model, episodic memories, like autobiographical memories, are explicit, self-related, event memories; like autobiographical memories, they fit into one category of the cube drawn in figure 2.3 rather than being a major division in a hierarchy as they are in Squire's hierarchy.

Episodic memories have numerous other properties, many of which can be viewed as independent processes (Tulving, 1983, p. 35, Table 3.1). When these are included, episodic memories become a subset of the category shown in figure 2.3. The most important of these properties for current purposes include the following. Episodic memories must come with a sense of reliving in the form of autonoetic consciousness or mental time travel (Rubin et al., 2003; Tulving, 1985). This depends on having a constructed event at recall, but not all event memories have a sense of reliving (Rubin & Umanath, 2015). Episodic memories must be recalled voluntarily (i.e., in retrieval mode; Tulving, 1984, pp. 230–231). Episodic memories must be for a single occurrence (Tulving, 1972, 1983, 2002), not a merging of information from similar occurrences, which is counter to the more process-oriented constructive approach to memory used to formulate dimensions (Rubin, 1988, 1995, 1998, 2006, 2014; Rubin & Umanath, 2015).

The combination of these and the other additional properties into a single theoretical entity has long been questioned by leading memory theorists (Anderson & Ross, 1980; McKoon & Ratcliff, 1979; McKoon et al., 1986; and in most commentaries in Tulving, 1984; for a review see Rubin & Umanath, 2015). Even though many current researchers would not subscribe to all these properties, they still govern most studies of episodic memory (e.g., items presented once for explicit voluntary recall that are judged as remembered instead of known). They also remain part of the dominant theory of memory, and reviewers still ask for clarification on whether a task is purely episodic or semantic or contains elements of both. The use of underlying processes instead of a single combined concept of episodic memory should help clarify both its behavioral and its neural basis.

The role of dimensions in organizing the effects of neuropsychological damage

Explicit self-reference event memories are autobiographical memories that, by definition, are lost in amnesia. Explicit non-self-reference event memories show a deficit in patients who cannot imagine a generic event and thus have a deficit in event memory (e.g., Hassabis et al., 2007). The two remaining explicit non-event categories that differ on self-reference are classified as semantic memory loss in the existing literature. These categories show loss with some neural damage, including that caused by Korsakov's syndrome (Butters & Cermak, 1986) and some cases of herpes simplex encephalitis (Wilson & Wearing, 1995). Moreover, consistent with the neural basis of event memory, the damage involved in these cases extends beyond the medial temporal and ventral stream areas involved in event memory. In addition, amnesics who lose event memory often still retain self-reference. For instance, Clive Wearing retained a sense of things and people related to him even though the memories indicating this were often confabulations (Wilson & Wearing, 1995). Thus, the dimensional approach helps to organize neuropsychological cases of memory loss in terms of dimensions developed to account for memory in general. Combined with added processes, including those for the individual senses, language, and narrative (Greenberg & Rubin, 2003), it could provide a more systematic view of neuropsychological damage than the existing hierarchy does.

Additional dimensions for understanding autobiographical memory

The three dimensions discussed cover the range of categories represented in Squire's hierarchy. However, for topics commonly studied in autobiographical memory research, additional dimensions are useful. The two dimensions I offer are not intended to be complete, but rather to show that the dimensional model could be extended as needed for other purposes. One reason to choose these dimensions is that they are a change from the basic systems model that will be considered in the next section.

Emotional intensity

A fourth dimension, not shown in figures 2.2 and 2.3, is emotional intensity (Talarico et al., 2004). Valence is not as easy to include as a dimension because the effects of valence are not as robust as those of emotional intensity, and because positive versus negative valence are not extremes of a single dimension (Bradley et al., 1992; Rubin & Talarico, 2009; Talarico et al., 2004). Rather emotional intensity would need to be divided into two dimensions, one for positive and one for negative emotions. This is a reasonable alternative, but one I do not pursue here.

Adding emotional content would double the number of categories to 16, as shown in figure 2.4. We have discussed eight of these already by assuming that they were not emotionally intense. In terms of categories, this leaves emotionally intense memories that may be self-reference or not, explicit or implicit, and event memories or not.

Explicit emotionally intense memories are commonly studied. Implicit emotionally intense memories that change one's emotional reaction without the memory itself reaching consciousness might be considered as underlying aspects of anxiety disorders if there is a specific memory at work, but one the person is not aware of. Implicit emotional intensity is a common aspect of memories for events and thus for complete scenes. For instance, a person might feel strong emotions without recalling any event that is responsible for the emotions in a particular place or experience symptoms of PTSD in a situation that has some general relation to an earlier trauma. Implicit emotional intensity can also occur for isolated objects that are not part of scenes, as in phobias.

Uncertainty

People believe they know what occurred in some memories; for other memories, including memories for imaginary events and events in the future, they are more uncertain. The certainty with which events are thought to occur underlies much of mental time travel, so I use it as shown in figure 2.5, as a more general dimension than past versus future (De Brigard & Gessell, 2016). The further an event is into the future or past or the less well-known its future location, the less certain and more schematic it becomes; moreover, the uncertainty increases faster into the future (Berntsen & Bohn, 2010; D'Argembeau & Van der Linden, 2004; Szpunar & McDermott, 2008; Spreng & Levine, 2006; Trope & Liberman, 2010).

Most of the differences in past versus future events that are not accounted for by uncertainty can be accounted for by the proposed emotional intensity dimension. Because alternative events in the future might actually happen, but alternative events in the past cannot occur, future events can be more emotionally intense. If the request is for unspecified or positive future events, positive valence increases (Berntsen & Bohn, 2010; D'Argembeau & Van der Linden, 2006; Finnbogadóttir & Berntsen, 2013; Newby-Clark & Ross, 2003). The effects are even larger for future events that are requested to be negative. For example, participants rated PTSD symptoms for their future negative events that were clearly in the clinical diagnosis range; for past negative events cued by the same topics, they were not (Rubin, 2014).

The standard past versus future literature in cognitive psychology (e.g., Berntsen & Bohn, 2010; Buckner & Carroll, 2007; D'Argembeau, 2012; Hassabis & Maguire, 2007; Schacter & Addis, 2007; Szpunar, 2010) evolved heavily from Tulving's (1985, 2002) theoretical development of mental time travel for explicit memory. Thus, most of the eight categories introduced by considering events without known content crossed with the eight categories shown in figure 2.2 have been explored, especially uncertain explicit self-reference memories. However, some have not. Uncertain implicit self-reference and non-self-reference memories have not been studied and may be involved in the emotions associated with fear and worry that come without an explicit awareness of why they arise. These are studied in fear conditioning and in clinical psychology but are not part of the standard past versus future memory literature and could be better integrated into it.

The basic systems model and its integration with the dimensional model

Similarities and difference of the dimensional and basic systems models

This section describes the overall basic systems model, emphasizing processes not already described. It examines how the dimensional and basic systems models integrate to provide a more comprehensive understanding of autobiographical memory at both a behavioral and neural level of analysis. The integration of these models is mostly an update of the basic system model as both models share the same fundamental neural-based, constructivist view of cognition. In both models, the emphasis is on the processes that produce memories. Moreover, the basic systems and dimensional model share many other assumptions including the emphasis on visual processes in the integration of memories.

Figure 2.6 depicts the basic system model (Rubin, 2005, 2006, 2012, 2015). This model, which considers memory and cognition in terms of basic systems, predates the dimensional model by a decade. It does not include event memory, and it was restricted to explicit episodic memories, including autobiographical memories. A major difference between the models is that the basic systems model started with major cognitive systems that had well-defined behavior and neural properties, such as the various sensory systems and language needed to account for all episodic and autobiographical memory. In contrast, the dimensional model first focused on the three dimensions needed to account for the organization of types of memories included in Squire's hierarchy, and then was extended to other dimensions that might be useful for autobiographical memory using emotional intensity and uncertainty as examples.

In addition, in the dimensional model, all dimensions, including emotional intensity and uncertainty, had to be general enough to be crossed with all the other dimensions already in the model, a requirement that could be met by almost all of the basic systems shown in figure 2.6. There are two exceptions. One is explicit memory, because epi-sodic and autobiographical memory by most definitions are forms of explicit memory and thus did not need a continuum. The other is the search system, which described conscious goal-directed search, but not other forms of memory retrieval. This system needs to be expanded to include the recall of explicit memories that are not the result of a conscious goal-directed search to allow for involuntary autobiographical memories (Berntsen, 2009).

Another difference is that the development and inclusion of event memory as an important process in memory altered the previous understanding of the roles of the dorsal (or where) system and the ventral (or what) system that were discussed exten-sively in the basic systems model. Knowing the location of an object within a scene can no longer be viewed as a dorsal stream function; rather, it becomes a ventral stream function that may involve interactions with the dorsal stream.

In the basic systems model, several neural regions were discussed for the coordin-ation or integration of the systems to construct memories. Each was based on consid-erable empirical support. A "dumb" system that was part of the hippocampal-based explicit memory system bound everything that occurred at the same time. A "smart" system that was part of the emotion system modulated the encoding of memories based on the discrepancy between what was expected and what occurred, interest, or emo-tional arousal. A "smarter" system that was part of the frontal search system searched for components of a memory when cued by other components and used inhibitory mechanisms to suppress dominant responses that did not fit all the criteria set by the known cues. Finally, a spatial coordination system located in primary visual cortex and the ventral stream coorordinated information that was spatially related, including what later became event memory. The spatial coordination system is based on both neural theories about vision (Zeki, 1993) and theories of behavior (Barsalou, 1999). All these forms of coordination among systems are still needed.

The role of individual difference in the dimensional and basic systems model

Experimental studies try to produce results that hold over a wide range of individ-uals. Research on individual differences focusing on how people differ is usually not integrated into this research (Cronbach, 1957). However, in this case, individual differ-ences in the extent to which the various processes were used informed both models and their application to clinical disorders. In one early study, undergraduates nominated 20 autobiographical memories that would be distinctive enough that the name they gave to each of the memories would allow it to be recalled later (Rubin et al., 2004). The par-ticipants recalled the 20 autobiographical memories and rated them on 17 scales com-monly used in autobiographical memory studies, including measures of reliving, belief, emotions, narrative, and sensory systems, as well ratings of overgeneral memories and the age of the memories. The recall and ratings of the 20 memories were done at two sessions separated by two weeks. The median correlation of the individuals' average rating on each of the 17 scales taken two weeks apart was 0.90. When the mean of 10 of the memories was correlated with the remaining 10 and the correlations, corrected to be comparable with that of the full set of 20 memories, the median did not decrease. Thus, there was considerable stability in the individuals' average rating on each scale, consistent with a constructive view of autobiographical memory, in which stable individual differences in cognitive style were important. Moreover, the stability was not caused by using the same memories, as it occurred when different subsets of the memories were compared.

In a study of PTSD, 75 participants diagnosed with PTSD and 45 controls rated word-cued, important, positive, and negative memories (Rubin et al., 2011). For all four types of memories, there were significant differences between the means of the PTSD and control groups on scales that correlated highly with PTSD symptom severity. These included emotional reactions as measured by ratings of emotional intensity and ratings of physiological reactions, the frequency that the memories occurred as measured by ratings of voluntary rehearsal and the frequency of involuntary memories, and ratings of centrality to the life story. The differences were large, averaging 1.24, 1.43, 1.04, 1.23, and 0.84 on the five 7-point scales, respectively. The differences were smaller and usually not significant on scales that did not correlate with PTSD symptom severity. Thus, there were substantial differences in the ratings of individual processes related to PTSD. Moreover, the difference occurred no matter if the memories were word-cued, important, positive, or negative. A similar study with undergraduates who varied in their PTSD symptom severity produced a similar pattern of results with smaller effects (Rubin et al., 2008). Such a replicable pattern of differences in the ratings for both traumatic and non-traumatic memories informs our understanding of individual differences in memory processes in PTSD by demonstrating a general tendency that affects memories that vary on valence and importance. This changes the focus from trauma memories being a special class of memories to one in which they can be understood using general processes that apply in varying degrees to all autobiographical memories.

Autobiographical memory as the explicit construction of self-relevant past scenes

Where does all this leave us? Based on considerable empirical evidence, there is reason to privilege event memory in autobiographical memory. Self-reference and explicit memory follow from most common definitions and theories of autobiographical memory. Once this is done, the three dimensions of the dimensional model become necessary processes to consider in the construction of autobiographical memory. However, they are not enough. Other dimensions, or processes, are needed for a comprehensive theory. Many of these can be drawn with minor modification from the basic systems model, such as, narrative, language, and sensory systems beyond those needed for event memory. In addition, integrating the two models provides mechanisms that the dimensional model lacked for the construction of memories. In particular, using the spatial coordination process from the basic systems model provides a mechanism for the event memory needed for the dimensional model.

When the models are combined, they provide a good account of many phenomena that is consistent with behavioral and neural results. These include how autobiographical memories that have properties related to each of the processes can be constructed, how they can vary over recalls and adapt to new information, goals, and situations that arise. They can also integrate accounts of variability in these processes both in individuals and in clinical syndromes.

As advances in our study of behavior and its neural basis continue, applications to more complex phenomena become tractable and the results more precise. The neurocognitive theory of autobiographical memory proposed here accounts for behavior in individuals with and without a variety of specific deficits in a way that converges with what is known about its neural basis. Moreover, autobiographical memory is given a clear conceptual location in relation to other kinds of memory that indicates dimensions along which it differs. This allows autobiographical memory to be separated from episodic memory in this conceptual space using specified properties of the two concepts.

Acknowledgments

I wish to thank Dorthe Berntsen, Kaitlyn Brodar, Roberto Cabeza, Dale Dagenbach, Emmaline Drew, Tobias Egner, Shana Hall, Kevin LaBar, Elizabeth Marsh, Simon Davis, the Memory at Duke Group, and the North Carolina Cognition Conference for comments and grant DNRF89 to the Center on Autobiographical Memory Research, Aarhus University.

References

Allport, G. W. (1955). *Becoming: Basic considerations for a psychology of personality*. New Haven: Yale University Press.

Anderson, J. R. & Ross, B. H. (1980). Evidence against a semantic–episodic distinction. *Journal of Experimental Psychology: Human Learning and Memory, 6*, 441–466.

Baldassano, C., Esteva, A., Fei-Fei, L., & Beck, D. M. (2016). Two distinct scene-processing networks connecting vision and memory. *eNeuro, 3*, ENEURO.0178–16.2016.

Barsalou, L. W. (1999). Perceptual symbol systems. *Behavioral and Brain Sciences, 22*, 577–660.

Bartlett, F. C. (1932). *Remembering: A study in experimental and social psychology*. London: Cambridge University Press.

Berntsen, D. (2009). *Involuntary autobiographical memories. An introduction to the unbidden past*. Cambridge: Cambridge University Press.

Berntsen, D. & Bohn, A. (2010). Remembering and forecasting: The relation between autobiographical memory and episodic future thinking. *Memory & Cognition, 38*, 265–278.

Berntsen, D. & Rubin, D. C. (2006). The centrality of event scale: A measure of integrating a trauma into one's identity and its relation to post-traumatic stress disorder symptoms. *Behaviour Research and Therapy, 44*, 219–231.

Boakes, R. A. (1989). How one might find evidence for conditioning in adult humans. In T. Archer & L.-G. Nilsson (eds.), *Aversion, avoidance and anxiety: Perspectives on learning and memory* (pp. 381–402). Hillsdale, NJ: Erlbaum.

Bradley, M. M., Greenwald, M. K., Petry, M. C., & Lang, P. J. (1992). Remembering pictures: Pleasure and arousal in memory. *Journal of Experimental Psychology: Learning, Memory, & Cognition, 18,* 379–390.

Brewer, W. F. (1974). There is no convincing evidence for operant or classical conditioning in adult humans. In W. B. Weimer & D. S. Palermo (eds.), *Cognition and the symbolic processes* (pp. 1–42). Hillsdale, NJ: Erlbaum.

Brewer, W. F. (1986). What is autobiographical memory? In D. C. Rubin (ed.), *Autobiographical memory* (pp. 25–49). Cambridge: Cambridge University Press.

Brown, A. S. (2003). A review of the déjà vu experience. *Psychological Bulletin, 129,* 394–413.

Brown, A. S. (2004). *The déjà vu experience.* New York: Psychology Press.

Buckner, R. L. & Carroll, D. C. (2007). Self-projection and the brain. *Trends in Cognitive Sciences, 11,* 49–57.

Burgess, N., Becker, S., King, J. A., & O'Keefe, J. (2001). Memory for events and their spatial context: Models and experiments. *Philosophical Transactions of the Royal Society of London Series B: Biological Sciences, 356,* 1493–1503.

Butler, A. C., Rice, H. J., Wooldridge, C. L., & Rubin, D. C. (2016). Visual imagery in autobiographical memory: The role of repeated retrieval in shifting perspective. *Consciousness & Cognition, 42,* 327–253.

Butters, N. & Cermak, L. S. (1986). A case study of the forgetting of autobiographical knowledge: Implications for the study of retrograde amnesia. In D. C. Rubin (ed.), *Autobiographical memory* (pp. 253–272). Cambridge: Cambridge University Press.

Cabeza, R., Prince, S. E., Daselaar, S. M., Greenberg, D. L., Budde, M., Dolcos, F., et al. (2004). Brain activity during episodic retrieval of autobiographical and laboratory events: An fMRI study using a novel photo paradigm. *Journal of Cognitive Neuroscience, 16,* 1583–1594.

Campbell, J. D., Assanand, S., & Di Paula, A. (2003). The structure of the self-concept and its relation to psychological adjustment. *Journal of Personality, 71,* 115–140.

Clark, R. E. & Squire, L. R. (1998). Classical conditioning and brain systems: The role of awareness. *Science, 280,* 77–81.

Clark, R. E. & Squire, L. R. (1999). Human eyeblink classical conditioning: Effects of manipulating awareness of the stimulus contingencies. *Psychological Science, 10,* 14–18.

Cleary, A. M., Ryals, A. J., & Nomi, J. S. (2009). Can déjà vu result from similarity to a prior experience? Support for the similarity hypothesis of déjà vu. *Psychonomic Bulletin & Review, 16,* 1082–1088.

Cronbach, L. J. 1975. Beyond the two disciplines of scientific psychology. *American Psychologist, 30,* 671–84.

Daselaar, S. M., Rice, H. J., Greenberg, D. L., Cabeza, R., LaBar, K. S., & Rubin, D. C. (2008). The spatiotemporal dynamics of autobiographical memory: Neural correlates of recall, emotional intensity, and reliving. *Cerebral Cortex, 18,* 217–229.

D'Argembeau, A. (2012). Autobiographical memory and future thinking. In D. Berntsen & D. C. Rubin (eds), *Understanding autobiographical memory: Theories and approaches* (pp. 311–330). Cambridge: Cambridge University Press.

D'Argembeau, A. & Van der Linden, M. (2004). Phenomenal characteristics associated with projecting oneself back into the past and forward into the future: Influence of valence and temporal distance. *Consciousness and Cognition, 13,* 844–858.

D'Argembeau, A. & Van der Linden, M. (2006). Individual differences in the phenomenology of mental time travel: The effect of vivid visual imagery and emotion regulation strategies. *Consciousness and Cognition, 15,* 342–350.

De Brigard, F. & Gessell, B. S. (2016). Time is not of the essence: Understanding the neural correlates of mental time travel. In: Klein, S. B., Michaelian, K. & Szpunar, K. K. (eds), *Seeing the future: Theoretical perspectives on future-oriented mental time travel* (pp. 153–179). New York: Oxford University Press.

Denny, B. T., Kober, H., Wager, T. D., & Ochsner, K. N. (2012). A meta-analysis of functional neuro-imaging studies of self- and other judgments reveals a spatial gradient for mentalizing in medial prefrontal cortex. *Journal of Cognitive Neuroscience, 24*, 1742–1752.

Dew, I. T. Z. & Cabeza, R. (2011). The porous boundaries between explicit and implicit memory: Behavioral and neural evidence. *Annals of the New York Academy of Science, 1224*, 174–190.

Ebbinghaus, H. (1885/1964). *Memory: A contribution to experimental psychology* (transl. H. A. Ruger & C. E. Bussenius). New York: Dover. (Original work published 1885.)

Eichenbaum, H., Dudchenko, P., Wood, E., Shapiro, M., & Tanila, H. (1999). The hippocampus, memory, and place cells: Is it spatial memory or a memory space? *Neuron, 23*, 209–226.

Epstein, R. & Kanwisher, N. (1998). A cortical representation of the local visual environment. *Nature, 392*, 598–601.

Finnbogadóttir, H. & Berntsen, D. (2013). Involuntary future projections are as frequent as involuntary memories, but more positive. *Consciousness and Cognition, 22*, 272–280.

Greenberg, D. L., Eacott, M. J., Brechin, D., & Rubin, D. C. (2005). Visual memory loss and autobiographical amnesia: A case study. *Neuropsychologia, 43*, 1493–1502.

Greenberg, D. L. & Rubin, D. C. (2003). The neuropsychology of autobiographical memory. *Cortex, 39*, 687–728.

Hassabis, D., Kumaran, D., Vann, S., & Maguire, E. (2007). Patients with hippocampal amnesia cannot imagine new experiences. *Proceedings of the National Academy of Sciences of the United States of America, 104*, 1726–1731.

Hassabis, D. & Maguire, E. A. (2007). Deconstructing episodic memory with construction. *Trends in Cognitive Sciences, 11*, 299–306.

Hoyle, R. H. (2006). Self-esteem and self-knowledge. In M. H. Kernis (ed.), *Self-esteem issues and answers: A sourcebook on current perspectives* (pp. 208–215). New York: Psychology Press.

Kanwisher, N. & Dilks, D. D. (2014). The functional organization of the ventral visual pathway in humans. In J. S. Werner & L. M. Chalupa (eds.), *The new visual neurosciences* (pp. 733–746). Cambridge, MA: MIT Press.

Kim, K. & Johnson, M. K. (2012). Extended self: Medial prefrontal activity during transient association of self and objects. *Social Cognitive and Affective Neuroscience, 7*, 199–207.

Larsen, S. F. (1988). Remembering without experiencing: Memory for reported events. In U. Neisser & E. Winograd (eds.), *Remembering reconsidered: Ecological and traditional approaches to the study of memory* (pp. 326–355). Cambridge: Cambridge University Press.

Leary, M. R. & Tangney, J. P. (2012). The self as an organizing construct in the behavioral and social sciences. In M. R. Leary & J. P. Tangney (eds.), *Handbook of self and identity* (2nd edn) (pp. 3–14). New York: Guilford Press.

Lovibond, P. F. & Shanks, D. R. (2002). The role of awareness in Pavlovian conditioning: Empirical evidence and theoretical implications. *Journal of Experimental Psychology: Animal Behavior Processes, 28*, 3–26.

Maguire, E. A. & Mullally, S. L. (2013). The hippocampus: A manifesto for change. *Journal of Experimental Psychology: General, 142*, 1180–1189.

Mandler, G. (1980). Recognizing: The judgment of previous occurrence. *Psychological Review, 87*, 252–271.

Mandler, G. (1994). Hypermnesia, incubation, and mind popping: On remembering without really trying. In C. Umilta & M. Moscovitch (eds.), *Attention and performance: Conscious and unconscious information processing* (pp. 3–33). Cambridge: MIT Press.

McIsaac, H. K. & Eich, E. (2002). Vantage point in episodic memory. *Psychonomic Bulletin and Review, 9*, 146–150.

McKoon, G. & Ratcliff, R. (1979). Priming in episodic and semantic memory. *Journal of Verbal Learning and Verbal Behavior, 18*, 463–480.

McKoon, G., Ratcliff, R., & Dell, G. S. (1986). A critical evaluation of the semantic–episodic distinction. *Journal of Experimental Psychology: Learning, Memory, and Cognition, 12*, 295–306.

Moran, J. M., Heatherton, T. F., & Kelley, W. M. (2009). Modulation of cortical midline structures by implicit and explicit self-relevance evaluation. *Social Neuroscience, 4*, 197–211.

Morel, N., Villain, N., Rauchs, G., Gaubert, M., Piolino P., et al. (2014). Brain activity and functional coupling changes associated with self-reference effect during both encoding and retrieval. *PLoS One*, *9*, e90488.

Mullally, S. L. & Maguire, E. A. (2013). Exploring the role of space defining objects in constructing and maintaining imagine scenes. *Brain and Cognition*, *82*, 100–107.

Neisser, U. (1967). *Cognitive psychology*. Englewood Cliffs, NJ: Prentice-Hall.

Neisser, U. (1976). *Cognition and reality: Principles and implications of cognitive psychology*. New York: Freeman.

Neisser, U. (1988). Five kinds of self-knowledge. *Philosophical Psychology*, *1*, 35–59.

Newby-Clark, I. R. & Ross, M. (2003). Conceiving the past and future. Personality and *Social Psychology Bulletin*, *29*, 807–818.

Nigro, G. & Neisser, U. (1983). Point of view in personal memories. *Cognitive Psychology*, *15*, 467–482.

Philippi, C. L., Duff, M. C., Denburg, N. L., Tranel, D., & Rudrauf, D. (2012). Medial PFC damage abolishes the self-reference effect. *Journal of Cognitive Neuroscience 24*, 475–481.

Pillemer, D., Steiner, K., Kuwabara, K., Thomsen, D. K., & Svob, C. (2015). Vicarious memories. *Consciousness and Cognition*, *36*, 233–245.

Posner, M. J. & Keele, S. (1970). Retention of abstract ideas. *Journal of Experimental Psychology*, *83*, 304–308.

Rice, H. & Rubin, D. (2011). Remembering from any angle: The flexibility of visual perspective during retrieval. *Consciousness and Cognition*, *20*, 568–577.

Rubin, D. C. (1988). Go for the skill. In U. Neisser & E. Winograd (eds.), *Remembering reconsidered: Ecological and traditional approaches to the study of memory* (pp. 374–382). Cambridge: Cambridge University Press.

Rubin, D. C. (1995). *Memory in oral traditions: The cognitive psychology of epic, ballads, and counting-out rhymes*. New York: Oxford University Press.

Rubin, D. C. (1998). Beginnings of a theory of autobiographical remembering. In C. P. Thompson, D. J. Herrmann, D. Bruce, J. D. Reed, D. G. Payne, & M. P. Toglia (eds.), *Autobiographical memory: Theoretical and applied perspectives* (pp. 47–67). Mahwah, NJ: Erlbaum.

Rubin, D. C. (2005). A basic-systems approach to autobiographical memory. *Current Directions in Psychological Science*, *14*, 79–83.

Rubin, D. C. (2006). The basic-systems model of episodic memory. *Perspectives on Psychological Science*, *1*, 277–311.

Rubin, D. C. (2012). The basic system model of autobiographical memory. In D. Berntsen & D. C. Rubin (eds.). *Understanding autobiographical memory: Theories and approaches* (pp. 11–32). Cambridge: Cambridge University Press.

Rubin, D. C. (2014). Schema driven construction of future autobiographical traumatic events: The future is much more troubling than the past. *Journal of Experimental Psychology: General*, *143*, 612–630.

Rubin, D. C. (2015). A basic systems account of trauma memories in PTSD: Is more needed? In L. A. Watson, D. Berntsen & D. C. Rubin (eds.). *Clinical perspective on autobiographical memory: Theories and approaches* (pp. 41–64). Cambridge: Cambridge University Press.

Rubin, D. C., Boals, A., & Berntsen, D. (2008). Memory in posttraumatic stress disorder: Properties of voluntary and involuntary, traumatic and non-traumatic autobiographical memories in people with and without PTSD symptoms. *Journal of Experimental Psychology: General*, *137*, 591–614.

Rubin, D. C., Dennis, M. F., & Beckham, J. C. (2011). Autobiographical memory for stressful events: The role of autobiographical memory in posttraumatic stress disorder. *Consciousness and Cognition*, *20*, 840–856.

Rubin, D. C. & Greenberg, D. L. (1998). Visual memory-deficit amnesia: A distinct amnesic presentation and etiology. *Proceedings of the National Academy of Sciences*, *95*, 5413–5416.

Rubin, D. C., Li, D., Hall, S. A., Kragel, P. A., & Berntsen, D. (2017 online). Taking tests in the magnet: Brain mapping standardized tests. *Human Brain Mapping*, *38*, 5706–5725.

Rubin, D. C., Schrauf, R. W., & Greenberg D. L. (2003). Belief and recollection of autobiographical memories. *Memory & Cognition*, *31*, 887–901.

Rubin, D. C. & Talarico, J. M. (2009). A comparison of dimensional models of emotion: Evidence from emotions, prototypical events, autobiographical memories, and words. *Memory, 17*, 802–808.

Rubin, D. C. & Umanath, S. (2015). Event memory: A theory of memory for laboratory, autobiographical, and fictional events. *Psychological Review, 122*, 1–23.

Schacter, D. L. & Addis, D. R. (2007). The cognitive neuroscience of constructive memory: Remembering the past and imagining the future. *Philosophical Transactions of the Royal Society of London B: Biological Sciences, 362*, 773–786.

Sheen, M., Kemp, S., & Rubin, D. C. (2001). Twins dispute memory ownership: A new false memory phenomenon. *Memory & Cognition, 29*, 779–788.

Singer, J. L. (1966). *Daydreaming: An introduction to the experimental study of inner experience.* New York: Random House.

Spreng, R. N., & Levine, B. (2006). The temporal distribution of past and future autobiographical events across the lifespan. *Memory & Cognition, 34*, 1644–1651.

Squire, L. R. (1987). *Memory and brain.* New York: Oxford University Press.

Squire, L. R. (1994). Declarative and nondeclarative memory: Multiple brain systems supporting learning and memory. In D. L. Schacter & E. Tulving (eds.), *Memory systems 1994* (pp. 203–231). Cambridge, MA: MIT Press.

Squire, L. R. (2004). Memory systems of the brain: A brief history and current perspective. *Neurobiology of Learning and Memory, 82*, 171–177

Szpunar, K. K. (2010). Episodic future thought: An emerging concept. *Perspectives on Psychological Science, 5*, 142–162.

Szpunar, K. K. & McDermott, K. B. (2008). Episodic future thought and its relation to remembering: Evidence from ratings of subjective experience. *Consciousness and Cognition, 17*, 330–334.

Talarico, J. M., LaBar K. S., & Rubin, D. C. (2004). Emotional intensity predicts autobiographical memory experience, *Memory & Cognition, 32*, 1118–1132.

Trope, Y. & Liberman, N. (2010). Construal-level theory of psychological distance. *Psychological Review, 117*, 440–463.

Tulving, E. (1972). Episodic and semantic memory. In E. Tulving & W. Donaldson (eds.), *Organization of memory* (pp. 381–402). New York: Academic Press.

Tulving, E. (1983). *Elements of episodic memory.* Oxford: Clarendon Press.

Tulving, E. (1984). Précis of elements of episodic memory. *Behavioral and Brain Sciences, 7*, 223–268.

Tulving, E. (1985). Memory and consciousness. *Canadian Psychology, 26*, 1–12.

Tulving, E. (2002). Episodic memory: From mind to brain. *Annual Review of Psychology, 53*, 1–25.

Wilson, B. A. & Wearing, D. (1995). Prisoner of consciousness: A state of just awakening following herpes simplex encephalitis. In R. Campbell & M. A. Conway (eds), *Broken memories: Case studies in memory impairment*, (pp. 14–30). Malden: Blackwell.

Zeki, S. (1993). *A vision of the brain.* Oxford: Blackwell.

3

The Self-Memory System Revisited

Past, Present, and Future

Martin A. Conway, Lucy V. Justice, and Arnaud D'Argembeau

Introduction

One of the central features of the self-memory system (SMS) model of autobiographical memory is that memory and goals are intricately and reciprocally linked (Conway, 1996, 2005, 2009; Conway & Pleydell-Pearce, 2000; Conway et al., 2004). In this chapter this interrelation is again considered, particularly with reference to the representation of the future, new findings are incorporated, and the brain basis of SMS is explored in some in detail. And we conclude by raising some fundamental questions about the nature of autobiographical memory. First, however, we outline the SMS.

The self-memory system

There are three key processes central to the SMS. The first is that memories are mental representations that are *constructed* out of autobiographical knowledge and episodic memories. Knowledge and episodic memories are organized in autobiographical memory knowledge structures in long-term memory (see figure 3.1) and transitory patterns of activation constantly arise and dissipate in these knowledge structures. These patterns of activation can coalesce into memories or the patterns of activation can themselves be channeled by control processes into specific memories. The second key process is that all patterns of activation in autobiographical memory knowledge structures are caused by *cues*. Cues can be anything from a sound, to a taste, to a smell, to a visual feature, to a feeling or a thought, even the conceptual structure of a problem (Schank, 1982), etc. The key point is that a cue maps onto specific items of knowledge in autobiographical memory knowledge structures and in so doing causes a rise in activation that then spreads, and dissipates as it spreads, to associated items of knowledge (Collins & Loftus, 1975). Third, *central control processes* (it is at this stage that goals enter into the memory construction process) can access the activation caused by cues, evaluate the activated knowledge, elaborate it and then use the elaborated cue to cause further activation in an iterative cycle of knowledge access, cue elaboration, and further knowledge activation as sought-for knowledge is eventually activated (Williams & Hollan, 1981). This iterative process creates a *complex cue* or what Norman

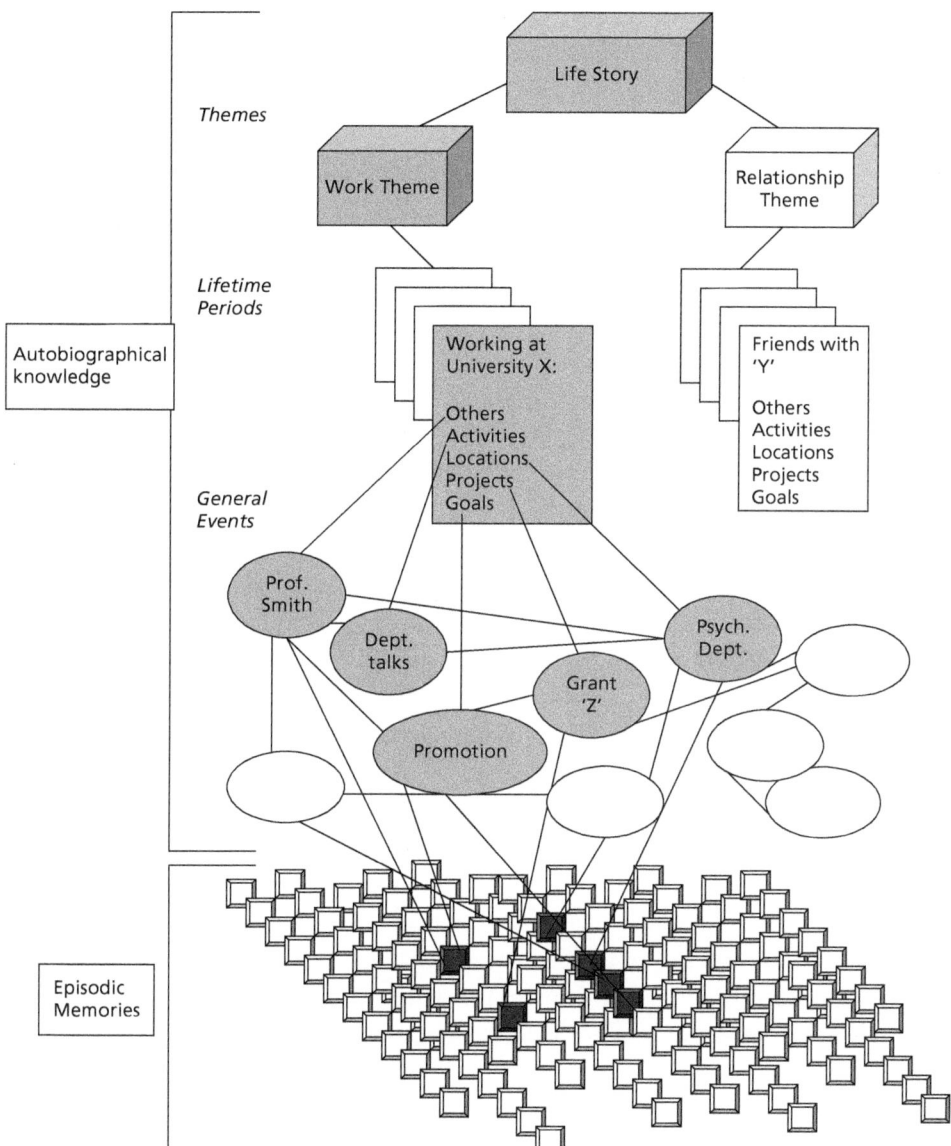

Figure 3.1 The self-memory system

Adapted with permission from Conway, M. A. 'Memory and the self,' *Journal of Memory and Language*, Volume 53, Issue 4, pp. 594–628, Figure 5, Copyright © (2005) Elsevier Ltd.

and Bobrow (1979) termed a *memory description*. Finally, it should be noted that all of this can occur non-consciously and without any conscious intention (what Schank, 1982, originally termed *remindings* and what later researchers have called *involuntary memories*, e.g. Berntsen, 2012). Indeed, in the SMS model it is only possible to become consciously aware of the *outputs* or *effects* of non-conscious processes, e.g. highly activated knowledge; it is not possible to become consciously aware of the processes themselves. Similarly it is not possible for control processes to modulate the search process directly—this can only be achieved by elaborating cues, although central control process may be able to inhibit activated knowledge or at least prevent it from entering conscious awareness (Barnier et al., 2004, 2007).

Figure 3.1 depicts how autobiographical knowledge and episodic memories may be represented in long-term memory (see Conway, 1996, and Conway & Pleydell-Pearce, 2000, for earlier versions). There are several features of figure 3.1, perhaps the most important being that the lines that connect knowledge representations, e.g. lifetime periods to general events, illustrate the action of cues. This action is transitory and occurs only when a cue is activated. Also the lower portion of figure 3.1 depicts episodic memories not as knowledge representations but rather as episodic representations. That is, as representations that contain details derived from single experiences, they are *experience-near* (Conway 2005). Episodic memories are accessed by cues; however, episodic memories may also have another additional form of organization and that is that they are represented contiguously, in groups (see Conway 2009), and so are organized along a temporal dimension. One implication of this is that when an episodic memory is accessed the accessibility of other temporally related episodic memories is raised. Nonetheless, when indexed by higher-order autobiographical knowledge structures their organization is primarily thematic and goal-orientated (see, for example, Anderson & Conway, 1993).

The nature of the representation of autobiographical memories as envisioned in the SMS model is based on findings from a very wide range of areas, from experimental psychology, neuropsychology, clinical psychology, and neuroscience (reviewed in Conway & Pleydell-Pearce, 2000, and Conway, 2005, 2009). This evidence will not be reviewed again here but some new findings that bear upon the model are covered in this chapter. However, another and compelling reason for our conception of the representation of autobiographical memory in the SMS was to preserve an important distinction in memory theory: the distinction between *stored* and *transitory* representations. Knowledge representation in the SMS allows the inferential and creative use of autobiographical memory, which is critically important in simulating future events (see ahead), reconceiving the past, imagination, and insight (Conway & Loveday, 2015; Conway et al., 2016). Consider a simple example. Suppose you are a participant in an autobiographical memory experiment and you are asked to recall memories that centrally feature *items of furniture*. Of course you and other participants in the experiment can do this. Indeed you probably can do so for a very wide range of ad-hoc categories (Barsalou, 1983), from memories of buying clothes to great meals you have had, but it does not follow that this is how the underlying knowledge structures are organized. According to the SMS model it rather more simply reflects your ability to use a cue to construct a wide range of specific memories. This is the creative use of memory, that Moscovitch (1992) memorably termed *working with memory*. From an evolutionary perspective this ability to use individual cues to construct a diverse range of autobiographical memories confers a considerable survival advantage because we can be reminded of diverse cue-relevant events that help guide us in the present in dealing with environmental challenges. Interestingly most of those challenges may relate to the social world and social interactions.

From the perspective of the memory researcher interested in how knowledge is represented in the mind, it does, however, pose a major difficulty and that is how to distinguish between what is stored and what is transitory or computed. The organization shown in figure 3.1 is based on a wide range of findings that converge to support it. Because these findings use many different techniques to probe the underlying knowledge, taken together they probably do—with at least some degree of accuracy—reflect the nature of the organization of autobiographical knowledge and episodic memories. Other approaches that often rely on a single technique or a narrow range of techniques often cannot determine whether their findings reflect the stored nature of autobiographical memory and/or its creative use. This most frequently arises when a single or narrow range of cues is used to probe autobiographical memory. For example, asking participants to recall memories of "important" events will lead to responses that depend on how people conceptualize the term "important." If they elaborate the cue 'important' to mean events that most people would find important, e.g. births, deaths, marriages, rites of passage, etc., then they will construct memories that are of such events. But it does not follow that autobiographical memory is organized in this way; rather, only that it can be used in this way. Thus, the stored-versus-transitory distinction is important in both what we do with our memories and how this varies with different types of cues. The SMS model identifies, to some extent, what is stored, and because of its cue-based nature supports the creative use of autobiographical memory.

The SMS is conceived as domains of knowledge representation at different levels of specificity. At the most abstract level is what Singer et al. (2004) termed the *conceptual self* (not shown in figure 3.1), which is a repository of personal beliefs, traits, and other self-referring attributes (see also Klein & Gangi, 2010). Knowledge represented in the conceptual self may consist of what we termed *self-images*. Such images may access beliefs about past selves, the current self, the future self, wanted and feared selves, which taken together we termed, after Markus & Nurius (1986), the *universe of possible selves* that form a central part of the conceptual self. Such representations might also be organized around a visual image or set of visual images forming knowledge structures that can be used as cues, or their details used as cues, to access other knowledge in more specific knowledge structures. For example, an image of oneself as a student, stored in the conceptual self, might access a lifetime period representation of "When I was at university." Note that this specific knowledge also instantiates the corresponding image in the conceptual self. Thus, it constrains the contents of the conceptual self. In a normally functioning autobiographical memory, knowledge at different levels constrains what knowledge may exist at other levels. In other words, the universe of possible selves is limited by the specific knowledge its cues can access. It is only in certain types of brain damage and psychological illness that this constraining function may malfunction or stop functioning altogether, giving rise to delusion, confabulation, and false beliefs.

Figure 3.1 illustrates the autobiographical knowledge structures with which the conceptual self interacts. The *life story* schema (Bluck & Habermas, 2000; McAdams, 2001;

see too Kris, 1952/1975) contains conceptual knowledge about the self over the life-span, providing an overall representation of a person's entire life. At a more specific level, knowledge in *lifetime periods* is generally of goals, people, places, activities, emotions, thoughts, etc., that were characteristic of the period. Note that lifetime periods, although having marked beginnings and endings, are not chronologically exclusive. For example, the lifetime period "When I was at university" might overlap or even be chronologically completely parallel with the lifetime period "When I lived with X." What distinguishes them is that they contain different knowledge—sometimes wholly so, sometimes there is much overlap—the main difference being in knowledge they represent about the goals of that particular lifetime period. Lifetime period knowledge can be used as cues to access knowledge in *general events*. General events are also of extended periods of time but shorter than lifetime periods, e.g. work projects, holidays, repeated events, etc. (see Conway & Bekerian, 1987; Barsalou, 1988). They too contain information about people, locations, activities, emotions, and so on, that define the period they represent. Knowledge represented in general events can be used as cues to access *episodic memories* (lower part of Figure 3.1). Episodic memories contain knowledge that derives from experience and some conceptual knowledge (see Conway, 2009). For example, a specific episodic memory contains episodic details, frequently in the form of (visual) images with some unifying conceptual knowledge, e.g. images of a cinema experience unified by the conceptual knowledge "When we went to see X."

This whole system of knowledge representation (Figure 3.1) can be viewed as sets of hierarchical partonomic autobiographical knowledge structures in which groups of episodic memories are parts of general events that are parts of lifetime periods, which themselves are parts of the life story. However, although some of this may be stored as knowledge structures in long-term memory, the SMS model views such structures as being largely transitory. By this view, patterns of activation caused by the effects of cues spreading between different levels of knowledge create transitory knowledge structures. Specific autobiographical memories are then transitory patterns of activation in the SMS and when they are specific they always feature activated episodic memories. It is important to recognize that patterns of activation are constantly arising and dissipating in the SMS and this occurs non-consciously outside awareness. These patterns of activation may sometimes form specific memories and occasionally they may enter consciousness, giving an experience of spontaneous memory retrieval (a phenomenon studied under the rubric of 'involuntary' memory, see Berntsen, 2012). Nonetheless the construction of specific autobiographical memories, especially the intentional rather than incidental construction, is frequently mediated by control processes prior to any conscious experience of a memory.

Although the process of memory construction is always the same, that is, driven by the activating effects of cues, conscious awareness of the retrieval process is variable. According to the SMS model we cannot be aware of the construction/retrieval process itself, which is always non-conscious, but we may be intermittently aware of inputs to and outputs from the process. Within the SMS, when a rememberer is aware of inputs and outputs of the construction process they undergo what is termed *generative*

THE BRAIN BASIS OF THE SMS 33

retrieval (Gilboa et al., 2006, termed this *strategic* retrieval, see 'Neurological injuries to the SMS'). The main idea of generative/strategic retrieval is that the rememberer can consciously evaluate outputs from the construction process and elaborate them into a more effective cue (Williams & Hollan, 1981, were the first to make a similar proposal based on protocol data collected during retrieval; see also Norman & Bobrow, 1979, and Haque & Conway, 2001). In contrast to generative retrieval is so-called *direct retrieval*, which simply refers to the situation in which a memory ""pops" into mind without the rememberer being aware of any output from the construction process. This can occur in intentional remembering when a person consciously attempts to recall a memory and is aware of the initial cue but unaware of any other aspects of the construction process until a specific autobiographical memory comes to mind. Direct retrieval is sometimes thought to be more rapid than generative retrieval and this may usually be the case, although there are instances where a memory cannot be intentionally recalled, only to pop into mind hours or even days later. Whatever the case, within the SMS model all acts of memory construction are considered to terminate in a moment of direct retrieval—it is not possible to be aware of what will come to mind before it comes to mind. That is to say, one cannot be aware of what a cue will activate prior to the effects of the activation.

The SMS is, then, a cue-driven model of the construction of autobiographical memories. Cues cause activation in the autobiographical knowledge base and that activation spreads and dissipates. This process takes place non-consciously, is continuous, and at any one time there are probably multiple sources of activation, some intersecting. This can give rise to *remindings* (Schank, 1982) when a memory spontaneously and incidentally comes to mind—a process within the SMS termed *direct retrieval*. In contrast, memory construction may be intentional, rather than incidental, and in this case executive/control processes elaborate cues and accessed knowledge into increasingly more effective cues. The outputs of the repeated search-and-elaborate cycles may become conscious or partly conscious—a process in the SMS model termed *generative retrieval*. Finally, because of the complexity of the autobiographical knowledge base, patterns of activation are distributed over widely interlocked neural networks. The next section explores the brain basis of these processes and their broad architecture.

The brain basis of the SMS

There have been several reviews of the many neuroimaging studies of autobiographical memories. Two early reviews (Conway et al., 2002; Maguire, 2001) focused largely on work dating to the 1990s in which, interestingly, a common control condition was what was then called 'resting'. In these studies, in the experimental condition participants retrieved autobiographical memories, whereas in the control condition they did nothing other than 'rest' in the scanner. Imaging data acquired in the control condition were subtracted from data collected in the experimental condition in order to determine activation unique to the construction of autobiographical memories. However, few differences were observed and we will return to this later as it transpires that the 'rest' condition is itself of particular interest. More recent reviews (Cabeza & St. Jacques, 2007; Conway & Piolino, 2009; Martinelli et al., 2013; McDermot et al., 2009; St. Jacques & De Brigard, 2015; Svoboda et al., 2006—see also Howe et al., 2018, chapter 5) have focused on the many neuroimaging studies conducted since 2000 using a wide range of procedures and control conditions. All these reviews, and indeed the earlier reviews, converge on approximately the same view of the brain basis of autobiographical memory and, as we shall see, one that is highly consistent with the SMS model.

Here we will mainly, but not solely, draw on the meta-analysis by Svoboda et al. (2006) of 24 neuroimaging studies of the construction of autobiographical memories and on the important meta-analysis of 38 neuroimaging autobiographical memory studies by Martinelli et al. (2013). Svoboda et al. identified what they termed a "core" network that emerged in the majority of studies along with secondary and tertiary regions that emerged in some studies but not others. The core network consisted of subsidiary regions activated largely in the left hemisphere and encompassing the medial and ventrolateral prefrontal, medial and lateral temporal, and retrosplenial/posterior cingulate cortices, and the temporal junction and cerebellum. The construction of specific autobiographical memories is a complex and—compared to other forms of cognition such as word recognition (Conway, 1996)—lengthy process. As Svoboda et al. observed, the data indicate that the involvement of frontal networks occurs early in the construction process and likely reflects an early phase of the search–evaluate–elaborate cycle of generating an effective cue. It seems likely that in this phase only general autobiographical knowledge is accessed (see the upper part of figure 3.1). Other more posterior networks only come online later in the construction process as a stable pattern of activation becomes established and a specific memory is formed.

There are large between- and within-individual differences in autobiographical memory retrieval, which is, in any case, highly sensitive to the (experimental) conditions under which memories are constructed. Given this variability it is perhaps surprising that it has been possible to identify a core network in the first place. The secondary network identified by Svobada et al. consisted of dorsolateral prefrontal cortex, superior medial and superior lateral cortex, anterior cingulate, medial orbitofrontal, temporopolar, and occipital cortices, thalamus, and amygdala. Regions in this network activated variably across studies, which may reflect differences in qualities such as memory vividness, degree of self-reference (importance), emotion, and even factors such as the age of a memory (retention interval). However, the broad pattern is clear: the construction of an autobiographical memory engages a whole series of neural networks in cortical and subcortical regions that become interlocked in the construction process.

Finally, consider the meta-analysis of Martinelli et al. (2013), which focused on those studies in which different types of autobiographical knowledge were imaged. Three broad domains of autobiographical knowledge were analyzed: episodic autobiographical memory (EAM), semantic autobiographical memory (SAM), and the conceptual self (CS). In figure 3.1 EAM is more simply termed episodic memory, and

SAM corresponds to autobiographical knowledge, general events, lifetime periods, etc. Knowledge relating to the CS (not shown in figure 3.1) consists of personality traits and beliefs about the self (Conway et al., 2004). It was found that the neural correlates of autobiographical knowledge showed a shift from posterior to anterior structures with increasing levels of abstraction. EAM was predominantly associated with activations in the limbic system (hippocampus and bilateral parahippocampal formation) and posterior midline cortical structures such as the precuneus and posterior cingulate. In contrast, activations associated with SAM were located in the temporo-parietal and parieto-frontal regions. Finally, activation unique to CS, essentially self-referential knowledge, was found only in the medial prefrontal cortex. This is part of a known mid-line cortical self-referential system—see, for example, D'Argembeau et al. (2007). Overall the findings of Martinelli et al.'s meta-analysis are highly consistent with those of Svoboda et al.'s (earlier) meta-analysis and consistent too with several other meta-analyses. The neuroimaging findings over many studies are therefore exactly what the SMS model predicts and are strong confirmation of the model. Figure 3.2, from Cabeza and St. Jacques's (2007) review, neatly sums up the complex autobiographical memory network (note that this is a simplified summary representation of the findings they reviewed).

What then of the 'rest' condition used in some of the early neuroimaging studies that did not find unique widespread activation of networks mediating autobiographical memory construction? It is important here to consider what might be occurring during a "rest" period; one cannot after all just switch the brain off. It is now evident that when participants are asked to rest, they start to daydream. This may involve planning, imaging future events, anticipating upcoming events, thinking about past events, imaging

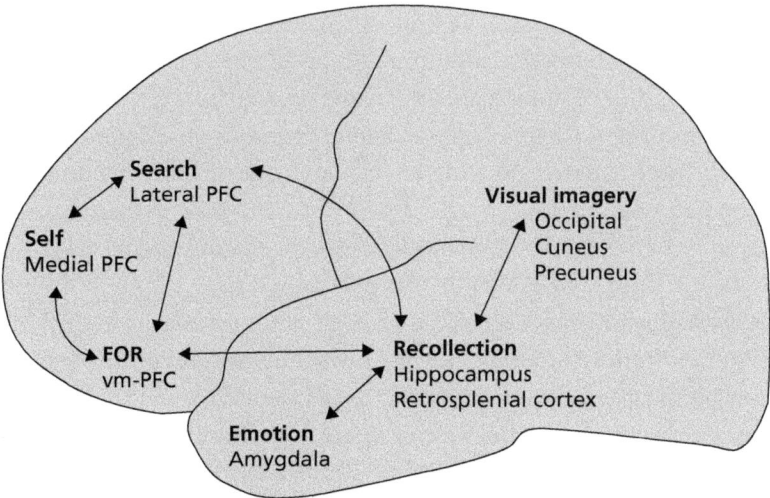

Figure 3.2 The autobiographical memory network.

Reproduced with permission from Cabeza & St. Jacques, 'Functional neuroimaging of autobiographical memory', *Trends in Cognitive Sciences*, Volume 11, Issue 5, pp. 219–227, Figure 5, Copyright © (2008) Elsevier Ltd.

more generally, thinking about others, etc. In short, they are activating networks that would be active if they were retrieving memories. Thus, when the patterns of activation present in the "rest" condition are subtracted from the patterns of activation in the autobiographical memory retrieval condition, they, in effect, cancel each other out. However, the interlocked set of networks active in rest have now been explored further (see, for example, Buckner et al., 2008) and have been found to form a frontal–temporal parietal–occipital network highly similar to the autobiographical network. Indeed, virtually the same network has been identified when people imagine the future (see Benoit & Schacter, 2015, for a recent review) and when any task entails a high degree of self-reference (see for instance, Humphreys & Sui, 2015). This complex and widely distributed network has been termed the *default* or core network and it becomes active when attention is oriented internally. Thus, the brain networks that support remembering and imagining are highly similar, leading Conway et al. (2016) to refer to this as the *remembering–imaging system* or, to extend the SMS model: *the self-memory and imaging system*. However one chooses to refer to it, the evidence from brain imaging is that remembering and imagining are interlinked in powerful ways.

According to the SMS model, when a memory is generatively retrieved, control processes should play a more prominent role than when a memory is subject to direct retrieval. Conway (1996) suggested that when episodic memories are directly accessed, then activation spreading (automatically) up through a hierarchical autobiographical memory knowledge structure, i.e. from episodic memories to a general event to a lifetime period, will be more rapid than an activation route spreading down from higher conceptual levels to episodic memories. This is because the route from episodic memories to autobiographical knowledge involves one-to-one mappings, whereas the route from higher conceptual personal knowledge to episodic memories typically involves one-to-many mappings that require evaluation, monitoring, and cue elaboration. It follows from this that there should be both similarities and differences in the neural substrates that mediate generative and direct retrieval. In an important neuroimaging study, Addis et al. (2012) found such similarities and differences. In order to prime direct retrieval Addis et al., in a pre-experimental phase, collected personal cues from participants that could be used to access episodic memories directly. In the imaging phase of the experiment, memory retrieval was cued either by personal cues, causing direct retrieval, or by words naming objects, causing generative retrieval (a procedure first used in behavioral experiments by Conway & Bekerian, 1987). In the generative condition early activation was detected in the left anterior middle and right inferior frontal gyri of the prefrontal cortex (PFC)—a result consistent with much other imaging research converging on the view that bilateral anterolateral PFC networks are activated in the early phase of generative retrieval. Importantly Addis et al. also found that subsequently there was activation of sites in the left lateral temporal cortex, an area considered to represent generic personal knowledge, i.e. general events (lifetime periods and the life story are most probably represented in frontal networks; see Conway & Piolino, 2009). Thus, Addis et al. conclude, "... these results converge with behavioral studies indicating that during generative retrieval, recovery of generic conceptual information precedes access of specific event memories" (p. 2919). Indeed, Addis et al. also found a temporal or phasic pattern of activation cycling between networks in the left lateral PFC, temporal cortex, and hippocampus—a pattern unique to generative retrieval. These neuroimaging findings are therefore strong support for the search–evaluate–elaborate model of generative retrieval proposed in the SMS model.[1]

What then of direct retrieval? The temporal sequence seen in generative retrieval was not present although activation of networks in the medial PFC, parietal cortex, and left hippocampus was greater in direct compared to generative retrieval. Interestingly activation of the right hippocampus was greater in generative compared to direct retrieval. Overall, however, activation of the various sites of the autobiographical memory retrieval network was greater in direct than in generative retrieval. Memories constructed in the direct condition were done so more quickly and were rated as more vivid than memories constructed in the generative condition. Thus, the patterns of memory activation caused by direct (personal) cues produced memories that phenomenologically were more distinct than memories constructed to generative cues. Possibly this is due to the direction of the spread of activation, as outlined earlier, with episodic to conceptual producing more distinct memories than conceptual to episodic. Whatever the case, the important outcome for the SMS is that generative and direct retrieval both take place in the autobiographical memory network but differ in the intensity of activation in different sites of the network. The main differences are that generative retrieval features more bilateral frontal activation than direct retrieval and there is a distinct time course to the patterns of activations in generative retrieval. All of which lends strong support to the SMS hypothesis that generative retrieval entails frontal or executive control and a cyclic cue search–evaluate–elaborate process, whereas direct retrieval does not feature this process, or at least not to the same extent.

In summary, neuroimaging research gives strong support to the main features of the SMS including its representation across multiple brain areas and in the complexities of the memory construction process. In the next section we shall see that brain injuries can impair this major, core, network.

Neurological injuries to the SMS

Neurological injuries offer interesting insights into the nature of the SMS (see Conway & Fthenaki, 2000) and the experience of remembering. In a study investigating recall over lifetime periods, Levine (2004) elicited memories, using the Autobiographical Interview Protocol, from individuals with frontotemporal dementia (FTD), progressive loss of neurons in the frontal and temporal lobes, and from healthy controls. Memories of controls contained more episodic details than the memories of FTD patients. Specifically, controls' memories contained more details of the event itself along

---

[1] Other behavioral research has opposed this aspect of the SMS, e.g. Uzer et al. (2012). However, because of methodological problems with that research we do not discuss it further here (see Conway & Sauer, 2015).

with more evaluative detail; controls' memories were more likely to contain descriptions of their thoughts and feelings of the event. Conversely, the memories elicited from FTD patients contained more semantic details, such as facts and metacognitive statements, argued to be perhaps a compensatory measure to the episodic deficits. These results were broadly replicated in a second study by Levine (2004). Patients with ventral prefrontal damage, as a result of focal lesions, also recalled reliably fewer internal details compared to controls although the memories from both groups contained a similar amount of semantic information. More generally Gilboa et al. (2006) argue that memory impairment following frontal injury leads to a deficit in what they term *strategic retrieval* (equivalent to generative retrieval). Depending on the nature of the injuries and which subcomponents of strategic retrieval are impaired, the ability to construct a detailed autobiographical memory may be attenuated, and in some cases disrupted strategic retrieval may give rise to confabulation (see also McCormick et al., 2017, for related findings).

Overall these neuropsychological findings implicate the frontal/temporal lobes in the recall of specific, evaluative, episodic detail from across the lifespan, and have been replicated and extended in a number of studies assessing autobiographical recall after brain injury in similar neural regions (Barr et al., 1990; Lah et al., 2004; Voltzenlogel et al., 2006). Additionally, Berryhill et al. (2007) assessed autobiographical recall of two patients with bilateral parietal lobe damage and found that, compared to controls, patients recalled reliably fewer episodic details. Also, patients showed a deficit in reporting time, perceptual, thought, and internal details. Therefore the patients' memories lacked specific, detailed descriptions, highlighting the role of the parietal networks in the recall of autobiographical memory.

In addition to reduced episodic detail, phenomenological characteristics of memory construction such as autonoetic consciousness (mental time travel), visual imagery and perspective taken in visual imagery have been shown to be disrupted following brain injury. For example, Piolino et al. (2007) elicited memories from across the lifetime of patients, predominantly with frontal lesions following traumatic brain injury (TBI). Broadly replicating findings from Levine (2004), TBI patients recalled fewer episodic memories than the control group and the memories that were recalled received lower episodic scores than the control counterparts. However, Piolino et al. (2006) also examined autonoetic consciousness using the Remember/Know paradigm (Tulving, 1985, 2002) and found that TBI patients reported fewer 'remember' responses than controls across all time periods, which the authors argue shows a lack of ability to mentally time travel across both recent and remote time periods to relive a specific event. Similarly, visual imagery, identified by Brewer (1988) as being the defining feature of autobiographical memory, has been shown to rely on posterior occipital cortical regions. Patients with damage to this region who as a consequence can no longer generate visual images have been found to have, as a secondary consequences, retrograde amnesia (Brown & Chobor, 1995; Conway, 1996; Ogden, 1993; Rubin & Greenberg, 1998). Typically these patients report difficulty recalling any pre-injury memories; on the other hand their conceptual autobiographical knowledge is often intact, that is, they can report some general events, lifetime periods, etc. Such a pattern of findings not only supports the claim that visual imagery is crucial for autobiographical recall, but indeed, indicates the role the posterior cortical regions play in autobiographical recall.

Piolino et al. also found that TBI patients described the visual imagery of their memories differently to the controls, such that they declared fewer "field" perspectives, particularly for early and recent memories, than controls. Further, TBI patients experienced difficulty when asked to attempt to switch perspectives (from observer to field) across all the lifetime periods tested, highlighting deficits in the phenomenological, subjective experience of autobiographical recall. Related phenomenological features of recall have also been found to be disrupted following other neurological injuries. For example, in patients who have undergone both left and right unilateral medial temporal lobe resection involving the amygdala, hippocampus, varying amounts of the temporopolar, perirhinal, entorhinal, and parahippocampal cortices. These patients reported by Noulhiane et al. (2008) completed an autobiographical memory task that was designed to elucidate and measure episodic memories across the entire lifetime and, paralleling Piolino et al. (2006), autonoetic consciousness was assessed using the Remember/Know paradigm. Note that this study also included an additional category of "Justified Remember", that was judged as present if participants could describe their memory with specificity and detail. Resection patients (no difference was found between right and left temporal resection) provided reliably fewer remember responses and more know responses than controls. Further, resection patients provided reliably fewer justified remember responses than the controls, pointing to a difficulty in encoding and recalling specific details and, in turn, a deficit in autonoetic consciousness. Overall, results highlight the bilateral involvement of the medial temporal lobe along with the frontal lobe in phenomenological measures of autobiographical recall across the lifespan.

A variety of neuropsychological research identifies multiple brain regions (the autobiographical memory network) involved in the recall of specific detailed autobiographical memories, and shows how the network also mediates the subjective experience of remembering and other phenomenological properties of recall. As noted earlier, an important feature of autobiographical remembering is that it supports planning and imagining the future—the intertwining of remembering and imagining (Conway et al., 2016). Interestingly it has been found that neuropsychological injuries can also impair this remembering–imagining system. Notably, a difficulty in imagining specific events that might occur in one's personal future has been documented in various patient populations with memory deficits, including amnesia (Tulving, 1985; Klein et al., 2002; Hassabis et al., 2007), Alzheimer's disease (Addis et al., 2009), depression (Williams et al., 1996), and schizophrenia (D'Argembeau et al., 2008). For instance, Rasmussen and Berntsen (2014) contrasted the recall and imagination of patients with a predominance of diffuse and frontal lobe lesions arising from moderate to severe traumatic brain injury (TBI) with healthy controls. Memories and future events were assessed for their episodic detail, autonoetic consciousness and phenomenological characteristics (feelings of (p)re-experiencing and feelings of mental time travel). In a separate study with amnesic patients, Cole et al. (2016) assessed the quality and quantity of episodic future thinking. As with the previous neuropsychological research, patients in both studies were found to recall fewer episodic details for both past and future events than controls. Interestingly, however, phenomenological ratings were not different for past or future events between groups, with feelings of (p)re-experiencing and autonoesis rated similarly in the Rasmussen and Berntsen study, whereas in the Cole et al. study these differences were present and patients performed poorly. Most likely such inconsistencies across studies are due to various factors including severity and location of injury.

The findings of the neuropsychological studies discussed here are highly consistent with the findings of the neuroimaging research reviewed earlier and converge to support the SMS model. Importantly, and additionally, the neuropsychological research also reveals much about the nature of subjective experience present when memories are constructed. The findings here are consistent with the SMS model, emphasizing episodic detail, the role of visual imagery and the (disrupted) nature of the complex generative/strategic memory construction process. What is new here and not part of the SMS model is the phenomenological experience of remembering that is so often impaired following brain injury. It may be that these experiences—perhaps they could be termed *cognitive feelings*—are most probably modulated by control processes that facilitate their expression or inhibition. Feelings of remembering may serve the very useful purpose of allowing a rememberer to know what mental state they are in mind, i.e. remembering or imagining (Conway et al., 2016).

Autobiographical knowledge and future-oriented thought

An important function of memory is to provide information that can be used to anticipate and plan for possible futures (Suddendorf & Corballis, 2007). Recent research has focused especially on the role of memory in the imagination of specific events or scenarios that might occur in one's personal future—often referred to as *episodic future thought* (Atance & O'Neill, 2001; Szpunar, 2010). The prevailing view is that episodic memory provides the constitutive elements or building blocks (e.g., details about objects, persons, locations, actions, and emotions) of imagined events, whereas semantic knowledge affords the conceptual framework or scaffold for constructing coherent scenarios (Irish & Piguet, 2013; Schacter & Addis, 2007). However, the mental representation of a specific event is not the sole ingredient of episodic future thinking. For imagined events to be perceived as possible future occurrences, they need to be placed in an autobiographical context (D'Argembeau, 2016). In this section, we review evidence demonstrating the role of autobiographical knowledge in imagining future events, and the next section proposes an extended version of the SMS that specifies the types of knowledge structures that support future-oriented thought.

Several lines of research indicate that autobiographical knowledge plays an important role in episodic future thinking (for review, see D'Argembeau, 2015). First, there is evidence that the construction of future scenarios is guided by general knowledge about oneself and one's life. For example, when asked to imagine future events in response to cue words, people frequently activate autobiographical knowledge before producing a specific event, and providing knowledge about personal goals facilitates the construction of specific events (D'Argembeau & Mathy, 2011). This suggests that activating general knowledge about goals and anticipated life events is an important first step in episodic future thinking, which then guides and constrains the construction of relevant scenarios. For example, when envisioning events that could occur next summer, a person might first consider the fact that she plans to go on vacation in France, and then she might progressively specify various event features (e.g., place, time, persons, objects, and actions) to construct specific scenarios (e.g., visiting a certain place during her trip).

Other studies have shown that autobiographical knowledge contributes to link and organize imagined future events in higher-order themes and sequences. To investigate the organizational structure of episodic future thoughts, D'Argembeau and Demblon (2012) used an event-cueing paradigm that required participants to produce pairs of future events, the rationale being that the types of relations characterizing the generated pairs of events reflect their organizational structure (Brown & Schopflocher, 1998). The results showed that events within each pair were commonly embedded in broader event sequences—termed event clusters—that link a set of envisioned events according to causal and thematic relations (see also Demblon & D'Argembeau, 2014). Furthermore, this study suggests that knowledge about personal goals plays an important role in structuring event sequences. Another study has shown that self-related future events cluster temporally around expected periods of identity developments, suggesting that future self-images also contribute to the organization of episodic future thoughts (Rathbone et al., 2011). These studies converge on the conclusion that self-images, goals, and other kinds of autobiographical knowledge provide a personal frame for integrating and organizing imagined future events. Furthermore, other recent findings have shown that autobiographical knowledge can also be used to locate imagined events on a personal timeline (Ben Malek et al., 2017).

A fundamental aspect of episodic future thinking is the subjective feeling of travelling into one's personal future to "pre-experience" possible occurrences—referred to as autonoetic experience (Arnold et al., 2011; D'Argembeau & Van der Linden, 2004; Klein, 2016). What shapes this sense of pre-experiencing is not yet fully understood, but there is evidence that connecting events with autobiographical knowledge plays an important role. For example, it has been found that autonoetic experience not only depends on the sensory–perceptual qualities of mental representations (e.g., their vividness) but also on the relevance of imagined events for personal goals (D'Argembeau & Van der Linden, 2012; Lehner & D'Argembeau, 2016). This suggests that the subjective feeling of pre-experiencing one's personal future depends, at least in part, on the extent to which imagined events can be placed in an autobiographical context. Furthermore, the subjective appraisal that an imagined event will actually occur in the future—referred to as belief in occurrence (Scoboria et al., 2014)—also depends on its connection to autobiographical knowledge (e.g., its link with other anticipated events and with general knowledge about oneself and one's life) (Ernst & D'Argembeau, 2017).

Neuroimaging studies provide further support to the idea that autobiographical knowledge, and especially knowledge about personal goals, is an integral part of episodic future thinking. To investigate brain regions supporting goal processing during episodic future thinking, D'Argembeau et al. (2010) asked participants to imagine future events related to their personal goals and future events that were plausible but unrelated to their goals. It was found that cortical midline structures, and notably the medial prefrontal cortex, were more activated when participants were thinking about goal-related than goal-unrelated events. Most neuroimaging studies of episodic future thinking did not explicitly investigate the contribution of goal-related processes (for review, see Schacter et al., 2012), yet if goal processing is an integral part of episodic future thinking, some of the detected brain activations should reflect goal-related processes. In support of this view, a meta-analysis of neuroimaging studies showed that episodic future thinking and goal processing were associated with overlapping activation in several brain regions, including the medial prefrontal cortex (Stawarczyk & D'Argembeau, 2015). An intriguing possibility is that the medial prefrontal cortex might mediate the integration of imagined experiences with higher-order autobiographical knowledge structures (including personal goals), thus contextualizing events within the individual's life story. Possibly this reflects one of the main functions of the remembering–imagining system: integrating imagining with memory. In line with this view, it has recently been found that the processing of future events that are part of the same cluster (i.e., events that are causally or thematically related to each other) is associated with medial prefrontal activation (Demblon et al., 2016).

In summary, the evidence reviewed above shows that, in addition to the construction of specific event representations (based on information gleaned from episodic and semantic memory), episodic future thinking recruits higher-order autobiographical knowledge, which guides the construction of imagined events, organizes them in broader themes and sequences, and contributes to the subjective sense of mentally visiting one's personal future. However, the precise nature of the different kinds of knowledge structures that support episodic future thinking, and how these knowledge domains are organized, has yet to be fully conceptualized. In the next section, we draw on the SMS framework to address these issues.

Future-oriented thought in the SMS

Drawing on the SMS and the evidence reviewed above, we propose that three main kinds of knowledge structures support episodic future thinking and, more generally, other forms of self-related prospection (see figure 3.3). The first knowledge structure contains abstract representations of the self in the future (i.e., ideas of what one might become, what one would like to become, and what one is afraid of becoming) (Markus & Nurius, 1986), which are conceived as part of the conceptual self, along

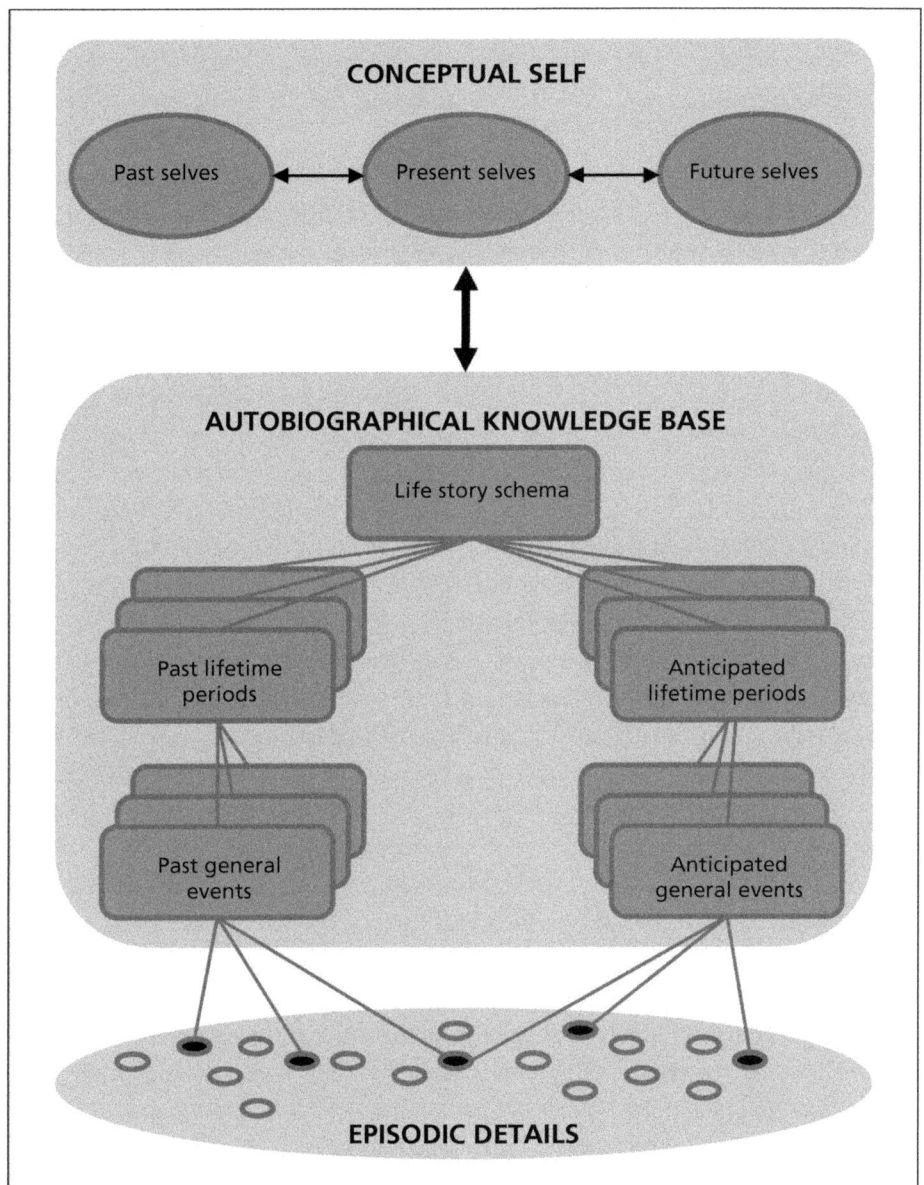

Figure 3.3 Knowledge structures in autobiographical memory and future thought.

with representations of present and past selves (Conway et al., 2004). This future-oriented part of the conceptual self is constituted by semantic knowledge about personal goals and anticipated self-attributes, such as traits (e.g., being self-assured), physical features (e.g., being in good shape), general abilities (e.g., speak well publicly), occupations (e.g., owner of a business), social roles (e.g., being a parent), and life styles (e.g., travel widely). Although the content of present, past, and future selves can differ in important ways, there is some continuity between the three kinds of self-representations—representations of present and past selves influence and constrain what is judged possible for the self in the future, and reciprocally, representations of future selves provide a context for interpreting current and past selves. This is illustrated in figure 3.3 by the double arrows that link past, present, and future selves within the conceptual self.

Goals and self-images that constitute the conceptual self are represented independently from, but interact with, knowledge structures that support the formation of future event representations—the autobiographical knowledge base and episodic memory system. The autobiographical knowledge base contains conceptual knowledge about one's life (Conway, 2005). In the present version of the SMS, we propose to extend the scope of this knowledge base to include representations about one's personal future (see figure 3.3). Within this framework, the life story schema provides an overall representation of a person's entire life that covers both the past and the future (McAdams, 2001). This life story is structured around a series of representations about the broad periods of one's life, not only in the past (e.g., "when I was in high school") but also periods that might characterize one's future life (e.g., "when I'll have moved to X," "when I'll own my own business"). Such lifetime periods include knowledge about the people, places, activities, objects, and goals associated with each period (Thomsen, 2015). Finally, at a more event-specific level, the autobiographical knowledge base contains conceptual representations of general events that occurred in the past or that one anticipates to occur in the future, including summary representations of repeated events (e.g., "taking children to school") and events extended in time (e.g., "going on vacation in France next summer") (Anderson & Dewhurst, 2009; D'Argembeau et al., 2011). As with autobiographical knowledge of the past, future-oriented autobiographical knowledge is organized in partonomic hierarchies, with representations of general events being part of anticipated lifetime periods that in turn constitute the future aspect of the life story schema. This knowledge may in part derive from cultural life scripts (i.e., shared knowledge about a series of events that represents a prototypical life course in a given culture, such as graduation, marriage, and having children (Berntsen & Bohn, 2010) or which may be more idiosyncratic in nature (i.e., based on personal experiences, interests, and goals).

Whereas the autobiographical knowledge base is conceived as including distinct representations for the past and the future (e.g., distinct lifetime periods), the same pool (or at least partly the same pool) of episodic details may be used for the construction of memories and future thoughts that represent specific events (Schacter & Addis, 2007; Suddendorf & Corballis, 2007). These episodic details may consist of components of prior experience (i.e., sensory–perceptual–conceptual–affective details) (Conway, 2009) that serve as the constitutive elements (e.g., places, objects, persons, actions, and so on) of remembered and imagined events. Most of these details may be derived from first-hand personal experiences but some may come from other sources of information, such as the experiences of friends or information gleaned from the media (Anderson, 2012). The idea that remembering and future thinking draw on the same pool of episodic details implies that the exact same element (e.g., a given place) could be used to reconstruct the memory of a past event and to generate the representation of a possible future event. On this view, episodic elements are "atemporal" in themselves and an event representation may only acquire a temporal dimension when it is linked to conceptual autobiographical knowledge structures that locate remembered or imagined events in the individual's life story.

The evidence reviewed in the previous section indicates that knowledge about personal goals plays a central role in structuring future-oriented thought. Goals are cognitive representations of desired states or outcomes (Austin & Vancouver, 1996), and personal goals refer to personally salient objectives that individuals pursue in their daily lives (Emmons, 1986; Klinger, 2013; Little, 1983). These goals focus on either a positive or negative possibility, and they serve a motivational function in guiding the individual toward potential positive outcomes or away from potential negative ones (Elliot & Friedman, 2007). Goal-related knowledge may be represented at different levels in the SMS. Indeed, one important dimension along which personal goals vary is their level of abstractness or generality: people pursue some goals that are very concrete and specific (e.g., striving to arrive at a certain meeting on time), whereas other goals are abstract and general (e.g., being a successful person). These different goal representations are organized in a hierarchy in which higher-order goals (e.g., becoming an artist) determine the content of lower-order goals (e.g., taking painting lessons) (Austin & Vancouver, 1996). Within this framework, episodic future thinking may be conceived as allowing the detailed representation of specific events, plans, and outcomes that are related to higher-order personal goals, which are represented at the level of the autobiographical knowledge base and conceptual self. In other words, an important function of episodic future thinking may be to provide a detailed (quasi-experiential) representation or simulation of what it would be like to be in a desired end-state, and to mentally try out various steps and envisage potential obstacles in achieving this state. According to this view, personal goals drive and constrain future event representations, which in turn motivate and guide goal pursuit.

In summary, we propose that future-oriented thought is supported by three main kinds of knowledge structures. Abstract representations of future goals and personal characteristics are part of the conceptual self, along with representations of present and past selves. Conceptual knowledge about broad lifetime periods and general events that one anticipates to occur in the future is organized in partonomic hierarchies in the autobiographical knowledge base, along with general knowledge about the periods and events of one's personal past. Finally, the episodic memory system contains a pool of experience-near details that can be used both for generating memories of specific past experiences and for constructing representations of specific future events. These different knowledge structures interact with each other and can be flexibly recruited to different degrees depending on situational demands. For example, when thinking about oneself in the distant future, most of the time it might be sufficient to access conceptual knowledge about one's goals and associated time periods to guide current decisions and behavior (e.g., to keep track of long-term goals and set priorities among potentially competing goals). On the other hand, when planning for near future events, it may be useful to construct more detailed event representations (using details sampled from the episodic memory system) to envision possible opportunities and obstacles in achieving one's goals.

The self-memory system: Where are we now?

In some respects it is a remarkable that a model of one of our most complex cognitive abilities, the ability to remember our selves, to be reminded in the present and to imagine the future—the SMS—should turn out to be so strongly supported by such a wide range of behavioral, neuroimaging, and neuropsychological data. Similarly, it is surprising that this model can also apply to future thinking and simulation. There remain, however, certain fundamental questions to be addressed by research, and in closing we consider four of them here (some of the other questions are addressed in other chapters in this book).

(i) *Cues.* The SMS views autobiographical memory, retrospective and prospective, as a highly dynamic system driven by the activating effect of cues. But what does it mean to say that a cue activates items of knowledge in long-term memory? Specifically, how does a single cue 'map' onto an item of knowledge? In other words, what is the process of access? How does it occur? At the neurological level it must be mediated by the firing of neurons, but how this might occur is unclear. For instance, how can a pattern of neural firing represent the lifetime period "When I was at university'? How can lifetime period knowledge such 'Graduation Day' be used to access episodic memories of events from that day? Thus, although the evidence reviewed definitively shows that cues play a central role in memory construction, exactly how they do so is unknown.

(ii) *Specificity.* A key feature of autobiographical memory research focuses on the specificity of memories. Specific episodic details have been termed 'experience-near'. But what does this mean? Episodic details do not replay the actual experience that they represent—they do not reinstate that experience. Somehow the details are derived from experience, perhaps over long periods of memory consolidation (integration of new knowledge with old), but how that derivation takes place is unknown.

(iii) *The problem of encoding.* What do we retain and why? Undoubtedly this is related to an individual's goals and how the complex goal structure selects and filters potential records of experience. There must also be a data-reduction issue here, as the brain, despite its assumed enormous capacity, cannot retain all experiences in detail. Presumably there is some mechanism for this. Some current views suggest that each time a memory is constructed a record is created of that construction (so-called "reconsolidation"). But if the brain retained all the records of all the patterns of activation that constantly arise in autobiographical memory, there could never be a stable memory system—and to at least some extent there is. Why and how we retain what we do is, therefore, also unknown.

(iv) *The formation of future-oriented autobiographical knowledge.* Whereas there is substantial evidence that people possess conceptual knowledge about their personal past, future-oriented autobiographical knowledge has been much less investigated. As outlined in the extended version of the SMS presented here, knowledge about personal goals and anticipated life events guides and constrains the construction of episodic future thoughts, but how this knowledge is formed initially remains to be investigated in detail. It is likely that the general scaffolding of a person's anticipated life is in part determined by culturally shared representations of major transitional events (cultural life scripts) and depends on more idiosyncratic goals and aspirations that are transmitted by parental figures or formed as a result of one's own life experiences. The development of future-oriented autobiographical knowledge and its role in prospective thought and goal pursuit remain, however, largely unexplored.

References

Addis, D. R., Knapp, K., Roberts, R. P., & Schacter, D. L. (2012). Routes to the past: Neural substrates of direct and generative autobiographical memory retrieval. *Neuroimage, 29*, 2908–2922.

Addis, D. R., Sacchetti, D. C., Ally, B. A., Budson, A. E., & Schacter, D. L. (2009). Episodic simulation of future events is impaired in mild Alzheimer's disease. *Neuropsychologia, 47*, 2660–2671.

Anderson, R. J. (2012). Imagining novel futures: the roles of event plausibility and familiarity. *Memory, 20*, 443–51.

Anderson, R. J. & Dewhurst, S. A. (2009). Remembering the past and imagining the future: Differences in event specificity of spontaneously generated thought. *Memory, 17*, 367–373.

Anderson, S. A. & Conway, M. A. (1993). Investigating the structure of autobiographical memories. *Journal of Experimental Psychology: Learning, Memory, and Cognition, 19*, 1178–1196.

Arnold, K. M., McDermott, K. B., & Szpunar, K. K. (2011). Individual differences in time perspective predict autonoetic experience. *Consciousness and Cognition, 20, 712–719.*

Atance, C. M. & O'Neill, D. K. (2001). Episodic future thinking. *Trends in Cognitive Science, 5*, 533–539.

Austin, J. T. & Vancouver, J. B. (1996). Goal constructs in psychology: Structure, process, and content. *Psychological Bulletin, 120*, 338–375.

Barnier, A.J., Conway, M.A., Mayoh, L., & Speyer, J. (2007). Directed forgetting of autobiographical memories. *Journal of Experimental Psychology: General, 136*, 301–322.

Barnier, A. J., Hung, L., & Conway, M. A. (2004). Retrieval-induced forgetting of emotional and unemotional autobiographical memories. *Emotion & Cognition, 18*, 457–477.

Barr, W. B., Goldberg, E., Wasserstein, J., & Novelly, R. A. (1990). Retrograde amnesia following unilateral temporal lobectomy, *Neuropsychologia, 28*, 243–255.

Barsalou, L. W. (1983). Ad hoc categories. *Memory & Cognition, 11*, 211–227.

Barsalou, L. W. (1988). The content and organization of autobiographical memories. In U. Neisser & E. Wonograd (eds), *Remembering reconsidered: Ecological and traditional approaches to the study of memory* (pp. 193–243). Cambridge: Cambridge University Press.

Ben Malek, H., Berna, F., & D'Argembeau, A. (2017). Reconstructing the times of past and future personal events. *Memory, 25*, 1402–1411.

Benoit, R. G. & Schacter, D. L. (2015). Specifying the core network supporting episodic simulation and episodic memory by activation likelihood estimation. *Neuropsychologia, 75*, 450–457.

Berntsen, D. (2012). *Involuntary memories: An introduction to the unbidden past.* Cambridge: Cambridge University Press.

Berntsen, D. & Bohn, A. (2010). Remembering and forecasting: The relation between autobiographical memory and episodic future thinking. *Memory & Cognition, 38*, 265–78.

Berryhill, M. E., Phuong, L., Picasso, L., Cabeza, R., & Olson, I. R. (2007). Parietal lobe and episodic memory: bilateral damage causes impaired free recall of autobiographical memory. *Journal of Neuroscience, 27*, 14415–14423.

Bluck, S. & Habermas (2000). The life story schema. *Motivation and Emotion, 24*, 121–147.

Brewer, W. F. (1988). Memory for randomly sampled autobiographical events. In U. Neisser & E. Winograd (eds.), *Remembering reconsidered: Ecological and traditional approaches to the study of memory* (pp. 21–90). Cambridge: Cambridge University Press.

Brown, J. W. & Chobor, K. L. (1995). Severe retrograde amnesia. *Aphasiology, 9*, 163–170.

Brown, N. R. & Schopflocher, D. (1998). Event clusters: An organization of personal events in autobiographical memory. *Psychological Science, 9*, 470–475.

Buckner, R. L., Andrews-Hanna, J. R., & Schacter, D. L. (2008). The brain's default network - Anatomy, function, and relevance to disease. *Annals of the New York Academy of Sciences, 1124*, 1–38.

Cabeza, R. & St. Jacques, P. (2007). Functional neuroimaging of autobiographical memory. *Trends in Cognitive Sciences*, 11, 219–227.

Cole, S. N., Morrison, C. M., Barak, O., Pauly-Takacs, K., & Conway, M. A. (2016). Amnesia and future thinking: Exploring the role of memory in the quantity and quality of episodic future thoughts. *British Journal of Clinical Psychology, 55*(2), 206-224.

Collins, A. M., & Loftus, E. F. (1975). A spreading activation theory of semantic processing. *Psychological Review, 82*, 407–428.

Conway, M. A. (1996). Autobiographical memories and autobiographical knowledge. In D. C. Rubin (ed.), *Remembering our past: Studies in autobiographical memory.* (pp. 67–93). Cambridge: Cambridge University Press.

Conway, M. A. (2001). Sensory-perceptual episodic memory and its context: autobiographical memory. *Philosophical Transactions of the Royal Society of London B: Biological Sciences, 356*, 1375–1384.

Conway, M. A. (2005). Memory and the self. *Journal of Memory and Language, 53*, 594–628.

Conway, M. A. (2009). Episodic memories. *Neuropsychologia, 47*, 2305–13.

Conway, M. A. & Bekerian, D. A. (1987). Organization in autobiographical memory. *Memory & Cognition, 15*, 119–132.

Conway, M. A. & Loveday, C. (2015). Remembering, imagining, & personal meanings. *Consciousness and Cognition, 33*, 574–581.

Conway, M.A., Loveday, C., & Cole, S.N. (2016). The remembering-imagining system. *Memory Studies, 9*, 256–265.

Conway, M. A. & Piolino, P. (2009). Tous les rouages de notre identite. *La Recherche, 432*.

Conway, M. A. & Pleydell-Pearce, C. W. (2000) The construction of autobiographical memories in the self-memory system. *Psychological Review, 107*, 261–288.

Conway, M. A., Pleydell-Pearce, C. W., Whitecross, & S. Sharpe, H. (2002). Brain imaging autobiographical memory. *The Psychology of Learning and Motivation, 41*, 229–264.

Conway, M.A. & Sauer, A. (2015). Introspecting on memory construction: misconceptions and flawed experiments. *Psychonomics Society Annual Meeting, Chicago 2015*. Abstracts, No. 27, p. 127.

Conway, M. A., Singer, J. A., & Tagini, A. (2004). The self and autobiographical memory: Correspondence and coherence. *Social Cognition, 22*, 495–537.

Coste, C., Navarro, B., Vallat-Azouvi, C., Brami, M., Azouvi, P., & Piolino, P. (2015). Disruption of temporally extended self-memory system following traumatic brain injury. *Neuropsychologia, 71*, 133–145.

D'Argembeau, A. (2015). Knowledge structures involved in episodic future thinking. In A. Feeney & V. A. Thompson (eds.), *Reasoning as memory* (pp. 128–145). Hove, UK: Psychology Press.

D'Argembeau, A. (2016). The role of personal goals in future-oriented mental time travel. In K. Michaelian, S. B. Klein, & K. K. Szpunar (eds.), *Seeing the future: Theoretical perspectives on future-oriented mental time travel* (pp. 199–214). New York: Oxford University Press.

D'Argembeau, A. & Demblon, J. (2012). On the representational systems underlying prospection: Evidence from the event-cueing paradigm. *Cognition, 125*, 160–167.

D'Argembeau, A. & Mathy, A. (2011). Tracking the construction of episodic future thoughts. *Journal of Experimental Psychology: General, 140*, 258–271.

D'Argembeau, A., Renaud, O., & Van der Linden, M. (2011). Frequency, characteristics, and functions of future-oriented thoughts in daily life. *Applied Cognitive Psychology, 25*, 96–103.

D'Argembeau, A., Ruby, P., Collette, F., Degueldre, C., Balteau, E., Luxen, A., Maquet, P., Salmon, E. (2007). Distinct regions of the medial prefrontal cortex are associated with self-referential processing and perspective-taking. *Journal of Cognitive Neuroscience, 19*, 935-944.

D'Argembeau, A., Stawarczyk, D., Majerus, S., Collette, F., Van der Linden, M., Feyers, D., & Salmon, E. (2010). The neural basis of personal goal processing when envisioning future events. *Journal of Cognitive Neuroscience, 22*, 1701–13.

D'Argembeau, A. & Van der Linden, M. (2004). Phenomenal characteristics associated with projecting oneself back into the past and forward into the future: influence of valence and temporal distance. *Consciousness and Cognition, 13*, 844–858.

D'Argembeau, A. & Van der Linden, M. (2012). Predicting the phenomenology of episodic future thoughts. *Consciousness and Cognition, 21*, 1198–206.

D'Argembeau, A., Raffard, S., & Van der Linden, M. (2008). Remembering the past and imagining the future in schizophrenia. *Journal of Abnormal Psychology, 117*, 247.

Demblon, J., Bahri, M. A., & D'Argembeau, A. (2016). Neural correlates of event clusters in past and future thoughts: How the brain integrates specific episodes with autobiographical knowledge. *NeuroImage, 127*, 257–266.

Demblon, J. & D'Argembeau, A. (2014). The organization of prospective thinking: Evidence of event clusters in freely generated future thoughts. *Consciousness and Cognition, 24*, 75–83.

Elliot, A. J. & Friedman, R. (2007). Approach-avoidance: A central characteristic of personal goals. In B. R. Little, K. Salmela-Aro, & S. D. Phillips (eds.), *Personal project pursuit: Goals, action and human flourishing*. Mahwah, NJ: Erlbaum.

Emmons, R. A. (1986). Personal strivings: An approach to personality and subjective well-being. *Journal of Personality and Social Psychology, 51*, 1058–1068.

Ernst, A. & D'Argembeau, A. (2017). Make it real: Belief in occurrence within episodic future thought. *Memory & Cognition, 45*, 1045–1061.

Gilboa, A., Claude, A., Stuss, D., Melo, B., Miller, S. & Moscovitch, M. (2006). Mechanisms of spontaneous confabulations: a strategic retrieval account. *Brain, 129*, 1399–1414.

Irish, M. & Piguet, O. (2013). The pivotal role of semantic memory in remembering the past and imagining the future. *Frontiers in Behavioral Neuroscience, 7*, 27.

Klein, S. B. (2016). Autonoetic consciousness: Reconsidering the role of episodic memory in future-oriented self-projection. *Quarterly Journal of Experimental Psychology, 69*, 381–401.

Haque, S. & Conway, M. A. (2001). Probing the process of autobiographical memory retrieval. *European Journal of Cognitive Psychology, 13*, 529–547.

Hassabis, D., Kumaran, D., & Maguire, E. A. (2007). Using imagination to understand the neural basis of episodic memory. *Journal of Neuroscience, 27*, 14365–14374.

Howe, M. L., Knott, L. M., & Conway, M. A. (2018). *Memory and miscarriages of justice*. Routledge: London.

Humphreys, G. W. & Sui, J. (2016). Attentional control and the self: The Self-Attention Network (SAN). *Cognitive Neuroscience, 7*, 5–7.

Klein, S. B. & Gangi, C. E. (2010). The multiplicity of self: neuropsychological evidence and its implications for the self as a construct in psychological research. *Annals of the New York Academy of Sciences, 1191*, 1–15.

Klein, S. B., Loftus, J., & Kihlstrom, J. F. (2002). Memory and temporal experience: The effects of episodic memory loss on an amnesic patient's ability to remember the past and imagine the future. *Social Cognition, 20*, 353–379.

Klinger, E. (2013). Goal commitments and the content of thoughts and dreams: basic principles. *Frontiers in Psychology, 4*, 415.

Kris, E. (1975). *Selected papers of Ernst Kris*. New Haven: Yale University Press.

Lah, S., Grayson, S., Lee, T., & Miller, L. (2004). Memory for the past after temporal lobectomy: impact of epilepsy and cognitive variables. *Neuropsychologia, 42*, 1666–1679.

Lehner, E. & D'Argembeau, A. (2016). The role of personal goals in autonoetic experience when imagining future events. *Consciousness and Cognition, 42*, 267–276.

Levine, B. (2004). Autobiographical memory and the self in time: Brain lesion effects, functional neuroanatomy, and lifespan development. *Brain and Cognition, 55*, 54–68.

Little, B. R. (1983). Personal projects: A rationale and method for investigation. *Environment and Behavior, 15*, 273–309.

Maguire E. A. (2001). Neuroimaging studies of autobiographical event memory. *Philosophical Transactions of the Royal Society of London, 356*, 1409–1419.

Markus, H. & Nurius, P. (1986). Possible selves. *American Psychologist, 41*, 954–969.

Martinelli, P., Sperduti, M., & Piolino, P. (2013). Neural substrates of the self-memory system: New insights from a meta analysis. *Human Brain Mapping, 34*, 1515–1529.

McAdams, D. P. (2001). The psychology of life stories. *Review of General Psychology, 5*, 100–122.

McCormick, C., Moscovitch, M., Valiante, T. A., Cohn, M., & McAndrews, M. P. (2017). Different neural routes to autobiographical memory recall in healthy people and individuals with left medial temporal lobe epilepsy. *Neuropsychologia, 110*, 26–36.

McDermott, K. B., Szpunar, K. K., & Christ, S. E. (2009). Laboratory-based and autobiographical retrieval tasks differ substantially in their neural substrates. *Neuropsychologia, 47*, 2290–2298.

Moscovitch, M. (1992). Memory and working with memory: a component process model based on modules and central systems. *Journal of Cognitive Neuroscience, 4*, 257–267.

Norman, D. A. & Bobrow, D. G. (1979). Descriptions an intermediate stage in memory retrieval. *Cognitive Psychology, 11*, 107–123.

Noulhiane, M., Piolino, P., Hasboun, D., Clemenceau, S., Baulac, M., & Samson, S. (2008). Autonoetic consciousness in autobiographical memories after medial temporal lobe resection. *Behavioural Neurology, 19*, 19–22.

Ogden, J. A. (1993). Visual object agnosia, prosopagnosia, achromatopsia, loss of visual imagery, and autobiographical amnesia following recovery from cortical blindness: Case MH. *Neuropsychologia, 31*, 571–589.

Rathbone, C. J., Conway, M. A., & Moulin, C. J. A. (2011). Remembering and imagining: the role of the self. *Consciousness & Cognition, 20*, 1175–1182.

Piolino, P., Desgranges, B., Clarys, D., Guillery-Girard, B., Taconnat, L., Isingrini, M., & Eustache, F. (2006). Autobiographical memory, autonoetic consciousness, and self-perspective in aging. *Psychology and aging, 21*(3), 510.

Piolino, P., Desgranges, B., Manning, L., North, P., Jokic, C., & Eustache, F. (2007). Autobiographical memory, the sense of recollection and executive functions after severe traumatic brain injury. *Cortex, 43*, 176–195.

Rasmussen, K. W. & Berntsen, D. (2014). Autobiographical memory and episodic future thinking after moderate to severe traumatic brain injury. *Journal of Neuropsychology, 8*, 34–52.

Rubin, D. C. & Greenberg, D. L. (1998). Visual memory-deficit amnesia: A distinct amnesic presentation and etiology. *Proceedings of the National Academy of Sciences of the USA, 95*, 5413–5416.

Schacter, D. L. & Addis, D. R. (2007). The cognitive neuroscience of constructive memory: remembering the past and imagining the future. *Philosophical Transactions of the Royal Society of London B: Biological Sciences, 362*, 773–786.

Schacter, D. L., Addis, D. R., & Buckner, R. L. (2007). Remembering the past to imagine the future: the prospective brain. *Nature Reviews Neuroscience, 8*, 657–661.

Schacter, D. L., Addis, D. R., Hassabis, D., Martin, V. C., Spreng, R. N., & Szpunar, K. K. (2012). The future of memory: remembering, imagining, and the brain. *Neuron, 76*, 677–94.

Schank, R. C. (1982). *Dynamic memory*. New York: Cambridge University Press.

Scoboria, A., Jackson, D. L., Talarico, J., Hanczakowski, M., Wysman, L., & Mazzoni, G. (2014). The role of belief in occurrence within autobiographical memory. *Journal of Experimental Psychology, General, 143*, 1242–1258.

St. Jacques, P. L. & De Brigard, F. (2015). Neural correlates of autobiographical memory: Methodological considerations. In D. R. Addis, M. Barense, & A. Durate (eds.), *Cognitive neuroscience of memory* (pp. 265–286). Chichester: Wiley–Blackwell.

Stawarczyk, D. & D'Argembeau, A. (2015). Neural correlates of personal goal processing during episodic future thinking and mind-wandering: An ALE meta-analysis. *Human Brain Mapping, 36*, 2928–2947.

Suddendorf, T. & Corballis, M. C. (2007). The evolution of foresight: What is mental time travel and is it unique to humans? *Behavioral and Brain Sciences, 30,* 299–351.

Svoboda, E., McKinnon, M. C., & Levine, B. (2006). The functional neuroanatomy of autobiographical memory: A meta-analysis. *Neuropsychologia, 44,* 2189–2208.

Szpunar, K. K. (2010). Episodic future thought: An emerging concept. *Perspectives on Psychological Science, 5,* 142–162.

Thomsen, D. K. (2015). Autobiographical periods: A review and central components of a theory. *Review of General Psychology, 19,* 294–310.

Trope, Y. & Liberman, N. (2003). Temporal construal. *Psychological Review, 110,* 403–421.

Tulving, E. (1985). Memory and consciousness. *Canadian Psychology/Psychologie canadienne, 26,* 1.

Tulving, E. (2002). Episodic memory: from mind to brain. *Annual Review of Psychology, 53,* 1–25.

Uzer, T., Lee, P. J., & Brown, N. R. (2012). On the prevalence of directly retrieved autobiographical memories. *Journal of Experimental Psychology: Learning, Memory, and Cognition, 38,* 1296–1308.

Voltzenlogel, V., Després, O., Vignal, J. P., Steinhoff, B. J., Kehrli, P., & Manning, L. (2006). Remote memory in temporal lobe epilepsy. *Epilepsia, 47,* 1329–1336.

Williams, D. M. & Hollan, J. D. (1981). The process of retrieval from very long-term memory. *Cognitive Science, 5,* 87–119.

Williams, J. M. G., Ellis, N. C., Tyers, C., Healy, H., Rose, G., & Macleod, A. K. (1996). The specificity of autobiographical memory and imageability of the future. *Memory & Cognition, 24,* 116–125.

4

Development and Organization of Autobiographical Memory Form and Function

Robyn Fivush and Theodore E. A. Waters

Introduction

When asked to narrate a significant life experience, one young college student responded:

> The summer before my senior year in high school, I enrolled in the summer program for high school students at [University 1] in [City 1]. I was excited to be in a big city (I am from a small town in [State 1]) and nervous to be away from home. When I arrived in [City 1], I was overwhelmed with all the hustle and fast pace of the city life. I spent one month there, taking a course in genetics. While [University 1] enriched my mind, the people I met there changed who I was and helped me discover who I wanted to be.
>
> I met many great people there, however there were two girls who I became particularly close with—one was [Person 1], a girl from [State 2]. She brought me around the city because she was familiar with it. We also lived together in the same suite. I instantly became attached to her within days of knowing her. [Person 1] was also in my particular class on genetics so we were also study buddies. She filled the void that was left when I left my comfort zone at home; my family and friends. Then there was Chelsea from [State 3]. The three of us became best friends over the course of those 4 weeks. We did everything from going to [Neighborhood 1] to get knock-off designer purses, to shopping almost daily at [Store 1], to getting lost (a lot) on the [Public Transit System]. Our friendship taught me so much. I learned how to allow people I barely knew into my life and allow them to know things about me that others do not. Although I only knew [Person 1] and [Person 2] for four weeks by the end of the program, I felt as if I had known them longer than some of my close friends. Even now, two years later, we still face-book each other with updates on our lives and I hope I will be able to see them again.

Although autobiographical memory is commonly defined as memories of our personal past experiences, as this example demonstrates, this simple definition belies the complexity and dynamism of both the content and structure of autobiographical memory.

Whereas in the memory literature, autobiographical memory is often studied as recall of factual information about specific episodic events, as this example makes clear, when individuals recall their past, the process involves a fluid movement among specific episodic events that occurred at a single point in time, recurring events that are experienced at multiple time points, extended events that stretch over long periods of time, and even semantic and conceptual information about the self, such as where one was born or that one is somewhat introverted, or values family. Further, information about the external actions that occurred are told in a context that privileges thoughts, emotions, and evaluations, how one understands and makes sense of these experiences in terms of who one is in the world, and moves fluidly through time, from past to present to future. This brief excerpt suggests that autobiographical memory is organized as multiply embedded subjective and temporal frameworks, and further, that narrating autobiographical experiences moves beyond chronological recounting to include functional information about self and relationships.

In this chapter, we expand current approaches to autobiographical memory through delineating the complexity of temporal frameworks for remembering and organizing our past. We argue that principles of narrative structure provide a critical tool for the creation of coherent and meaningful autobiographical memories. Although autobiographical memory is not represented exclusively in linguistic or narrative form (see, e.g. Rubin, 2005), the developing ability to construct coherent narratives facilitates the ability to understand both specific episodic events and organize those events to create an overarching life story, or autobiography (Fivush et al., 2011). Thus we need to consider the narrative organization of autobiography at multiple levels, the specific event, recurring events, extended events, and the entire life narrative. Moreover, children learn the forms and functions of autobiographical narratives through participating in everyday social interactions that model these forms and highlight their cultural value (Fivush, 2013). We begin by defining autobiographical memory, moving from its initial conception as episodic memory to include multiple temporal horizons, and we then describe the development of autobiographical narratives within sociocultural interactions beginning early in development. In making these arguments, we further demonstrate that the functions of autobiographical memory, in particular functions of defining self and relationships with others, necessitate a more fluid and dynamic organization that links events together across time.

Defining autobiographical memory

In 1972, Tulving made the now classic distinction between episodic and semantic memory. Whereas semantic memory was generalized information, or knowledge, about the world (e.g., the Eiffel tower is in Paris), episodic memory was of specific experiences that happened at a particular time and place (e.g., the day I visited the Eiffel tower and got stuck in the elevator). Episodic memory was differentiated from semantic memory in two ways: first, it was pinpointed in a specific temporal and spatial context, and, second, it included the phenomenological sense of reliving, of remembering the self-engaging in the event. This historical distinction laid the groundwork for equating episodic memory, defined as an experience subjectively recalled as occurring in a specific time and place, with autobiographical memory, memory of one's personal past. But even early on, theorists realized that autobiographical memory could not be fully defined as episodic memories of the past. Larson (1991) defined autobiographical memory as memory of personal experiences embedded in the context of one's life. Within that broad category of memory, Brewer (1988) outlined four potential basic classes of autobiographical memory: personal memory, autobiographical facts, generic personal memory, and a self-schema. Personal memories describe unique single events, or experiences, in one's life. They often prompt a feeling of reliving the experience during recollection, including strong visual and affective components. Autobiographical facts are declarative fragments typically reported without accompanying mental imagery (e.g., the date of your birth). Generic personal memories contain information from a repeated set of similar experiences (recurring events). Brewer suggested that because these memories consist of a combination of multiple similar experiences, they lack the element of uniqueness attributed to personal memories. Last of all, the self-schema contains a large body of generic autobiographical information, and provides an integrated set of beliefs about one's self (e.g., "I enjoy going to the movies with friends").

Brewer (1988) provided a necessary description of what autobiographical memory is the memory of. Autobiographical memory is not simply a list of facts, nor an unconnected series of unique personally meaningful episodes, but it is instead a broad set of specific and generic facts and experiences with varying levels of vividness derived from both unique and recurring personal experiences. Beyond the basic contents of autobiographical memory, Conway and Pleydell-Pearce (2000) proposed a model of the basic structure and organization of the contents of autobiographical memory that includes both specific-level event knowledge and more generalized events and life periods. Indeed, Barsalou (1988) demonstrated more than two decades ago that when college students were asked to recall what they did over their summer break they produced a variety of distinct event types that varied in terms of time scale and level of specificity/schematization. When recalling the past, individuals move seamlessly among multiple specific episodes, as informed by larger life themes, and embedded within recurring and extended events, as our narrative example at the beginning of this chapter illustrates.

Autobiographical memory researchers also began to consider the functions of autobiographical memory. In 1982, Neisser challenged researchers to consider how memories were used in the everyday world, and in 1988 Alan Baddeley famously asked of autobiographical memory, "But what the hell is it for?" These theorists spurred research from a more ecological perspective, querying the functions of recalling specific details of a personal past, and suggested that autobiographical memory was not simply about accurate recall of the past in order to direct future behavior, but also served more socioemotional functions. Theorists from social and personality psychology furthered arguments that autobiographical memories were as much about defining who we are as what we should do (see especially Bluck, 2003; Greenwald, 1980; McAdams, 1996).

Bringing these threads together, some researchers of autobiographical memory began to consider how the structure and functions of autobiographical memory provide complementary ways of understanding how and what individuals recall of their personal past. Indeed, Conway and Pleydell-Pearce (2000) posit that autobiographical memory is about defining the self and achieving both local and life goals (see also Conway et al., 2004). Conway and colleagues posit a hierarchical organization with life themes at the top of the hierarchy, and event-specific knowledge at the bottom. Yet these frameworks are posited as retrieval guides with the ultimate goal still being recall of specific episodes as the index of autobiographical memory. The overwhelming majority of research on autobiographical memory remains focused on individuals' recall of specific episodes, and being able to retrieve a specific event located at a specified time in a particular place remains the "gold standard" of autobiographical recall (Williams & Broadbent, 1986). Similarly, within the developmental literature, the advent of autobiographical memory is usually conflated with the development of episodic memory, and empirical questions focus on when in development infants can recall specific episodes located in time and space (see Bauer, 2006; Bauer et al., 2010, for an excellent theoretical and empirical review of this literature). The underlying assumption is that the ability to recall specific details of an experience located in a specific temporal–spatial nexus is the hallmark of "true" autobiographical memory.

We take a different approach. We argue that autobiographical memory is not equivalent to episodic memory, that it follows a different developmental trajectory, that it serves different functions, and that it is organized in different ways. More specifically, we argue that Tulving's (1972) equivalence of episodic memory with autobiographical memory is both too broad and too narrow. It is too broad in that not all episodic memories are autobiographical, and it is too narrow, in that not all autobiographical memories are episodic (see Fivush, 2010; and Fivush & Graci, in press; and Fivush & Waters, 2013, for additional theoretical arguments). To foreshadow our arguments, we present a sociocultural developmental account of autobiographical memory that privileges how memories are shared through language in social interaction to achieve social and emotional goals. It is in the very process of sharing memories that memories take on narrative form that integrates event information with personal meaning to become autobiographical. As we will argue, it is through sharing events with others that children learn the forms and functions of narrating experiences in coherent and detailed ways, and begin to organize and represent their personal experiences in narrative form (Fivush, 2013; Fivush et al., 2006). With development, narratives of recurring events and unique experiences are embedded within larger life narratives that encompass a sense of coherence and meaning across a lifetime (Fivush et al., 2011; Habermas & Reese, 2015). In this chapter, we begin early in development, with the emergence of narrative organization across the preschool years, and show developmentally how autobiographical memory becomes a fluid system moving seamlessly among temporal horizons in the service of defining self and relationships.

The sociocultural model of autobiographical memory narratives

Narratives are the key cultural tool for organizing an autobiography. In 2004, Nelson and Fivush laid out a sociocultural developmental model of autobiographical narrative memory based on Vygotsky's (1978) developmental theories. Vygotsky argued that children are socialized to become competent members of their culture, and that the tools, skills, and values of the culture are internalized through participating in adult-guided activities. Literacy is a good example, as it is clearly a vital skill in industrialized modern cultures. Well before infants can understand what these squiggles may mean, they are surrounded by the tools of literacy: letters and numbers are emblazoned on their clothes, their toys, refrigerator magnets, and so on, and adults are singing alphabet songs and playing rhyming games with them before they can even speak. Soon after, they are expected to participate in these activities, learning letters and numbers, and engaging with adults in songs and rhymes. The heavy presence and focus on these kinds of activities brings children into this mediated literate world, and provides the necessary tools to achieve the cultural value of being literate.

Just as literacy is valued in industrialized Western cultures, so is being able to tell one's personal story. Whether it is meeting new friends, writing a college essay, engaging in a job interview, or meeting a possible romantic partner, individuals are expected to have a coherent and compelling narrative of who they are and how they came to be that way. This is perhaps especially valued in industrialized Western cultures, where individuals move from place to place, constantly meet new people, and need to define themselves across times and places as a coherent person (Fivush, 2010; McAdams, 2015; Nelson, 2003). These skills and values are already on display as soon as infants enter the world. Parents whisper stories of the family into infants' ears (Fiese et al., 1995), and begin to engage them in telling their own narrative as soon as they can talk. Preschoolers are encouraged to tell Mommy what they did at daycare, and tell Grandma about the birthday party. In preschool, children sit in story circles and tell what they did over the weekend, or about a special event. By middle school children are writing their autobiography, and by adolescence, individuals are challenged to create a life narrative that frames their past, present, and future self in terms of motivations, commitments, roles, and values (Erikson, 1968; McAdams, 2001).

In these ways, cultures pull individuals into storying their life, and narratives provide the organizational framework, both for specific episodes, and to link disparate experiences together into a coherent narrative of who one is and who one might become across extended periods of time, perhaps a lifetime. This account clearly privileges language, and more specifically, narrative, as a cultural tool for creating and organizing individual autobiography. Narratives move beyond a simple chronology of actions in the world in at least four ways (Bruner, 1990; Chafe, 1990; Fivush, 2011; Labov & Waletzky, 1997; Ricouer, 1991). First, narratives carve the unremitting flow of experience into meaningful units with beginnings, middles, and ends. Second, these units can be at multiple levels of spatial and temporal organization, from a specific activity located in a specific time and place (breakfast this morning at home) to a lifetime period (when I lived in Minneapolis). In this way, narratives place experiences within simultaneously embedded spatial and temporal contexts that can be both local, and more general, creating a temporal hierarchy that organizes experiences across the lifetime (e.g., Conway & Pleydell-Pearce, 2000). Third, narratives include more than a recounting of actions in the world; narratives include intentions, thoughts, and emotions of self and of other, creating human causes and consequences. By integrating actions in the world with inner states and reactions, narratives create a sense of agentic self, experiences do not simply happen, they happen *to and because of me*, and thus define who I am. Finally, because narratives are social, both in their content, such that other people's inner worlds are also described, and in practice, in that they are socially shared, narratives define relationships over time. Culturally mediated canonical narrative forms develop gradually as children participate in social interactions that model and frame narrative tellings of personal experience. Moreover, through participating in social reminiscing, children are further internalizing the cultural functions of autobiographical narrative, to define self through one's personal experiences, and to create social bonds across time through creating a shared history and engaging in shared reminiscing (Fivush et al., 2006; Beike et al., 2016).

In the remainder of this chapter, we flesh out these arguments in three sections. First, we describe the emergence of narrative organization in early childhood, showing how children learn the forms and functions of autobiographical narratives in socially mediated interactions. Second, we delineate how initial narrative organization expands, especially through adolescence and early adulthood, to encompass larger life periods and the creation of a life narrative that provides coherent themes of self and relationships across discrete experiences. Third, we review recent research from our laboratory that demonstrates how adults differentiate both the forms and functions of narrating specific episodes, recurring events, and extended events. This research supports the argument that autobiographical memory is a complex intertwining of multiple levels of temporally organized experiences serving multiple self and social functions. We conclude that narrative forms and functions of autobiographical memory are dynamic, and that autobiographical memory is best conceptualized as an iteratively organized series of narrative timelines that simultaneously include specific episodes, recurring events, and extended events, all in the service of defining a self in relation to others.

The emergence of narrative organization

Narrating episodes

Although it is clear that even infants have temporally organized representations (see Bauer, 2006, for a review), language permits a new form of temporal organization through narrative that allows children to recall experiences in more coherent ways (Nelson, 1998). Children begin to reference past events almost as soon as they begin to use language at all, at about 14–16 months of age (Eisenberg, 1985; Uehara, 2015), indicating that they are motivated to share their experiences with others. However, before 3 years of age, references to past events are quite fleeting, and most often refer either to recurring events, such as a bedtime routine, or to specific events that had occurred on that day (Nelson, 2006). For example, the child might look up from play and say "Berries!," arguably referring to what they ate for breakfast. References to past experiences become more frequent and refer to more distant events across the first few years of life, and by 3 years of age children can verbally recall specific details of events that occurred as long as 6 months in the past (e.g. Bauer et al., 2000; Fivush et al., 1987; Nelson & Ross, 1980), as well as provide coherent accounts of recurring events, such as grocery shopping or going to McDonald's (Nelson & Gruendel, 1986).

Importantly, children are already differentiating between specific and recurring events in their verbal accounts. At 2–3 years of age, verbal recall of specific past events is not quite coherent. Very young children rarely place the recalled event in time and space, and do not link actions together in any coherent fashion. Although they may recall actions in accurate chronological order, they do not provide any temporal or causal links between actions in their verbal reports. Before the age of 3 years, children rarely use the past tense appropriately, and confuse past experiences and future expectations in their narratives (Nelson, 2006; Uehara, 2015). The ability to provide more coherent narrative accounts of specific past experiences develops quite rapidly from age 3 to 5 years, and by the end of the preschool years most children, at least in Western cultures, are able to provide fairly coherent narrative accounts of specific personally experienced events (see Reese et al., 2011, for a full theoretical and empirical discussion). Moreover, these narratives almost always include an evaluative component, commenting on internal states and motivations (Haden et al., 1997; McCabe & Peterson, 1991). Thus we see a clear progression in narrative form across the preschool years from a relatively unstructured list of details to a temporally organized narrative that includes explicit links among actions and integrates inner states in ways that indicate self-agency and reaction to the event.

In contrast, even 3-year-olds provide coherent accounts of recurring events. Moreover, these events are told in the timeless present tense, even well after children have mastered past tense usage, and most often told in the impersonal "you do" or generalized "we do" rather than the personal "I did" (see Nelson & Gruendel, 1986, for a full review). Scripted accounts usually do not include any evaluative information or refer to any inner states, suggesting that they are oriented toward accounting for how the world works, serving the function of predicting and directing future behavior. This early differentiation of event types suggests that it is not linguistic or cognitive skill alone that accounts for these differing narrative forms, but rather that children are already differentiating these types of events in their representations, and perhaps even using them for different functions.

An important question raised in this literature is whether narrative forms simply reflect children's developing ability to represent events in more coherent and temporally organized ways, or whether narrative forms help children to organize their experiences. A definitive answer to this question is empirically difficult to assess, but there is some suggestion that narrative is not merely a medium of expression. For example, children's expressive language and narrative ability at time of experience limits what they can subsequently recall about the event, such that children have difficulty recalling aspects of events that they did not have the language to express at time of experiences (Peterson & Rideout, 1998; Simcock & Hayne, 2002). Perhaps more relevant, there is a great deal of evidence that individual differences in the narrative forms to which children are exposed in early development have long-lasting effects on children's developing autobiographical memory, an issue to which we now turn.

Maternal narrative style

In line with the sociocultural developmental model of autobiographical memory, the development of coherent verbal narratives occurs within everyday social interactions in which families reminisce about their past experiences together and is highly modulated by these social interactions. Mothers (for pragmatic and theoretical reasons most research is with mothers, but see Fivush & Zaman, 2013, for a review of research with fathers as well) vary along a dimension of elaboration. Highly elaborative mothers reminisce more frequently about their past with their young children, and they engage in more detailed and more coherently organized reminiscing than less elaborative mothers. For example, here is one mother reminiscing about a sad event with her 4-year-old daughter:

MOTHER: Well, one thing that made you really sad is when your best friend Sheila moved away, right?
DAUGHTER: (nods)
MOTHER: Yeah, and did we watch all her things go on the moving truck?
DAUGHTER: (nods)
MOTHER: Uh-huh, and do you remember why she had to move away?
DAUGHTER: ... Because Sheila's Dad had to work.
MOTHER: Sheila's Daddy was going to start working at a new job ... And do you still miss Sheila when you think about it? Yes?
DAUGHTER: Yes.
MOTHER: It makes you sad. Doesn't it?
DAUGHTER: (nods)
MOTHER: But is she still your friend even far away?
DAUGHTER: (nods)
MOTHER: Yes! What can you do even though she's far away?
DAUGHTER: Give her a happy letter with a (drawing) on it.
MOTHER: Give her a happy letter, right, and we have a drawing, don't we?

As can be seen in this example, the mother introduces the event, and, although the daughter is engaged in responding to the mother, the daughter initially offers little information. But the mother continues to structure her questions in such a way that the story unfolds. When the daughter does recall some information, the mother weaves it into the emerging narrative. Note also that the mother talks about what happened, why it happened, and how the daughter felt about it, thus creating a story with meaning for self and relationships. Finally, the end of the story moves the events into the present and the future, creating a more extended personal timeline. In all these ways, the mother has helped the child weave the limited recalled details into a coherent and meaningful narrative. More highly elaborative mothers both model and teach their children to tell more coherently organized narratives. And, indeed, longitudinal research across the preschool years demonstrates that children of more highly elaborative mothers come to tell more coherent and detailed narratives than children of less elaborative mothers (see Fivush et al., 2006, for a review). More specifically, mothers who place experiences in more specific temporal and spatial context, when reminiscing with their toddler, have preschoolers who subsequently provide more contextual information in their own personal narratives (Peterson et al., 1999). And mothers who use more temporal and causal links in their co-narrations, such as "and then," "and so," and "because," have children who use more of these temporal and causal links in their own narratives later in development (Fivush, 1991; Haden et al., 1997). The specificity of the relations between the kinds of temporal spatial language mothers use in early co-narrations and how children integrate these same narrative devices in their later narratives indicates that children are learning specific narrative skills in these early interactions.

Importantly, these early mother–child reminiscing conversations also help children to use their memories more functionally. Children of mothers who reminisce in more highly elaborative ways show a more differentiated sense of self at the end of the preschool years, show higher understanding of theory of mind (the idea that self and others have beliefs, desires, thoughts, and so on), and better emotion regulation than children of mothers who are less elaborative when reminiscing (Laible & Thompson, 2000; Reese et al., 2007). Most intriguing, these effects are specific to reminiscing contexts. Mother–child reminiscing predicts unique variance in children's developing understanding of self and emotion compared to mother–child talk in other contexts (Laible, 2004; Bird & Reese, 2006). That elaborative reminiscing is uniquely related to these developing social and emotional skills suggests that mothers are helping their children to use their past experiences in functional ways to define and regulate self, emotions, and relationships. In fact, when asked why they reminisce about the past with their young children, mothers report engaging in this activity in order to help their child understand who they are and to enhance emotional bonds (Kulkofsky et al., 2009).

The examination of parent–child reminiscing reveals the emerging functions of autobiographical memory, as more elaborative event narratives begin to define self and regulate emotions, and generalized events provide frameworks for understanding routines and relationships, and for predicting future events. But, as yet, children are not linking individual events, either specific or scripted, into larger units that cross time and create a coherent personal history

From narrative episodes to life narratives

As children develop through middle childhood and adolescence, they begin to form longer and larger life narratives, linking events together into a personal timeline. Moreover, these developments continue to be situated within sociocultural contexts that provide both the forms and functions of this type of extended autobiographical narrative (Fivush et al., 2011; Habermas & Reese, 2015). Theoretically, two critical developmental transitions happen during this developmental period. First, as children enter middle childhood, about age 8–10 years, they begin to learn the cultural forms of a life script (Berntsen & Rubin, 2004); second, as children transition into adolescence, they begin to use this life script as a template to create a personal life narrative that links discrete personal experiences into a story of self (Habermas & Bluck, 2000).

Life scripts

Cultures provide structural templates for what a typical life looks like, including the expected events, such as schooling, graduation, getting married, having children, and so on, as well as the temporal sequencing of these events. Although somewhat culturally specific, adults in a wide variety of cultures studied provide very similar events and timing of events that define a typical life of an individual born into that culture (e.g., Berntsen & Rubin, 2004; Bohn & Berntsen, 2008; Thomsen & Berntsen, 2008). Bohn and Berntsen (2008) demonstrated that children learn these cultural scripts in middle childhood, before they begin to link their own personal stories into a life narrative. It seems that learning the cultural life script provided the organizational structure for children to begin to tell their own life story in a more coherent, extended way as children with greater knowledge of the cultural life script told more organized and coherent life stories. However, cultural life script knowledge did not predict coherence of single event narratives. Thus the creation of one's own life story is structured by culturally provided life scripts that define, organize, and constrain how we recall our lives (Fivush, 2010).

Life narratives and narrative identity

As children transition into adolescence, they are faced with the task of developing a healthy adult identity (Erikson, 1968; McAdams, 2001). With increasing cognitive and social skills, adolescents become capable of more complex perspective-taking, and more abstract and hypothetical thinking, setting the stage for the development of a more extended abstract sense of identity (Habermas & Bluck, 2000). With these new skills, adolescents are also challenged by their sociocultural environment to think about who they are and who they want to be (Habermas & Reese, 2015). Adolescents must now consider life tasks, including professional and personal choices that confront them with the need to create a more coherent sense of identity that persists across time. Thus, there is a major impetus to forming a more coherent extended life narrative of how individuals become the person they are and who they will be into the future. Moreover, these developing life narratives have the explicit function of defining self as coherent and continuous over time (e.g., McAdams, 1996, 2001).

Two skills especially develop during middle childhood and into adolescence that are crucial for the development of a life narrative, temporal reasoning, and autobiographical reasoning (Habermas & Reese, 20015). Whereas preschoolers can easily sequence actions within specific episodes and temporally organized scripted events, they have difficulty with temporally organizing events in relation to each other. Friedman and his colleagues (see Friedman, 1992, 1993, for reviews) have done extensive research documenting that the ability to sequence a series of events into a coherent timeline is actually quite a difficult task that develops gradually across middle childhood. Young children, 6–8 years old, can accurately sequence two unique events in time, but are confused by recurring events. So if asked which event was most recent, their birthday or Christmas, two events that occur annually, 8-year-old children cannot easily figure this out. By age 10 years, child can sequence these kinds of recurring events, but still have surprising difficulty with calendar time, and will make sequencing errors when asked to place multiple events on a conventional calendar timeline. It is not until age 12 years that we see adult levels of temporal understanding, which is a clear cornerstone of the developing ability to create a coherent life narrative that integrates events into a personal timeline.

Autobiographical reasoning, as conceptualized by Habermas and his colleagues (e.g., Habermas & Bluck, 2000; Habermas & Köber, 2015; Habermas et al., 2010), builds on the development of temporal sequencing of life events, to include causal and autobiographical links among experiences. Whereas children in middle childhood are beginning to create more extended temporal sequences of life events, it is not until adolescence that individuals are able to create personally meaningful links among their experiences. These links include creating causal connections between events (e.g., "Because I went to computer camp, I became really interested in building robots, and that led me to join the computer club at school and build a robot for the science fair"), as well as autobiographical connections between events and self-understanding (e.g., "Winning the science fair was really important to me because it made me realize that if I work hard, I can achieve my goals").

Importantly, temporal, causal, and autobiographical reasoning develop in parentally scaffolded interactions. Just as mothers' scaffold coherent narratives of single events during the preschool years in ways that facilitate children's developing event representations, mothers continue to expand their scaffolding to help their children develop more extended life sequences. In a series of longitudinal studies by Habermas and his colleagues (Habermas & de Silveira, 2008; Habermas & Köber, 2015; Habermas et al., 2010), they have demonstrated that early in middle childhood, when children are about 8–10 years of age, mothers focus on helping their children accurately sequence life events in time. By adolescence, mothers are focusing less on temporal sequence per se, and more on causal and autobiographical reasoning. Furthermore, tracing these skills across time, children are learning these skills by participating in these structured life narratives with their mothers. Thus, 8-year-olds cannot temporally structure their life story on their own, but need the help of their mothers to create the timeline. By age 12 years, adolescents can create the timeline for themselves, but need their mothers to complicate this timeline with causal reasoning that links events together. Even at age 16 years, adolescents are still somewhat dependent on their mothers to create complex life narratives that integrate causal and autobiographical reasoning. It is not until age 20 years that young adults can independently construct complicated life narratives that define self over time.

Thus, through middle childhood and adolescence, children are expanding their autobiographical narrative repertoire to include more extended life experiences that link disparate events together into personally meaningful sequences. Moreover, these developments continue to occur within sociocultural contexts that value certain ways of telling a life and linking events together. Thus, as individuals enter adulthood, autobiographical narratives are not necessarily single experiences located in time and space, but include multiple types of events—single, extended, and scripted—all of which have developed in sociocultural contexts that highlight both form and function.

Form and function of single, recurring, and extended events

From early childhood through middle childhood and adolescence, we see the development of both scripted and episodic narrative representations of experience. Interestingly, in both early and middle childhood, scripted representations seem to develop before more specific, episodic narratives. Both develop within sociocultural contexts that provide the narrative templates for these forms, as well as in more local social interactions in which parents, and especially mothers, scaffold the narrative with the child in ways that both bring children into the world of narratives and help them learn the specific skills of narration for organizing their experience. Thus far, we have focused on learning the forms of narrative autobiographical memory, and have only touched on the functions. But, as noted by Baddeley (1988) more than three decades ago, we need to think seriously about what functions this form of memory might serve.

Functions of autobiographical memory and narrative

Theory on the functions of autobiographical memory has largely settled on the three core functions of self-definition, relationship maintenance and social closeness, and directing behavior (e.g., Bluck & Alea, 2002; Hyman & Faries, 1992; Nelson, 2003; Pillemer, 1998, 2003; Robinson & Swanson, 1990; Waters, et al., 2014). Empirical research examining the existence of these functions has increasingly provided support for the three basic functions of autobiographical memory (self, social, and directive). Further, research has found support for the three functions in cross-cultural samples and comparisons (e.g., Maki et al., 2015; Reese & Neha, 2015; Wang et al., 2015).

Several studies have also examined the extent to which using autobiographical memories to serve self, social, or directive functions is adaptive. For example, examining the directive function of autobiographical memories, Kuwabara et al. (2011) found that school-aged children who generated more autobiographical memories during problem-solving also generated more potential solutions for the problems during a laboratory-based task. This result supported the prediction that individuals who are more adept at recruiting autobiographical memories to serve a basic function—directive in the present case—show an adaptive advantage. Several studies have also suggested that individuals who use memories to serve social functions tend to report closer and more satisfying relationships. For example, Alea and Vick (2010) found that individuals who claimed to rehearse memories that defined their relationship with their romantic partner more often reported higher levels of marital satisfaction (see also Alea & Bluck, 2007). Waters (2014) examined associations between all three functions of autobiographical memory and multiple domains of psychological well-being. Results indicated that all three functions positively predicted well-being in terms of a sense of purpose and more positive intimate relationships. These results suggest that the ability to use our autobiographical memories can be highly adaptive across multiple domains of adjustment.

Different forms for different functions?

Most research on functions of autobiographical memory rely on self-report questionnaires of how individuals use their memories in everyday situations. But how might different temporal forms of autobiographical remembering relate to different functions? Guided by Barsalou's (1988) earlier work, Waters and colleagues (Fivush & Waters, 2013; Waters et al., 2014; Waters & Fivush, 2015) argued that there are three organizationally related but distinct categories of autobiographical memories—single, recurring, and extended events—and that these organizational forms lend themselves to different functions. Single events are defined as unique and fixed in a specific time and place (e.g., a wedding). Recurring events, in contrast, are not unique but are generally occurring during a similar time and place across instances, and are more like scripted representations (e.g., Christmas dinner at the family home). Extended events represent larger continuous temporal periods in life that can span weeks or even years (e.g., my time working for the United Nations).

These different forms of autobiographical memories are freely produced and endorsed by individuals in multiple research contexts. For example, Barsalou (1988) found that during free recall about 20% of the autobiographical content recalled was related to specific events, 30% to recurring events, and 10% to extended events, with the remaining 40% being general autobiographical information (e.g., likes/dislikes). Barsalou (1988) found that cued recall produced even higher proportions of recurring or extended events, combining for roughly 60% of autobiographical information being recalled. These findings suggest that autobiographical memories are fluidly and dynamically organized and accessed along multiple temporal dimensions.

Given these multiple temporal organizations, Waters et al. (2014) asked whether different temporal forms of autobiographical memory might serve different functions. Thus, they examined autobiographical memory functions served by single, recurring, and extended events across two studies of emerging adults. They argued that single events, because of their uniqueness, would be best suited for self-definition (especially in industrialized Western cultures where uniqueness and individuality are valued). Recurring and extended events, however, might be better suited for the social function because they capture longer periods of time and are thus better able to communicate the development and value of a relationship in the larger context of one's life. To examine these hypotheses, Waters et al. (2014) elicited autobiographical narratives of single, recurring, and extended events, and coded them for the expression of the functions they served. They also collected self-report questionnaire data on the functions each event served. The result indicated that different event types were easily accessed and narrated and that they differentially served the functions of autobiographical memory. Specifically, single events were most strongly associated with the self function compared to recurring events. Recurring events were relatively high on the social function in comparison to single events. Interestingly, extended events were high on all three functions of autobiographical memory.

To illustrate these different forms and functions, we present examples of each narrative type. The first is a participant asked about a single episodic experience:

After 11th grade, I traveled to [Country 1] on a volunteer surgical trip with a group of surgeons. [This trip had left tons of lasting memories] but the most lasting experience was at a particular village, for a clinic session, there were easily 1000 people in line waiting for medical help, and some people had traveled for over a day at the notice that 8 [Country 2] doctors were available. I was working with my father, a [Doctor—Specialty 1] as a translator. At the end of the day, we had to leave in order to catch a boat crossing [Lake 1], and there were still over 300 people in line. As we were packing up, mothers would push their way in, begging for help for their children with tears flowing. We tried to see any patients that seemed dire, but we just could not stay any longer. Suddenly, a mother carrying her son came in crying—he was not breathing. We halted everything and were able to resuscitate him. The most lasting and vivid memory from the experience was watching the tears of fear turn into tears of joy in the mother's eyes. She looked at me and said a simple "[thank you]" but she did not need to. Her eyes explained it all. I have always known I wanted to be a doctor, but any doubts I had fell to the ground with that [Resident of Country 1]'s tears. Since then my priority in almost all things I do is to become a Dr. so that maybe one day I can receive that "[thank you]" and deserve it.

The narrator clearly focuses on a specific episodic event—the day that this child's life was saved—and provides a good deal of specific episodic content. But note that even in recalling this episodic event, the event is first placed in a larger life context, specified on a personal timeline (after 11th grade) and a larger spatial context (this clinic in this village in this country). Note also that the narrative does not finish at the end of the episode, but pulls back again to provide a larger temporal context of where this person is in their life now. Further, the links between this specific experience and this person's values and life goals is made explicit, thus demonstrating how this memory serves the function of self-definition. Contrast this narrative with a narrative of a recurring event:

> One recurring event in my life is my family watches Jeopardy every night at dinner. This is really the only time I spend with my family, as we are all busy people. Every time I watch it with my family I feel safe and at home. I feel comforted in knowing my family is with me. When I went away to college, I still try to watch Jeopardy every night and I feel the connection to my family despite the distance between us. I can hear my Dad say "Why do we watch this? You're all terrible at it, the news is more interesting and relevant anyways." I can hear my brother saying "You didn't put it in the form of a question. My point," or "Ooooh, so close, it counts, point for me," and I can hear my mom from the other room saying "Good job! I'm impressed you knew that one." These memories bring me back to my childhood and back home. That feeling of being at home has helped me get through my first year of college.

This narrative is also highly detailed, but note that the specified time and place are the generalized "at home at dinner" reflecting a more scripted generalized representation. The narrative certainly serves some self-defining functions, but the overriding function is connection to family, and how this social closeness functions to keep the narrator feeling safe.

Extended events were a complex interplay of specific and recurring episodes across time, as the narrative at the beginning of this chapter illustrates. The event is the summer before senior year at high school, but narrated within this multiple month event are several specific episodes as well as events that occurred on a regular basis throughout the summer. Interestingly, extended events served both self and social functions equally.

In support of these different temporally organized experiences being differentiated in recall, individuals also use different linguistic markers for these different types of events. More specifically, episodic events tend to be told in the personal past, "I did," whereas recurring events tend to be told in the timeless plural, "We do" (Waters & Fivush, 2016). These differences mirror what we see early in development in terms of linguistic differentiation between episodes and scripts, and suggests that these different forms reflect different ways of using autobiographical representations: one focused on the personal self and one focused on extended relationships. These findings further suggest that individuals are easily able to access and recall events at different temporal levels, although we further note that, even within these different forms, individuals move easily among temporal frameworks. Moreover, although certain forms were more highly associated with certain functions, all three narrative types served multiple functions. Thus these data demonstrate both the fluidity and the distinction of autobiographical forms and functions. When recalling personal experiences, individuals move easily among these differing temporal horizons, but focusing on one horizon over another facilitates certain forms of recall that serve related functions.

Conclusions

Autobiographical memory defines who we are in relationship to others in the world. In addition to providing essential information to direct our behavior in adaptive ways, autobiographical memory functions to create a coherent and continuous sense of self and relationships over time (e.g., Conway et al., 2004). As such, we have argued for expanding our understanding of the forms and functions of autobiographical memory to include multiple temporal horizons. Further, by taking a sociocultural developmental approach, we have shown that these different temporal horizons develop at different rates across childhood, and are socially scaffolded in their forms through sharing memories with others. Early in development, mothers help preschoolers create more coherent and elaborated narratives of episodic experiences, and by the end of the preschool years children are able to recall specific episodes and recurring scripted events in coherent, but differentiated ways. These two forms being differentiated so early in development suggests that children may be using them for different functions, and there is preliminary evidence that episodic representations are used to define self and regulate emotions, whereas scripted representations are used to direct behavior. Importantly, at this early stage in development children are as yet unable to link disparate events together into more extended temporal timelines. With the social and cognitive advances of adolescence, and especially with the continued scaffolding of parents, adolescents begin to create more extended life scripts and personal life narratives. Thus, by adulthood, autobiographical memory has developed into a complex interplay among episodes, recurring events, and extended events. Adults are easily able to differentiate episodes, recurring events and extended events in their recall when specifically asked to, but when asked to spontaneously narrate their experiences, all three temporal horizons are interleaved, suggesting that autobiographical memory is simultaneously embedded within multiple temporal frameworks. Perhaps most intriguing, adults may use different autobiographical forms for different functions. Our approach to examining autobiographical memory as it develops along multiple temporal horizons and serves multiple functions indicates the need to expand our theoretical understanding of the organization of autobiographical memory to account for these social, cultural, and developmental factors.

References

Alea, N. & Bluck, S. (2007). I'll keep you in mind: The intimacy function of autobiographical memory. *Applied Cognitive Psychology*, *21*, 1091–1111.

Alea, N. & Vick, S. C. (2010). The first sight of love: Relationship-defining memories and marital satisfaction across adulthood. *Memory*, *18*, 730–742.

Baddeley, A. D. (1988). But what the hell is it for? In M. M. Grunebert, P. Morris, & R. N. Sykes (eds.), *Practical aspects of memory: Current research and issues*, Vol. 1: *Memory in everyday life* (pp. 3–18). Oxford: John Wiley & Sons.

Barsalou, L. W. (1988). The content and organization of autobiographical memories. In U. Neisser & E. Winograd (eds.), *Remembering reconsidered: Ecological and traditional approaches to the study of memory*. New York: Cambridge University Press.

Bauer, P. J. (2006). Event memory. *Handbook of child psychology*. New York: John Wiley & Sons.

Bauer, P. J., Larkina, M., & Deocampo, J. (2010). Early memory development. *The Wiley–Blackwell handbook of childhood cognitive development*, 2, 153–179.

Bauer, P. J., Wenner, J. A., Dropik, P. L., & Wewerka, S. S. (2000). Parameters of remembering and forgetting in the transition from infancy to early childhood. *Monographs of the Society for Research in Child Development*, 65 (Serial No. 263).

Beike, D. R., Brandon N. R., & Cole, H. E. (2016). Is sharing specific autobiographical memories a distinct form of self-disclosure? *Journal of Experimental Psychology: General*, 145, 434–450.

Berntsen, D. & Rubin, D. C. (2004). Cultural life scripts structure recall from autobiographical memory. *Memory and Cognition*, 32, 427–442.

Bird, A. & Reese, E. (2006). Emotional reminiscing and the development of an autobiographical self. *Developmental Psychology*, 42, 613–626.

Bluck, S. (2003). Autobiographical memory: Exploring its functions in everyday life. *Memory*, 11, 113–124.

Bluck, S. & Alea, N. (2002). Exploring the functions of autobiographical memory: Why do I remember the autumn? In J. D. Webster & B. K. Haight (eds.), *Critical advances in reminiscence work* (pp. 61–75). New York: Springer.

Bohn, A. & Berntsen, D. (2008). Life story development in childhood: The development of life story abilities and the acquisition of cultural life scripts from late middle childhood to adolescence. *Developmental Psychology*, 44, 1135–1147.

Brewer, W. F. (1988). Memory for randomly sampled autobiographical events. In U. Neisser & E. Winograd (eds.), *Remembering reconsidered: Ecological and traditional approaches to the study of memory*. Cambridge: Cambridge University Press, pp. 21–90.

Bruner, J. (1990). *Acts of meaning*. Cambridge, MA: Harvard University Press.

Chafe, W. (1990). Some things that narratives tell us about the mind. In B. K. Britton & A. D. Pelligrini (eds.), *Narrative thought and narrative language* (pp. 79–98). Hillsdale, NJ: Erlbaum.

Conway, M. A. & Pleydell-Pearce, C. W. (2000). The construction of autobiographical memories in the self-memory system. *Psychological Review*, 107, 261–288.

Conway, M. A., Singer, J. A., & Tagini, A. (2004). The self in autobiographical memory: Correspondence and coherence. *Social Cognition*, 22, 491–529.

Eisenberg, A. (1985). Learning to describe past experience in conversation. *Discourse Processes*, 8, 177–204.

Erikson, E. H. (1968). *Identity: Youth and crisis*. New York: Norton.

Fiese, B. H., Hooker, K. A., Kotary, L., Scwagler, J., & Rimmer, M. (1995). Family stories in the early stages of parenthood. *Journal of Marriage and the Family*, 57, 763–770.

Fivush, R. (1991). The social construction of personal narratives. *Merrill-Palmer Quarterly* 37, 59–81.

Fivush, R. (2010). Speaking silence: The social construction of silence in autobiographical and cultural narratives. *Memory*, 18, 88–98.

Fivush, R. (2011). The development of autobiographical memory. *Annual Review of Psychology*, 62, 559–582.

Fivush, R. (2013). Maternal reminiscing style: The sociocultural construction of autobiographical memory across childhood and adolescence. In P. J. Bauer & R. Fivush (eds.), *Handbook of the development of children's memory*. New York: Wiley–Blackwell.

Fivush, R., Bohanek, J. G., & Zaman, W. (2011), Personal and intergenerational narratives in relation to adolescents' well-being. In T. Habermas (ed.), *The development of autobiographical reasoning. New Directions for Child and Adolescent Development*, 131, 45–57.

Fivush, R. & Graci, M. E. (2017). Autobiographical memory. In J. Wixted (ed.), *Learning and memory: A comprehensive reference* (2nd edn; online). Elsevier.

Fivush, R., Gray, J. T., & Fromhoff, F. A. (1987). Two-year-old talk about the past. *Cognitive development, 2,* 393–409.

Fivush, R., Habermas, T., Waters, T. E. A., & Zaman, W. (2011). The making of autobiographical memory: Intersections of culture, narratives and history. *International Journal of Psychology, 46,* 321–345.

Fivush, R., Haden, C. A. & Reese, E. (2006). Elaborating on elaborations: The role of maternal reminiscing style in cognitive and socioemotional development. *Child Development, 77,* 1568–1588.

Fivush, R. & Waters, T. E. (2013). Sociocultural and functional approaches to autobiographical memory. *The handbook of applied memory. Sage,* 221–238.

Fivush, R. & Zaman, W. (2013). Gender and autobiographical consciousness. In P.J. Bauer & R. Fivush (eds.), *The handbook of children's memory development.* New York: Wiley–Blackwell.

Friedman, W. J. (1992). Children's time memory: The development of a differentiated past. *Cognitive Development, 7,* 171–187.

Friedman, W. J. (1993). Memory for the time of past events. *Psychological Bulletin, 113,* 44–66.

Greenwald, A. G. (1980). The totalitarian ego. *American Psychologist, 35,* 603–618.

Habermas, T. & Bluck, S. (2000). Getting a life: The emergence of the life story in adolescence. *Psychological Bulletin, 126,* 748–769.

Habermas, T. & de Silveira, C. (2008). The development of global coherence in life narratives across adolescence: Temporal, causal, and thematic aspects. *Developmental Psychology, 44,* 707–721.

Habermas, T. & Köber, C. (2015). Autobiographical reasoning in life narratives buffers the effect of biographical disruptions on the sense of self-continuity. *Memory, 23,* 664–674.

Habermas, T., Negele, A., & Mayer, F. B. (2010). "Honey, you're jumping about"—Mothers' scaffolding of their children's and adolescents' life narration. *Cognitive Development, 25,* 339–351.

Habermas, T. & Reese, E. (2015). Getting a life takes time: The development of the life story in adolescence, its precursors and consequences. *Human Development, 58,* 172–201.

Haden, C. A., Haine, R. A., & Fivush, R. (1997). Developing narrative structure in parent–child reminiscing across the preschool years. *Developmental Psychology, 33,* 295–307.

Hyman, I. E. & Faries, J. M. (1992). The functions of autobiographical memory. In M. A. Conway, D. C. Rubin, H. Spinnler, & J. W. A. Wagenar (eds.), *Theoretical perspectives on autobiographical memory* (pp. 207–221). Dordrecht: Kluwer.

Kulkofsky, S., Wang, Q., & Koh, J. B. K. (2009). Functions of memory sharing and mother–child reminiscing behaviors: Individual and cultural variations. *Journal of Cognition and Development, 10,* 92–114.

Kuwabara, K. J., Rouleau, T. J., & Pillemer, D. B. (2011). Children's use of autobiographical memories during social problem-solving. Poster presented at the biennial meeting for the Society of Research on Child Development, Montreal, Canada.

Labov, W. & Waletzky, J. (1997). Narrative analysis: Oral versions of personal experience. *Journal of Narrative and Life History, 7,* 3–38.

Laible, D. (2004). Mother–child discourse in two contexts: Links with child temperament, attachment security, and socioemotional competence. *Developmental Psychology, 40,* 979–992.

Laible, D. J. & Thompson, R. A. (2000). Mother–child discourse, attachment security, shared positive affect, and early conscience development. *Child Development, 71,* 1424–1440.

Maki, Y., Kawasaki, Y., Demiray, B., & Janssen, S. M. (2015). Autobiographical memory functions in young Japanese men and women. *Memory, 23,* 11–24.

McAdams, D. P. (1996). Personality, modernity, and the storied self: A contemporary framework for studying persons. *Psychological Inquiry, 7,* 295–321.

McAdams, D. P. (2001). The psychology of life stories. *Review of General Psychology, 5,* 100–122.

McAdams, D. P. (2015). Tracing three lines of personality development. *Research in Human Development, 12,* 224–228.

McCabe, A. & Peterson, C. (1991). *Developing narrative structure.* Hove, UK: Psychology Press.

Neisser, U. (ed.) (1982). *Memory observed: Remembering in natural contexts*. San Francisco: W. H. Freeman.

Nelson, K. (2003). Self and social functions: Individual autobiographical memory and collective narrative. *Memory, 11*, 125–136.

Nelson, K. (2006). *Narratives from the crib*. Boston: Harvard University Press.

Nelson, K. (1998). *Language in cognitive development: The emergence of the mediated mind*. Cambridge: Cambridge University Press.

Nelson, K. & Fivush, R. (2004). The emergence of autobiographical memory: A social cultural developmental model. *Psychological Review, 111*, 486–511.

Nelson, K. & Gruendel, J. (1986). *Event knowledge: Structure and function in development*. Hillsdale, NJ: Erlbaum.

Nelson, K. & Ross, G. (1980). The generalities and specifics of long-term memory in infants and young children. *New Directions for Child and Adolescent Development, 10*, 87–101.

Peterson, C., Jesso, B., & McCabe, A. (1999). Encouraging narratives in preschoolers: An intervention study. *Journal of Child Language, 26*, 49–67.

Peterson, C. & Rideout, R. (1998). Memory for medical emergencies experienced by 1-and 2- year-olds. *Developmental Psychology, 34*, 1059.

Pillemer, D. B. (1998). Momentous events: Vivid memories. Cambridge, MA: Harvard University Press.

Pillemer, D. B. (2003). Directive functions of autobiographical memory: The guiding power of the specific episode. *Memory, 11*, 193–202.

Reese, E., Bird, A., & Tripp, G. (2007). Children's self-esteem and moral self: Links to parent–child conversations regarding emotion. *Social Development, 16*, 460–478.

Reese, E., Haden, C. A., Baker-Ward, L., Bauer, P., Fivush, R., & Ornstein, P. A. (2011). Coherence of personal narratives across the lifespan: A multidimensional model and coding method. *Journal of Cognition and Development, 12*, 424–462.

Reese, E. & Neha, T. (2015). Let's kōrero (talk): The practice and functions of reminiscing among mothers and children in Māori families. *Memory, 23*, 99–110.

Ricoeur, P. (1991). Life in quest of narrative. In D. Wood (ed.), *On Paul Ricoeur: Narrative and interpretation* (pp. 20–33). London: Routledge.

Robinson, J. A. & Swanson, K. L. (1990). Autobiographical memory: The next phase. *Applied Cognitive Psychology, 4*, 321–335.

Rubin, D. C. (2005). A basic-systems approach to autobiographical memory. *Current Directions in Psychological Science, 14*, 79–83.

Simcock, G. & Hayne, H. (2002). Breaking the barrier? Children fail to translate their preverbal memories into language. *Psychological Science, 13*, 225–231.

Thomsen, D. K. & Bernsten, D. (2008). The cultural lie script and life story chapters contribute to the reminiscence bump. *Memory, 16*, 420–435.

Tulving, E. (1972). Episodic and semantic memory. In E. Tulving & W. Donaldson (eds.), *Organization of memory* (pp. 382–403). New York: Academic Press.

Uehara, I. (2015). Developmental changes in memory-related linguistic skills and their relationship to episodic recall in children. *PloS One, 10*, e0137220.

Vygotsky, L. S. (1978). *Mind in society: The development of higher psychological processes*. Cambridge, MA: Harvard University Press.

Wang, Q., Koh, J. B. K., Song, Q., & Hou, Y. (2015). Knowledge of memory functions in European and Asian American adults and children: The relation to autobiographical memory. *Memory, 23*, 25–38.

Waters, T. E. A. (2014). Relations between the functions of autobiographical memory and psychological wellbeing. *Memory, 22*, 265–275.

Waters, T. E. A., Bauer, P. J., & Fivush, R. (2014). Autobiographical memory functions served by multiple event types. *Applied Cognitive Psychology, 28*, 185–195.

Waters, T. E. A. & Fivush, R. (2015). Relations between narrative coherence, identity, and psychological well-being in emerging adulthood. *Journal of Personality, 83*, 441–451.

Waters, T. E. A. & Fivush, R. (2016). The content and organization of specific, recurring, and temporally extended autobiographical event narratives. Presented at the 6th International Conference on Memory, Budapest, Hungary, July 17–22, 2016.

Waters, H. & Waters, E. (2006). The attachment working models concept: Among other things, we build script-like representations of secure base experiences. *Attachment and Human Development*, *8*, 185–197.

Williams, J. M. & Broadbent, K. (1986). Autobiographical memory in suicide attempters. *Journal of Abnormal Psychology*, *95*, 144.

5

Culture in the Organization of Autobiographical Memory

Qi Wang

Introduction

Our beliefs, motivations, and goals influence how we perceive and interpret things around us, and in turn, how we remember our experiences (Conway, Justice, and D'Argembeau, this volume, chapter 3; Conway & Pleydell-Pearce, 2000). These beliefs, motivations, and goals may originate from factors as idiosyncratic as our physiological or mood states, our personality traits, or our personal aspirations. More importantly, from the current perspective, these beliefs, motivations, and goals may be deeply conditioned by our culture and therefore widely shared among individuals of the same community. As a result, our memories often reflect the prevailing ideologies, dominant themes, and current concerns in our time and culture (Wang, 2013a). Our memories are both an individual construction and a cultural product.

In this chapter, I first outline a cultural dynamic theory as the framework to understand and predict the effects of cultural variables on the organization of autobiographical memory. The theory posits that autobiographical memory is an open system that emerges, develops, and transforms under the multitude of influences of culture (for a detailed discussion, see Wang, 2016a). I then discuss the organization of autobiographical memory and apply the theoretical model of the cultural dynamic theory to discuss the influence of culture on the organizational components of autobiographical memory. To illustrate the overarching influence of culture on remembering, I further discuss parallel findings of episodic memory as typically assessed in laboratory settings with non-personal materials (e.g., words or stories), and those of vicarious memory for events that happened to other people. I will demonstrate that although these types of memories vary in the degree of personal relevance or self-involvement, their organizational components are similarly and inevitably conditioned by cultural variables as the cultural dynamic theory predicts. Throughout my discussion, I focus on existing research involving the comparison between Westerners, particularly European-Americans, and East Asians, who are heterogeneous themselves. However, the cultural dynamic theory should also apply to other cultural groups for the understanding of the dynamic impact of culture on remembering.

A cultural dynamic theory of autobiographical memory

The cultural dynamic theory of autobiographical memory is inspired by dynamic systems theories that view human development as a result of dynamic interaction between person and context (Thelen & Smith, 2006). It comprises three major themes: First, autobiographical memory takes place in the dynamic transaction between an active individual and his or her changing environment. Second, autobiographical memory is situated in culturally conditioned time and space over a multitude of timescales. Third, autobiographical memory develops in the process of children acquiring cultural knowledge about the self and the purpose of the past through early socialization (see figure 5.1). Together, these integrative themes provide an explanatory framework to synthesize existing data and a coherent guide to further systematic investigation (Wang, 2016a).

Theme 1: Autobiographical remembering takes place in the dynamic transaction between an active individual and his or her changing environment that constitutes multiple levels of social, cultural, and historical variables. Individual and group differences in autobiographical memory emerge as a result of the transaction.

This theme highlights the culturally constructive nature of autobiographical memory, whereby the process of remembering takes place not in isolation, in the individual mind, but is thoroughly contextual. Cultural is conceptualized as a dynamic, multi-faceted system that comprises and further takes effect through different dimensions, variables, and levels (Holland & Quinn, 1987; Wang & Brockmeier, 2002). Many cultural elements further evolve as a result of individual development and historical transformation. Autobiographical memory is an open system that is deeply immersed in the cultural milieu and thus shaped by a variety of cultural forces. Furthermore, individuals play an active role in the process of cultural learning, being in constant transaction with their environments and selectively internalizing aspects of culture into their own repertoires of beliefs, motivations, and goals (Wang, 2013a). In the end, autobiographical memory takes shape as a joint product of the individual and the cultural agenda of the society. This theme thus predicts individual and group differences in memory as a result of pertaining cultural variables.

Theme 2: Autobiographical memory is being continually constructed in time and space conditioned by culture, over a multitude of timescales from seconds to a lifetime. Culture thus exerts influence over the course of remembering, affecting every stage from perception and encoding, to consolidation and retention, to retrieval.

This theme highlights the dynamic process of remembering that is shaped by culture from the beginning to the end. Given their culturally situated beliefs, motivations, and goals, individuals from different cultures often perceive and interpret event information differently so that cultural variations may emerge in what, how, and whether

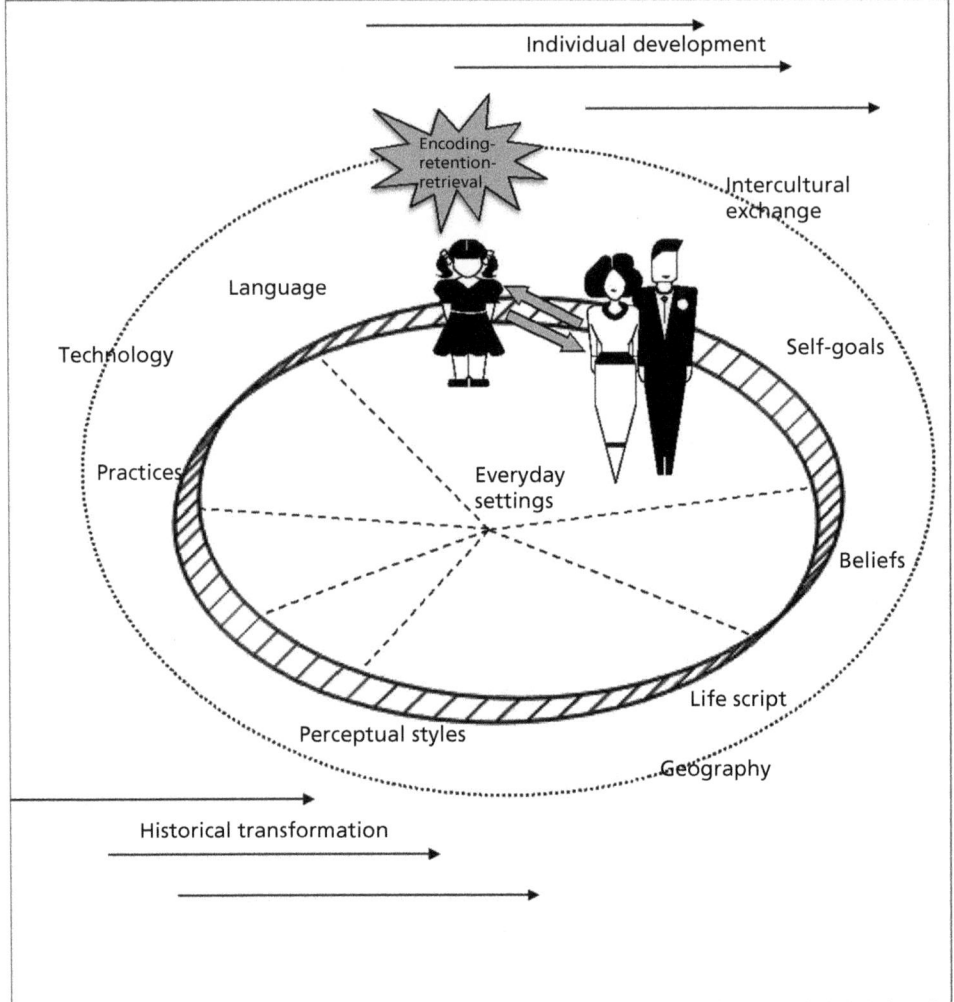

Figure 5.1 The cultural dynamic system of autobiographical memory.

Reproduced with permission from Q. Wang 'Remembering the self in cultural contexts: A cultural dynamic theory of autobiographical memory.' *Memory Studies*, Volume 9, Issue 3, pp. 295–304. Copyright © (2016) SAGE Publications.

event information becomes encoded and consolidated in memory. These culturally situated beliefs, motivations, and goals may further guide individuals to selectively retrieve from memory what is most important or salient to them and thus determine whether and how much the encoded information remains accessible at recall. Cultural variables can further influence post-encoding remembering and memory reconstruction during an extended period of retention, such that memories may change over time in light of new cultural experiences and evolving perspectives. The cultural templates of life stories, or narrative templates (Wertsch, 2008), may further constrain the ways of thinking, recounting, and sharing personal experiences and, in turn, ways of remembering the past (Wang, 2013a). This theme thus predicts cultural differences at every stage of remembering.

Theme 3: Autobiographical memory develops in the process of children acquiring cultural knowledge about the self and the purpose of the past from their everyday actions and interactions with parents and important others. As a result, cultural differences in remembering emerge early in ontogeny.

This theme highlights the mediation role of early socialization practices that institutionalize cultural values, beliefs, and ideologies to impart culture-specific modes of autobiographical remembering in children. Parents and other socialization agents uphold beliefs and goals endorsed by their culture when engaging their children in everyday mnemonic activities. Through this process, the culturally endorsed beliefs and goals are eventually internalized by children into their own memory operations. One such practice that has been shown to be particularly important for the development of autobiographical memory is parent–child sharing memories (Fivush & Waters, this volume, chapter 4; Nelson & Fivush, 2004). Parents discuss past events with their children, where they model to children what to remember, how to remember, and why to remember it, thus instilling in children purposes and ways of remembering the personal past appropriate to their cultural assumptions (Wang & Brockmeier, 2002). This theme predicts the early emergence of cultural differences in children's autobiographical memory and variations in early mnemonic practices that give rise to the differences.

In sum, the cultural dynamic theory construes autobiographical memory as an open system that emerges, develops, and transforms under the multitude of influences of culture. It provides a framework to understand and predict the effects of cultural variables on autobiographical remembering. Instead of viewing any particular ways of remembering as "better" or "more advanced" than others, the theory further emphasizes that memories and the practices of remembering are conditioned by culture to serve goals and purposes important to specific cultural contexts (Alea & Wang, 2015). The ultimate stance of autobiographical remembering reflects individuals' responses, conscious or unconscious, to varied cultural expectations. From the current perspective, the theory can shed important light on cultural influences on the organization of autobiographical memory.

Organization of autobiographical memory

Researchers have provided several theoretical accounts for the organization of autobiographical memory. For instance, Conway and colleagues propose that autobiographical memories are organized in a hierarchical self-memory system (SMS) that comprises temporally defined life periods, general events, and specific episodic details (Conway, Justice, & D'Arembeau, this volume, chapter 3; Conway & Pleydell-Pearce, 2000).

Different from this view that emphasizes general-event or temporal associations, Mace (2010) highlights conceptual associations within the autobiographical memory system, in which memories are organized as conceptual classes of events and the activation of one memory can spread to other memories in its associative network. Brown and colleagues argue that memories are organized by "historically defined autobiographical periods," which are engendered by important social events (e.g., war, earthquake) that substantially impact on the fabric of daily living (Zebian & Brown, 2014). Schulkind and Woldorf (2005) suggest that autobiographical memories may be primarily organized in terms of their emotional valence. Taking a lifespan perspective, Habermas and Bluck (2000) provide a comprehensive account of the story-organization of autobiographical memories, maintaining that memories are constructed into coherent life stories through temporal, biographical, causal, and thematic connections.

To tease apart these theoretical accounts of autobiographical memory organization is beyond the scope of this chapter. It is likely that, as suggested in Habermas and Bluck (2000)'s life story framework, there exist multiple organizational dimensions for autobiographical memory, be it temporal, causal, conceptual, or emotional. To delineate the influence of culture on memory organization, I discuss components of memory that reflect the various organizational dimensions, including objective components, subjective components, and structural components.

Objective components of memory refer to the factual details of when, where, who, and what. Obviously, these elements of a memory event are only relatively "objective" in that they can be overly observed and recorded. Such observations, however, are not photographic but subject to personal interpretations—and to cultural influence, a point that I will elaborate below in "Memories of varied personal relevance". In research, the objective components of memory are often investigated in terms of what information and how much of the information is remembered. Some of the variables include memory accessibility, i.e., the extent to which individuals retrieve memories and the details of the memories from the recent and distant past (i.e., memory density, detailedness), and memory content focus, i.e., the extent to which memory information concerns rememberers themselves versus others and social interactions (i.e., self-focus versus other focus).

Different from objective components of memory that focus on *what* happened, subjective components of memory focus on individuals' personal reactions in memory events. They concern the idiosyncratic perceptions, thoughts, emotions, and evaluative reflections of the rememberer. These internal states mostly cannot be overtly observed but are only accessible to the rememberer. By making the memory "personal," they are considered to be the defining feature of autobiographical memory (Bauer, 2007). I will show, however, that cultures hold different attitudes toward subjective experience and expression, further influencing the extent to which individuals focus on their internal states in remembering.

Structural components of memory, by definition, concern how objective and subjective elements are structured or put together in a memory. One particularly important structure component concerns episodic specificity—the extent to which individuals represent a past event in episodic details that situate the event in a specific time and place in the past (e.g., "Today, I finished all the work that my teacher asked me to do"), relative to semantic knowledge and other general details that provide background information to the memory (e.g., "I have a new teacher at school"; Levine et al., 2002; Wang et al., 2014). In addition, based on their interpretations of what happened, individuals may draw temporal–causal connections between event elements (e.g., "I took the kids to the zoo, *because* my husband was busy packing up the garage"), and add elaborations to enhance the richness of event details (e.g., "The hot air balloon ride was *sooooo* cool!"). These structural components of memory, including specificity, causality, and elaboration, although seemingly fundamental to remembering, are also subject to cultural influences.

Notably, the objective, subjective, and structural components of memory are intertwined memory elements that often overlap in memory recall. Nevertheless, these components take different forms and functions in the remembering of a past event: Whereas the objective components supply the factual ingredient to a memory, the subjective and structural components render the memory with coherence and personal meaning (Bauer, 2007; Habermas & Bluck, 2000; Wang, 2013a). These organizational components are not specific to autobiographical memory; they also constitute other types of memory that differ from autobiographical memory in their personal relevance, namely, episodic memory and vicarious memory.

Memories of varied personal relevance

By definition, episodic, vicarious, and autobiographical memories all concern the conscious recollection of specific events that took place at a particular time and place in the past, involving such information as what (event content), where (location), and when (temporal occurrence; Tulving, 2002). They are discussed separately here not because they are different "kinds" of memory necessarily supported by unique neurocognitive mechanisms, but because they vary in personal relevance or self-involvement. Parallel findings of cultural influences on these memories may provide converging evidence for the important role of culture in memory organization.

The term episodic memory is used here to refer to memory in laboratory research that is typically assessed by first presenting participants with some information such as words, photos, objects, or episodes and later testing the participants' memory of the presented information through recall or recognition tasks (Tulving, 2002). The to-be-remembered material usually has little relevance or importance to the self and the memory has no personal meaning attached. Vicarious memory, on the other hand, refers to memory for events that happened to other people, oftentimes people important in the rememberer's life. Although it is not about events that one has directly experienced, vicarious memory is often held with great personal and emotional commitment and associated with vivid recollections (Galanidou & Dommasnes, 2008; Miller, 2009; Pratt & Fiese, 2004). There is then autobiographical memory, which encompasses significant personal experiences and knowledge of the self and, consequently, is vital for personal identity and psychological well-being (Conway & Pleydell-Pearce, 2000; Pillemer, 1998). Thus, the degree of personal relevance or self-involvement increases from episodic memory to vicarious memory and to autobiographical memory.

Whereas some memory researchers make no distinction between episodic and auto-biographical memories that both entail mentally travelling back in time (e.g., Tulving, 2002), others emphasize the personal importance of autobiographical memories as a key reason for the endurance of such memories (e.g., Bauer, 2007; Conway et al., this volume, chapter 3; Nelson & Fivush, 2004). Regardless of the theoretical view, research on epi-sodic memory provides an important means of examining cultural effects on memory by allowing the control for individual and group variations in the to-be-remembered material and by eliminating possible interference of previous retrievals. Notably, there are interesting similarities between autobiographical memory and episodic memory for fictional stories. Just like autobiographical memories, memories for stories embed a temporal–causal structure and involve the rememberers' interpretations (e.g., of the de-tails of the story and the story characters' mental states) to make the story coherent and meaningful. Story memories thus similarly consist of objective, subjective, and struc-tural components. In addition, research has suggested that the binding of event infor-mation into a cohesive narrative for fictional and autobiographical events may involve similar neural processes (Rosenbaum et al., 2009; Spreng et al., 2009).

Vicarious memory has attracted little attention from memory researchers until re-cently. Just like autobiographical memories for personal events, vicarious memories for events experienced by others similarly consist of objective, subjective, and structural components. Pillemer and colleagues further argue that vicarious and autobiograph-ical memories share similar phenomenological and functional qualities and that con-ceptions of autobiographical memory should not be limited to specific past events that happened directly to the self but be expanded to include past events that happened to other people (Pillemer et al., 2015). Nonetheless, given its indirect source of infor-mation and lower self-relevance, vicarious memories are generally less vivid, clear, and emotional and serve less prominent functions than autobiographical memories (Larsen & Plunkett, 1987; Pillemer et al., 2015).

Cultural beliefs and practices have been shown to influence a variety of cognitive processes from attention, perception, and memory to categorization, reasoning, and problem solving, with the information ranging from being of no personal relevance to that of highly significant to the individual (Kitayama & Cohen, 2007). Therefore, des-pite the difference between the three types of memory in self-involvement, culture may have parallel influences on the organizational components of episodic, vicarious, and autobiographical memories (see figure 5.2).

To apply the cultural dynamic theory to understand the influence of culture on memory organization, I present findings of autobiographical memory and supplement them with existing findings of episodic memory (for stories) and vicarious memory. I analyze each of the memory organizational components in turn and discuss cross-cultural evidence in correspondence to the three themes of the theory to demonstrate

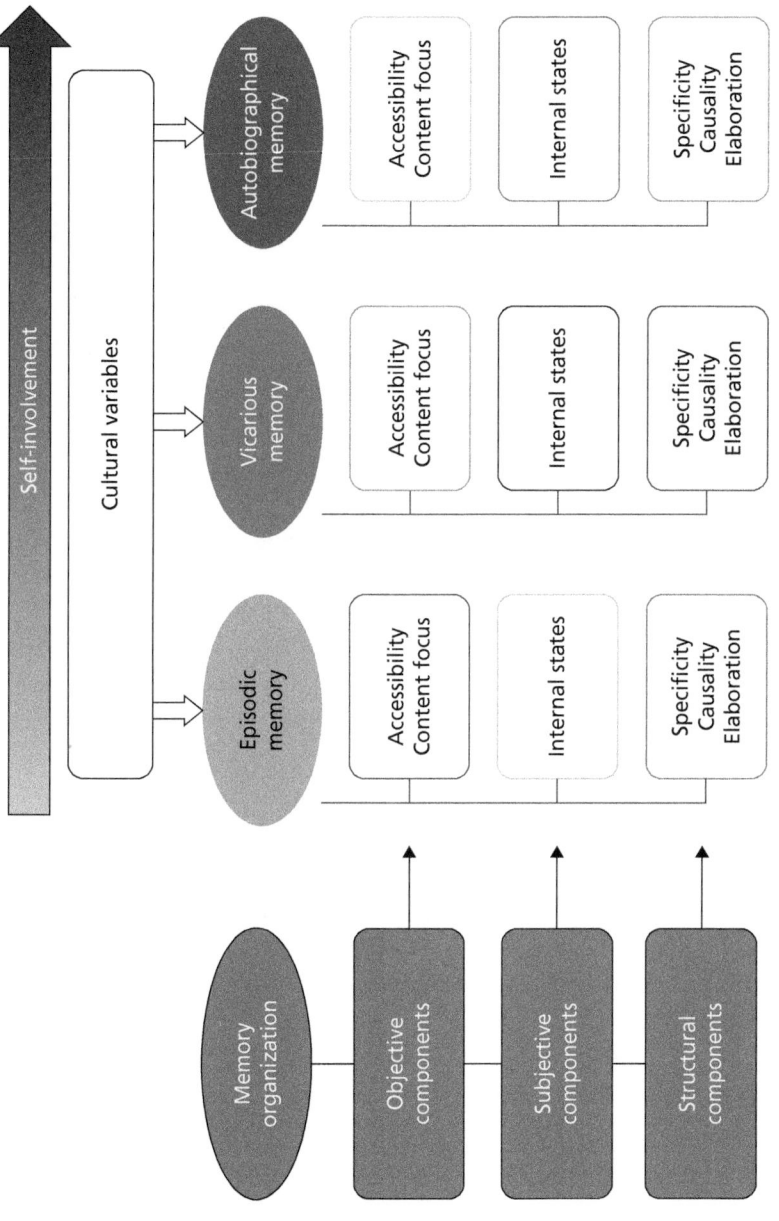

Figure 5.2 Culture in the organization of memories of varied self-involvement.

that (1) there are individual and cultural variations in the memory components as a result of pertaining cultural variables; (2) the cultural influences can be observed at both encoding and recall; and (3) the cultural differences emerge early and originate from early narrative interactions between parents and children.

Culture and the objective components of memory

For the objective components, cross-cultural research pertaining to memory accessibility has shown that European-American adults and children often access a greater number of memories as well as more distant and more detailed memories, including earliest childhood memories, than do their Asian counterparts (e.g., Han et al., 1998; Mullen, 1994; Peterson et al., 2009; Wang, 2001a, 2006a; Wang et al., 2004). Pertaining to memory content focus, when asked to recall recent or distant personal events, European-American adults and children focus more on their own roles and perspectives than Asians and Asian-Americans, who recall more information about other people and social interactions (e.g., Han et al., 1998; Wang, 2001a, 2004; Wang & Conway, 2004). How do we explain these cultural differences? Here I elaborate on the influence of cultural self-goals on memory content focus as an example. For a detailed cultural analysis of memory accessibility, please see Wang (2013a).

Martin Conway and colleagues have proposed that working self-goals serve an executive role in modulating the process of remembering (Conway & Pleydell-Pearce, 2000; Conway et al., this volume, chapter 3). These currently activated and salient self-goals channel cognitive resources to encode and consolidate goal-consistent information into memory and later prioritize selective retrieval of such information at recall, thus profoundly influencing what events and what aspects of the events are remembered. Important from the current perspective, fundamental self-goals such as autonomy and relatedness, although they exist universally, are variably emphasized in different cultures (Wang, 2013a). The culturally prioritized self-goals often remain chronically activated and readily guide the remembering process. Thus, in cultures that prioritize autonomous self-goals, most notably European-American culture, people may focus on event information concerning their own roles and perspectives that accentuates the uniqueness and agency of the individual. Such information is likely to be well represented in memory and highly accessible during recall. By contrast, in cultures that prioritize relational self-goals, such as East Asia, people may focus on and remember information about collective activities and significant others.

In line with this theoretical analysis, cross-cultural research has shown that whereas European-American adults and children (as young as preschool age) often recall memories of unique personal experiences with idiosyncratic details and cast themselves as the central character of the story (e.g., successes, fears, nightmares), East Asian adults and children often recall memories focusing on the roles of others and social interactions (e.g., school activities, family outings, disputes with neighbors; Han et al., 1998; Wang, 2001a, 2004, 2006a, 2008; Wang & Conway, 2004). The culturally prioritized self-goals are further related to individual differences in memory content focus. Regardless of culture, individuals who exhibit heightened autonomous self-goals also recall more self-focused memories, compared with those who exhibit heightened relational self-goals whose memories tend to be more socially oriented (Wang, 2001a, 2004). Parallel cultural differences have been found in episodic memory for stories and vicarious memory (Wang, 2006a; Wang & Ross, 2005).

The notion that culture influences story memory is not new, as demonstrated over 80 years ago in Frederic Bartlett's study with Cambridge University students (Bartlett, 1932). Bartlett found that, when asked to read and later recall a folktale from Native American culture, "The War of the Ghosts," his "educated and rather sophisticated" participants failed to remember many of the supernatural elements and unusual terms and events that were foreign to them. These foreign elements of the folktale were often reconstructed in memory to appear in forms common to the participants' social group. For example, a participant replaced "canoe" with "boat" and hunting seals with "fishing" in his recall. Furthermore, with the retention interval lengthened, the strangeness of the folktale was completely gone, and the content and style of the recalled stories became increasingly familiar and stereotyped in line with the participants' cultural norms. Bartlett contended that memory is an act of reconstruction influenced by what he termed "schemata"—mental structures that represent people's general knowledge about the world. He further claimed that the wealth of customs, institutions, and traditions of a group constitute lasting social schemata that serve as the basis for memory reconstruction, whereby "social organization gives a persistent framework into which all detailed recall must fit, and it very powerfully influences both the manner and the matter of recall" (Bartlett, 1932, p. 296).

More recently, Michael Ross and I examined culture differences in the content of story memory in terms of its focus on the main character versus peripheral characters, in parallel with studies of autobiographical memory (Wang & Ross, 2005). We asked European-American and Asian-American college students to read a cartoon book that had only illustrations but no words, to encourage personal interpretations of events. Participants then received a surprise memory test shortly after the reading, being asked to recall as precisely as they could what they remembered about the story. Compared with their Asian counterparts, European Americans recalled more information about the protagonist and introduced fewer peripheral characters in their story memories.

Furthermore, in a study that examined both autobiographical and vicarious memories (Wang, 2006a), I asked European-American and Taiwanese college students to recall earliest childhood memories in response to cue words of self, mother, family, friend, and surroundings. Not surprisingly, in both cultural groups, vicarious memories for mother, family, and friend were more socially oriented in content than memories for self or surroundings. However, across all memories, European-Americans focused more on their own roles than did Taiwanese, who emphasized more the roles of others. Indeed, European-Americans often cast themselves as the central character even when recalling memories of important others.

In addition to influencing memory content at retrieval, as the findings of cultural differences in autobiographical, episodic, and vicarious memories have revealed, do cultural self-goals also influence memory encoding? Michael Ross and I set out to test this question through experimental priming of self-goals (Wang & Ross, 2005). We asked European-American and Asian college students to describe themselves as either unique individuals (i.e., autonomous-self prime) or as members of social groups (i.e., relational-self prime). We then examined their subsequent memories of earliest childhood experiences and of a fictional story. If cultural self-goals only influence memory retrieval, then a main effect of priming condition would be expected, such that the retrieved memory content is semantically consistent with the self-primes. If culture self-goals only influence memory encoding, a main effect of culture on memory content would be expected that is not qualified by priming effects. However, if culture self-goals influence both memory encoding and retrieval, there would be main effects of both culture and priming condition.

Findings lend support to the encoding–retrieval hypothesis. Priming did influence the content focus for both the earliest memory and the fictional story. Participants who attended to their autonomous self-goals prior to the recall reported more self-focused and protagonist-focused memories, whereas those who attended to their relational self-goals recalled more socially oriented memories. Yet the priming effects did not eliminate or even reduce the magnitude of cultural differences in either memory: European-Americans recalled more self-focused and protagonist-focused memories than did Asians regardless of priming. These findings provide experimental evidence for the influence of cultural self-goals on memory content focus.

They further suggest that cultural self-goals not only filter the information people retrieve from memory, but that they may also directly act upon memory encoding by affecting people's attention, perception, emotion, and meaning analysis during an ongoing event, thus determining how, what, and whether event information is encoded in memory (Wang, 2013a, 2016).

Cultural discrepancies in memory content focus may be traced back to early narrative interactions between parents and their young children. Cross-cultural studies have consistently revealed differences in the content focus of parent–child memory sharing in line with the prevailing cultural self-goals orientated toward autonomy versus relatedness (Miller et al., 1997; Mullen & Yi, 1995; Wang, 2001b; Wang et al., 2000). Memory sharing between European-American mothers and children often takes a child-centered approach, where the child remains the focal point of the conversation and the mother frequently refers to the child's roles and perspectives in the past event. By contrast, memory sharing in East Asian families often takes a mother-centered, hierarchically organized approach in which mothers set the direction of the conversation and frequently refer to social interactions and group activities in the past event. Similarly, when telling stories together, European-American mothers focused more on the protagonist than did Chinese mothers, who paid more attention to social interactions and behavioral expectations (Wang et al., 2000). Parallel cultural differences have also been observed in parent–child discussion of vicarious events (Wang, 2013a).

Taken together, as the cultural dynamic theory predicts, memory content focus as an important objective component of memory exhibits systematic variations in line with culturally prioritized self-goals that emphasize autonomy versus relatedness. Such variations reflect cultural influences on memory not only at recall but also at encoding. They further originate from early narrative interactions between parents and children.

Culture and the subjective components of memory

Subjective components such as emotions, desires, and preferences are considered to be the defining feature of autobiographical memory (Bauer, 2007) and the literary genre of autobiography and other life-writings in general (Wang, 2013a; Weintraub, 1975). Yet cultures hold different attitudes toward subjective experience and expression, which can, in turn, influence their manifestation in memory. In Western—particularly European-American—cultures where a great emphasis is placed on individuality and agency, individuals are encouraged to attend to and express their inner attributes such as emotions, preferences, and beliefs that are considered to be vital ingredients of personal experience and salient indicators of one's distinctiveness from the social world (Halberstadt et al., 2001; Markus & Kitayama, 1991). By contrast, in East Asian cultures where there is a paramount concern with social harmony and group interests, a great emphasis is placed on moderation of all matters of the heart (Mauss et al., 2010). Individuals are encouraged to attend to social norms and regulate their behaviors that may have direct consequences for group functioning, and to control and minimize emotions and other subjective experiences because they can be socially divisive (Halberstadt et al., 2001; Wang, 2006b).

In line with these different cultural beliefs and expectations, studies have shown that when recalling autobiographical events, European-American adults and children more frequently referred to their thoughts, feelings, and desires than did their Asian and Asian-American counterparts (e.g., Wang, 2001a; Wang & Conway, 2004; Wang & Ross, 2005). For instance, in one study of autobiographical memory in middle-aged adults from China and the USA (all European-Americans), Martin Conway and I asked participants to each recall twenty memories from any period of their lifetime (Wang & Conway, 2004). Regardless of which life period the memories came from, Americans referred more frequently to their own thoughts and emotions in the memory events than did Chinese. Similar cultural differences in the recall of internal states have also been observed in adults' memories of recent events (e.g., Chua et al., 2005) and very-long-term memories, such as earliest childhood recollections (Wang, 2001a), whereby European-American adults more frequently described their emotions, personal opinions, and agency in the past events than did Chinese and Taiwanese. Furthermore, the cultural differences in attending to subjective experiences in memory events emerge as early as preschool age (Han et al., 1998; Wang, 2004). For example, when asked to recall recent autobiographical events, European-American 4-, 6-, and 8-year-olds made more spontaneous references to emotions, personal preferences, and opinions than did their Chinese counterparts, regardless of age (Wang, 2004).

Paralleling these cultural differences in autobiographical memory, studies have further found that, when recalling memories of a fictional story (Wang & Ross, 2005) or vicarious memories about significant others (Wang, 2006a), European-American adults referred more frequently to the needs, desires, and opinions of the story protagonist or those of their own than did Asian-Americans and Taiwanese. Similar cultural differences have also been observed in children's story memories. Jessica Han, Michelle Leichtman, and I showed Korean, Chinese, and European-American 4- and 6-year-olds a cartoon story, "Bear goes to the Market," and interviewed them the next day about their memories of the story (Han et al., 1998). For both age groups, European-American children had higher overall usage of internal state language, which included talk about emotion, cognition, preferences, and evaluations, than did their Korean and Chinese peers. Importantly, children of the three cultures recalled specific elements of the story (e.g., the color of Bear's outfit) with equal accuracy after a day-long interval, suggesting that basic memory capacity or mnemonic skills did not vary across cultures. Instead, the dynamic influence of culture takes place in the constructive process of remembering during which people perceive, interpret, and retrieve information in line with their cultural beliefs and goals (Wang, 2013a).

Do these cultural differences in subjective components of memory at recall also reflect differences in memory encoding? In the study described earlier by Wang and Ross (2005), main effects of both culture and priming condition emerged in participants' references to internal states in their story memories, and a main effect of culture but not priming condition emerged in participants' personal memories. These findings suggest that cultural self-goals and the associated cultural attitudes toward subjective experiences serve both as a constructive filter affecting the way information is initially encoded and represented in memory, and as a reconstructive filter that shapes memory at the time of retrieval. Priming effects were more pervasive for story memories than for personal memories probably because new, unrehearsed memories are more susceptible to such manipulations than are older, well-established memories.

Early socialization practices further give rise to the cultural differences in subjective components of memory. Research examining the way in which mothers share memories with their young children has shown that European-American mothers more frequently encourage children to describe their thoughts, preferences, wishes, and perceptions than do Japanese, Korean, and Chinese mothers, who focus more on children's behaviors in connection with social norms and expectations (Martini, 1996; Miller et al., 1997; Mullen & Yi, 1995; Wang, 2001b; Wang et al., 2000). For example, my colleagues and I observed that compared with Chinese mothers, European-American mothers often made more comments on the child's or the story protagonist's needs, preferences, judgments and opinions when sharing memories and telling stories (Wang, 2001b; Wang et al., 2000). These cultural differences in mother–child conversations appear to play out even when the subject under discussion is highly emotional. For example, Robyn Fivush and I (Fivush & Wang, 2005) examined Chinese and European-American mother–child conversations about positive and negative emotionally salient events (e.g., birthday parties, conflict with parents or peers). We found that whereas the sheer volume of conversations did not differ between cultures, American mothers dwelled on lengthy discussions about the causes of emotions experienced by their children and others, whereas Chinese mothers quickly switched to pinpoint the social and behavioral implications of emotions to their children.

Taken together, as the cultural dynamic theory predicts, people in Western and East Asian cultures vary in their inclination to attend to and recall their subjective experiences in memory events. This is in line with their respective cultural emphases on inner attributes as the defining elements of a unique sense of self and the authenticity of the individual, versus being an indication of personal weakness and a potential social threat that needs to be strictly controlled (Halberstadt et al., 2001; Mauss et al., 2010; Wang, 2006b). The cultural differences in subjective components of memory are consistent across memories of varying personal relevance, are reflected in both memory encoding and retrieval, and are sustained by early narrative interactions between parents and children.

Culture and the structural components of memory

Pertaining to the structural components of memory, studies have shown that when asked to recall autobiographical events from the recent or distant past, European-American adults and children often provide more elaborate and coherent memories about what happened, organize the information in a clearer causal sequence, and recall more specific event details, in contrast to their Asian counterparts who often provide bare-bone accounts of the past events with a greater focus on general information (Chae et al., 2006; Han et al., 1998; Wang et al., 2014; Wang & Song, 2018). I focus here on memory specificity to illustrate the ways in which culture variables operate in remembering.

Research has consistently revealed cultural differences in the extent to which people remember specific episodes and their details versus general events (for a review, see Wang, 2009). European-American adults and children retrieve more frequently unique, one-time episodes (e.g., "One time I won a prestigious award"), compared with their Asian counterparts who more often recall general or routine events (e.g., "My family attended this community event every Sunday") (e.g., Han et al., 1998; Wang, 2001a, 2004; Wang & Conway, 2004). Also, Westerners exhibit easier access to a greater number of specific memories than do East Asians for both distant events (e.g., childhood; Peterson et al., 2009; Wang, 2001a; Wang et al., 2004) and very recent events (e.g., yesterday or today; Oishi et al., 2011; Wang, 2009a). For example, when asked to recall as many childhood memories (of events occurring before the age of 5 years) as they could within 5 minutes, European-American and British participants recalled twice as many specific events as did Chinese (Wang et al., 2004). Oishi et al. (2011) observed that when asked to list all the activities they engaged in on the previous day, both Korean retirees and non-retirees reported approximately two-thirds the number of activities as did American retirees and non-retirees. Furthermore, when recalling specific episodes, European-American adults and children often reported more event-specific details than do Asians, who often included more general information (Wang et al., 2011, 2014; Wang & Song, 2018). These cultural differences in memory specificity are further extended to the construction of future events (Wang et al., 2011, 2014).

Paralleling cultural differences have been found in story memories and vicarious memories. When recalling a fictional story, European-Americans provided more specific descriptions about definite episodes in the story (e.g., "Bear didn't get to buy the big cake") and fewer general descriptions concerning broad impressions of the story (e.g., "All characters had red eyes" and "The pages were in different colors"), compared with their Asian counterparts (Wang & Ross, 2005). When recalling memories about significant others, European-Americans were more likely to report memories of specific episodes than Taiwanese, who more often recalled routine events (Wang, 2006a).

Whereas most studies of autobiographical memory focus on personal events from individuals' own lives, we conducted a study to examine European-American and Korean preschoolers' memories for a staged event, thus keeping the to-be-remembered event constant across groups (Chae et al., 2006). A researcher visited children in their classroom and played with them a "Pizza Game," which was administered in an identical way for the two cultural groups. Approximately one week following the event, a second researcher interviewed children individually about the event in a free recall (with an open-ended question) and a prompted recall task (with direct questions pertaining to specific aspects of the event, e.g., "How many toppings did you put on the pizza?"). Compared with Korean children, American children recalled more details of the staged event not only during free recall but also in the prompted recall task that provided cues for specific answers. These results suggest that the culture effect on memory may take place not just during retrieval or in the verbal report of an event but at encoding and consolidation processes as well. Compared with Korean children, American children might have encoded more details about the event and the details might have been better consolidated so that they could be more effectively cued later.

Research on perceptual styles has further shed light on cultural influences on memory specificity during encoding (Wang, 2009b, 2013b). Research by Nisbett and colleagues has shown that Asians often engage in holistic perceptual processes, attending to relationships and similarities among objects and events, whereas Westerners tend to engage in analytic perceptual processes, focusing on salient features of individual objects and events (Nisbett & Miyamoto, 2005; Norenzayan et al., 2007). Compared with Westerns, Asians are better at detecting relationships between events (Ji et al., 2000), experience greater difficulty in separating objects from their surroundings (Kitayama et al., 2003), and pay more attention to relationships in the field (Masuda & Nisbett, 2001). These cultural differences in perceptual styles may influence how people perceive and encode discrete events from a continuous stream of activity (Zacks & Swallow, 2007). The holistic processing of information in Asians may lead them to view different objects and events as interrelated and thus perceive fewer discrete episodes in a continuous flux of information. By comparison, European-Americans, attending to salient properties of individual objects and events, may analytically segment the information into a greater number of unique episodes.

This is indeed what we have found. In one study (Wang, 2009b), Asian and European-American college students were presented with a narrative text. They were asked to segment the text into discrete events, indicating wherever, in their judgment, one meaningful event ended and another event began. As expected, Asians perceived and thus encoded fewer discrete episodes than did European-Americans. The cultural difference in event perception and encoding has direct consequences for memory. At an immediate recall test following reading the narrative text, Asians recalled fewer event episodes from the text than did European-Americans (Wang, 2009b). In another study, cultural influences on encoding and recall were examined using a random sampling method (Wang, 2013b). European-American and Asian-American participants were sent a text message three times a day during a one-week period and were asked to record as soon as they received the message what was happening during the past 30 minutes. At the end of the week, they received a surprise memory test for the events that they had recorded. The immediate event entry reflected the amount of episodic detail being perceived and encoded, and the delayed recall tabulated retention and retrieval. Among Asians, those who moved to the USA at an earlier age and were therefore likely more Americanized perceived and subsequently recalled more event details than those who had moved at an older age.

Furthermore, the differential attention to, and recall of, specific events and their details are culturally motivated (Wang, 2009a). Autobiographical memories of specific episodes with idiosyncratic details (e.g., "wining a spelling bee competition") are considered to be a vital ingredient for the establishment of individuality and autonomy that is highly valued in Western cultures. By contrast, generic memories (e.g., "going to church every Sunday") often imply social conventions, rules, and regularities and therefore are important for people in East Asian cultures that embrace social harmony and collective solidarity. Indeed, even within a single culture, people with a greater autonomous orientation exhibit greater episodic specificity than those with a greater relational orientation. Research has shown that children and adults who dwelled more on personal attributes and predilections when describing themselves (i.e., an autonomous orientation) were also more likely to recall specific memories, compared with those who dwelled more on social roles and group memberships when describing themselves (i.e., a relational orientation), regardless of cultural group (Wang, 2001a, 2006c; Wang et al., 1998).

The influence of culture on memory specificity can be further traced back to early family socialization. Compared with Korean, Japanese, and Chinese mothers, European-American mothers more frequently engage in high-elaborative conversations with their preschool-age children, where they dwell upon specific episodes, supplement children's responses with rich and embellished information, and provide ample support to scaffold children's participation (Minami & McCabe, 1995; Mullen & Yi, 1995; Wang, 2001b; Wang et al., 2000). Such conversations model to children how to construct elaborate stories about themselves. By contrast, Asian mothers tend to initiate low-elaborative conversations and often ask redundant questions without providing embellished information or following up on children's responses (e.g., "Who went to the park with us? ... Who else? ... And who else?"). Such conversations seem not to focus on remembering the past but more on reinforcing the position of the mother as an authority figure. The different maternal styles of memory conversations are directly echoed in children's memory reports. During memory sharing, European-American children frequently volunteer new and descriptive information about the event under discussion, assuming a collaborative partnership with their mothers. By contrast, Asian children tend to play a passive role in responding to their mothers' inquiries and often contribute no new information (Wang, 2001b; Wang & Fivush, 2005; Wang et al., 2000).

European-American mothers' use of a high-elaborative conversational style early on, compared with Asian mothers' low-elaborative style, directly facilitated their children's memory recall (Wang, 2006c, 2007). In a cross-cultural longitudinal study (Wang, 2007), for example, European-American, Chinese, and Chinese-American immigrant mothers and their children discussed shared past experiences three times at home, when the children were 3, 3.5, and 4.5 years of age. Across all time points, European-American mothers carried out more elaborate conversations than mothers of the two Chinese groups. Mothers' provision of event details facilitated children's memory both concurrently and over the long term, such that European-American children recalled more specific details of the memory events than did their Chinese peers. Interestingly, mothers' provision of specific details was positively associated with their endorsement of autonomy and individuality, and negatively related to their endorsement of relatedness.

Taken together, as the cultural dynamic theory predicts, there are systematic cultural differences in episodic specificity and other structural components of memory. Asians consistently exhibit lower specificity than European-Americans, whereby they are more inclined to recall general routine events even when explicitly instructed to recall specific episodes. Cultural variables such as perceptual styles and value orientations modulate the encoding process, influencing whether and how event information is structured and represented in memory and further determining the type of event information being recalled. Furthermore, maternal styles of memory sharing serve as an important developmental mechanism that gives rise to cultural differences in memory specificity.

Conclusions

The cultural dynamic theory provides an important framework to understand the influence of culture on memory organization (Wang, 2016a). As the theory predicts, the constructive processes of remembering, rather than taking place merely inside an individual's mind or brain, are thoroughly immersed in a social–historical–cultural milieu that consists of a multitude of influencing factors or variables. These cultural variables operate on the objective, subjective, and structural components of autobiographical memory organization, influencing what information and how much of the information we remember, whether we attend to our inner psychological experiences in the past events, and how we structure our memories in line with our cultural expectations. These cultural variables affect not only how we recall our past experiences, but also what we perceive as our experiences unfold, by focusing our attention to some aspects of the experiences to the neglect of others. The influences of culture thus take place even before the process of remembering begins and continue to manifest in our memory construction and reconstruction. Such influences are further sustained by mnemonic practices in the family and in the society more generally (Wang, 2013). Parents, in line with their cultural beliefs about the purpose of remembering, scaffold a communicative context in which they instill, consciously or unconsciously, in their young children culture-specific ways of remembering the personal past. This encul-turation process perpetuates cultural influences on autobiographical memory across generations.

Furthermore, as my analysis illustrates, the dynamic influence of culture is not limited to autobiographical memory but also applies to episodic memory of no personal importance and vicarious memory of relatively more personal importance. The parallel cultural influences on the organizational components of episodic, vicarious, and autobiographical memories highlight the overarching role of culture in shaping the processes of remembering. They demonstrate the vital importance of integrating culture into research in order to fully understand human memory and cognition (Wang, 2016b). Furthermore, the parallel findings suggest that the cultural dynamic theory may be useful for researchers to study the influence of culture on other types of memory and related cognitive constructs that have been typically assumed to be immune to culture or that have not been systematically examined in relation to culture, such as working memory, prospective memory, collective memory, and more.

In support this proposal, for instance, a recent line of fruitful inquiry concerns foresight, or episodic future thinking, where individuals use autobiographical memory as raw materials to simulate possible future episodes (Schacter, 2012). Conceivably, given that Westerners remember their autobiographical experiences in greater episodic detail and specification (e.g., Han et al., 1998; Wang, 2001a, 2004; Wang & Conway, 2004), they can utilize the rich sensory–perceptual–emotional details stored in their memory "data base" to simulate potential future events, and consequently should be able to generate more detailed future events, when compared with Asians. In studies with both adults and children, we have obtained just this result (Wang et al., 2011, 2014). The cultural differences in future simulation are further mirrored in parent–child conversations about future events (Sahin-Acar & Leichtman, 2015), as the cultural dynamic theory predicts. Thus, to construe other types of memory and related cognitive constructs as open systems under the multitude of influences of culture—just like autobiographical memory—may provide researchers with new perspectives and new ways of investigation.

Acknowledgments

This article is partly based upon work supported by Grant BCS-0721171 from the National Science Foundation, Grant R01-MH64661 from the National Institute of Mental Health, and Hatch Grants from the US Department of Agriculture to the author.

References

Alea, N. & Wang, Q. (2015). Going global: The functions of autobiographical memory in cultural context. *Memory, 23*, 1–10.

Bartlett, F. C. (1932). *Remembering: A study in experimental and social psychology.* Cambridge: Cambridge University Press.

Bauer, P. (2007). *Remembering the times of our lives: Memory in infancy and beyond.* Mahwah, NJ: Erlbaum.

Chae, Y., Kulkofsky, S., & Wang, Q. (2006). What happened in our Pizza Game? Memory of a staged event in Korean and European American preschoolers. In M. A. Vanchevsky (ed.), *Frontiers in cognitive psychology* (pp. 71–89). New York: Nova Science Publishers.

Chua, H. F., Leu, J., & Nisbett, R. E. (2005). Culture and diverging views of social events. *Personality and Social Psychology Bulletin, 31*, 925–934.

Conway, M. & Pleydell-Pearce, C. W. (2000). The construction of autobiographical memories in the self-memory system. *Psychological Review, 107*, 261–288.

Fivush, R. & Wang, Q. (2005). Emotion talk in mother-child conversations of the shared past: The effects of culture, gender, and event valence. *Journal of Cognition and Development, 6*, 489–506.

Galanidou, N. & Dommasnes, L. H. (eds.) (2008). *Telling children about the past: Interdisciplinary approaches.* Ann Arbor, MI: International Monographs in Prehistory.

Habermas, T. & Bluck, S. (2000). Getting a life: The emergence of the life story in adolescence. *Psychological Bulletin, 126*, 748–769.

Halberstadt, A. G., Denham, S. A., & Dunsmore, J. C. (2001). Affective social competence. *Social Development, 10*, 79–119.

Han, J. J., Leichtman, M. D., & Wang, Q. (1998). Autobiographical memory in Korean, Chinese, and American children. *Developmental Psychology, 34*, 701–713.

Holland, D. & Quinn, N. (eds.) (1987). *Cultural models in language and thought.* NY: Cambridge University Press.

Ji, L., Peng, K., & Nisbett, R. E. (2000) Culture, control, and perception of relationships in the environment. *Journal of Personality and Social Psychology, 78*, 943–955.

Kitayama, S. & Cohen, D. (eds.) (2007). *Handbook of cultural psychology.* New York, NY: Guilford Publications.

Kitayama, S., Duffy, S., Kawamura, T., & Larsen, J. T. (2003). Perceiving an object and its context in different cultures: A cultural look at New Look. *Psychological Science, 14*, 201–206.

Larsen, S. F. & Plunkett, K. (1987). Remembering experienced and reported events. *Applied Cognitive Psychology, 1*, 15–26.

Levine, B., Svoboda, E., Hay, J. F., Winocur, G., & Moscovitch, M. (2002). Aging and autobiographical memory: Dissociating episodic from semantic retrieval. *Psychology and Aging, 17*, 677–689.

Oishi, S., Kurtz, J. L., Miao, F. F., Park, J., & Whitchurch, E. (2011). The role of familiarity in daily well-being: Developmental and cultural variation. *Developmental Psychology, 47*, 1750–1756.

Mace, J. H. (2010). Understanding autobiographical remembering from a spreading activation perspective. In J. H. Mace, J. H. Mace (eds.), *The act of remembering: Toward an understanding of how we recall the past* (pp. 183–201). Wiley–Blackwell.

Markus, H. & Kitayama, S. (1991). Culture and the self: Implications for cognition, emotion, and motivation. *Psychological Review, 98*, 224–253.

Martini, M. (1996). 'What's New?' at the dinner table: Family dynamics during mealtimes in two cultural groups in Hawaii. *Early Development and Parenting, 5*, 23–34.

Masuda, T. & Nisbett, R. E. (2001). Attending holistically versus analytically: Comparing the context sensitivity of Japanese and Americans. *Journal of Personality and Social Psychology*, *81*, 922–934.

Mauss, I. B., Butler, E. A., Roberts, N. A., & Chu, A. (2010). Emotion control values and responding to an anger provocation in Asian-American and European-American individuals. *Cognition and Emotion*, 24, 1026–1043.

Miller, P. J. (2009). Stories have histories: Reflections on the personal in personal storytelling. *Taiwan Journal of Anthropology*, *7*, 67–84.

Miller, P. J., Wiley, A. R., Fung, H. & Liang, C. H. (1997). Personal storytelling as a medium of socialization in Chinese and American families. *Child Development*, *68*, 557–568.

Minami, M. & McCabe, A. (1995). Rice balls and bear hunts: Japanese and North American family narrative patterns. *Journal of Child Language*, *22*, 423–445.

Mullen, M. K. (1994). Earliest recollections of childhood: A demographic analysis. *Cognition*, *52*, 55–79.

Mullen, M. K. & Yi, S. (1995). The cultural context of talk about the past: Implications for the development of autobiographical memory. *Cognitive Development*, *10*, 407–419.

Nelson, K. & Fivush, R. (2004). The emergence of autobiographical memory: A social cultural developmental theory. *Psychological Review*, *111*, 486–511.

Nisbett, R. E., & Miyamoto, Y. (2005). The influence of culture: Holistic versus analytic perception. *Trends in Cognitive Sciences*, *9*, 467–473.

Norenzayan, A., Choi, I., & Peng, K. (2007). Perception and cognition. In H. Kitayama & D. Cohen (eds), *Handbook of Cultural Psychology* (pp. 569–594). New York: Guilford Publications.

Oishi, S., Kurtz, J.L., Miao, F.F., Park, J., & Whitchurch, E. (2011). The role of familiarity in daily well-being: Developmental and cultural variation. *Developmental Psychology*, *47*, 1750–1756.

Peterson, C., Wang, Q., & Hou, Y. (2009). "When I was little": Childhood recollections in Chinese and European Canadian grade school children. *Child Development*, *80*, 506–518.

Pillemer, D. B. (1998). *Momentous events, vivid memories*. Cambridge, MA: Harvard University Press.

Pillemer, D. B., Steiner, K. L., Kuwabara, K. J., Thomsen, D. K., & Svob, C. (2015). Vicarious memories. *Consciousness and Cognition*, *36*, 233–245.

Pratt, M. & Fiese, B. (eds.) (2004). *Family stories and the life course: Across time and generations*. Mahwah, NJ: Erlbaum.

Rosenbaum, R., Gilboa, A., Levine, B., Winocur, G., & Moscovitch, M. (2009). Amnesia as an impairment of detail generation and binding: Evidence from personal, fictional, and semantic narratives in K. C. *Neuropsychologia*, *47*, 2181–2187.

Sahin-Acar, B. & Leichtman, M. D. (2015). Mother–child memory conversations and self-construal in Eastern Turkey, Western Turkey and the USA. *Memory*, *23*, 69–82.

Schacter, D. L. (2012). Adaptive constructive processes and the future of memory. *American Psychologist*, *67*, 603–613.

Schulkind, M. D. & Woldorf, G. M. (2005). Emotional organization of autobiographical memory. *Memory & Cognition*, *33*, 1025–1035.

Spreng, R.N., Mar, R.A., & Kim, A.S.N. (2009). The common neural basis of autobiographical memory, prospection, navigation, theory of mind and the default mode: A quantitative meta-analysis. *Journal of Cognitive Neuroscience*, *21*, 489–510.

Thelen, E. & Smith, L. B. (2006). Dynamic systems theories. In R. M. Lerner & W. Damon (eds), *Handbook of child psychology* (6th edn): Vol. 1, *Theoretical models of human development* (pp. 258–312). Hoboken, NJ: Wiley.

Tulving, E. (2002). Episodic memory: From mind to brain. *Annual Review of Psychology*, *53*, 1–25.

Wang, Q. (2001a). Culture effects on adults' earliest childhood recollection and self-description: Implications for the relation between memory and the self. *Journal of Personality and Social Psychology*, *81*, 220–233.

Wang, Q. (2001b). 'Did you have fun?' American and Chinese mother–child conversations about shared emotional experiences. *Cognitive Development*, *16*, 693–715.

Wang, Q. (2004). The emergence of cultural self-constructs: Autobiographical memory and self-description in European American and Chinese children. *Developmental Psychology*, *40*, 3–15.

Wang, Q. (2006a). Earliest recollections of self and others in European American and Taiwanese young adults. *Psychological Science*, *17*, 708–714.

Wang, Q. (2006b). Developing emotion knowledge in cultural contexts. *International Journal of Behavioral Development*, *30* (Suppl. 1), pp. 8–12.

Wang, Q. (2006c). Relations of maternal style and child self-concept to autobiographical memories in Chinese, Chinese immigrant, and European American 3-year-olds. *Child Development*, *77*, 1794–1809.

Wang, Q. (2007). 'Remember when you got the big, big bulldozer?' Mother–child reminiscing over time and across cultures. *Social Cognition*, *25*, 455–471.

Wang, Q. (2008). Being American, being Asian: The bicultural self and autobiographical memory in Asian Americans. *Cognition*, *107*, 743–751.

Wang, Q. (2009a). Once upon a time: Explaining cultural differences in episodic specificity. *Social and Personality Psychology Compass*, *3*, 413–432.

Wang, Q. (2009b). Are Asians forgetful? Perception, retention, and recall in episodic remembering. *Cognition*, *111*, 123–131.

Wang, Q. (2013a). *The autobiographical self in time and culture*. New York: Oxford University Press.

Wang, Q. (2013b). Gender and emotion in everyday event memory. *Memory*, *21*, 503–511.

Wang, Q. (2016a). Remembering the self in cultural contexts: A cultural dynamic theory of autobiographical memory. Special issue: Memory and Connection: Remembering the Past and Imagining the Future in Individuals, Groups, and Cultures. *Memory Studies*, *9*, 295–304.

Wang, Q. (2016b). Why should we all be cultural psychologists? Lessons from the study of social cognition. *Perspectives on Psychological Science*, *11*, 583–596.

Wang, Q. & Brockmeier, J. (2002). Autobiographical remembering as cultural practice: Understanding the interplay between memory, self and culture. *Culture & Psychology*, *8*, 45–64.

Wang, Q., Capous, D., Koh, J. B. K., & Hou, Y. (2014). Past and future episodic thinking in middle childhood. *Journal of Cognition and Development*, *15*, 625–643.

Wang, Q. & Conway, M. A. (2004). The stories we keep: Autobiographical memory in American and Chinese middle-aged adults. *Journal of Personality*, *72*, 911–938.

Wang, Q., Conway, M. A., & Hou, Y. (2004). Infantile amnesia: A cross-cultural investigation. *Cognitive Sciences*, *1*, 123–135.

Wang, Q. & Fivush, R. (2005). Mother–child conversations of emotionally salient events: Exploring the functions of emotional reminiscing in European American and Chinese families. *Social Development*, *14*, 473–495.

Wang, Q., Hou, Y., Tang, H., & Wiprovnick, A. (2011). Traveling backward and forward in time: Culture and gender in the episodic specificity of past and future events. *Memory*, *19*, 103–109.

Wang, Q., Leichtman, M. D., & Davies, K. I. (2000). Sharing memories and telling stories: American and Chinese mothers and their 3-year-olds. *Memory*, *8*, 159–178.

Wang, Q., Leichtman, M. D., & White, S. H. (1998). Childhood memory and self-description in young Chinese adults: The impact of growing up an only child. *Cognition*, *69*, 73–103.

Wang, Q. & Ross, M. (2005). What we remember and what we tell: The effects of culture and self-priming on memory representations and narratives. *Memory*, *13*, 594–606.

Wang, Q. & Song, Q. (2018). He says, she says: Mothers and children remembering the same events. *Child Development*, *89*, 2215–2229.

Weintraub, K. J. (1975). Autobiography and historical consciousness. *Critical Inquiry*, *1*, 821–848.

Wertsch, J. (2008). Collective memory and narrative templates. *Social Research*, *75*, 133–156.

Zebian, S. & Brown, N. R. (2014). Living in history in Lebanon: The influence of chronic social upheaval on the organization of autobiographical memories. *Memory*, *22*, 194–211.

Zacks, J. M. & Swallow, K. M. (2007). Event segmentation. *Current Directions in Psychological Science*, *16*, 80–84.

6

Form Follows Function

Autobiographical Memory in Ecological Context

Susan Bluck, Nicole Alea, and Emily L. Mroz

Introduction

This chapter examines the structure of autobiographical memory from the functional perspective. We take our title from an oft-quoted phrase, *form follows function*. That phrase originates from the field of architecture but has taken hold more generally in popular culture as it applies across a variety of situations and disciplines. In fact, that was the author's original idea. In his early writing, Sullivan (1896) suggests that the idea that structure is guided by function is highly generalizable, even a law of nature:

> Whether it be the sweeping eagle in his flight, or the open apple-blossom, the toiling work-horse, the blithe swan, the branching oak, the winding stream at its base, the drifting clouds, over all the coursing sun, form ever follows function, and this is the law. Where function does not change, form does not change. The granite rocks, the ever-brooding hills, remain for ages; the lightning lives, comes into shape, and dies, in a twinkling. It is the pervading law of all things organic and inorganic, of all things physical and metaphysical, of all things human and all things superhuman, of all true manifestations of the head, of the heart, of the soul, that the life is recognizable in its expression, that form ever follows function (Sullivan, 1896, p. 408).

Within the memory literature, the idea that form follows function has held sway to different extents across time: it fits well, for example, with the ecological approach to cognition proposed in the 1960s (Gibson, 1966). Since all readers may not be familiar, we begin with a discussion of the tenets that provide the foundation for the functional perspective, reviewing its distant and more recent history. The remainder of the chapter then presents several issues and controversies that arise when taking a functional approach to examine the form, or structure, of autobiographical memory.

Foundations of the functional approach

Researchers who embrace a functional approach generally agree that autobiographical memories are "transitory dynamic mental constructions" (Conway & Pleydell-Pearce,

2000, p. 261). As such, they are shaped by, and can change in, different contexts. In keeping with that, the functional approach holds that personal memories are adaptive (Bruce, 1989; Robinson & Swanson, 1990): they do not serve merely as records of events (Conway et al., 2004; Mace, 2007). Verbatim recall of life's events is certainly recognized as important in certain situations (e.g., eyewitness testimony: Wells & Quinlivan, 2009; classroom settings: Roediger & Karpicke, 2006). Focusing solely on the mechanics of memory accuracy and performance, however, is seen as lacking ecological validity (Neisser, 1978) and as distracting researchers from asking important questions about how memory operates and is organized. In fact, remembering the personal past fully and with complete accuracy may not be congruous with a flexible, functional memory system that helps humans to nimbly navigate daily life (Newman & Lindsay, 2009). Instead, the functional approach suggests that memories of one's personal experiences in an ever-changing environment are certainly records of lived experience but are integratively constructed so as to be both accessible and adaptive (Kihlstrom, 2009). The generation of a given autobiographical memory at retrieval thus relies on a hierarchical structure with multiple levels of activation being guided by the current goals of the *working self* (self-memory system (SMS) model; Conway & Pleydell-Pearce, 2000; Conway, Justice, & D'Arembeau, this volume).

The functional approach is thereby consonant with the SMS model: the memory system is organized not only to represent the world but to serve the functions necessary for an individual to survive and flourish given the complex reality of their everyday environment (Neisser, 1986).

In brief, the functional approach has several foundational tenets, including: (i) remembering past events occurs commonly as part of daily life, (ii) specific psychosocial functions of remembering can be determined (e.g., self, social, directive), (iii) how memories are recalled and used depends on one's ecological context, (iv) remembering the personal past is responsive to changes over time, and (v) the form or structure of autobiographical memory follows the functions it serves, so as to facilitate access. A review of some distant roots and more recent history illustrates these tenets.

The distant history of the functional approach

Long before the ecological movement took hold in cognitive psychology, scholars across disciplines had been considering the functions that remembering the personal past serves in human lives. Such writings (e.g., Bartlett, 1932; Bergson, 1911; Kuhlmann, 1907) sometimes directly, sometimes only implicitly, provided the groundwork for the mid-twentieth century emergence of the functional approach to autobiographical memory (e.g., Baddeley, 1988; Neisser, 1978).

William James (1890) initially considered the adaptive functions of autobiographical memory through a thought experiment: imagining what life would be like for a person without it. He suggested that an individual stripped of his or her current set of personal memories would essentially be a different person, thereby illustrating memory's self-function. Similarly, memory has been discussed in philosophy as a way to bind the self together, allowing a continuous sense of identity even in the face of long passages of time or over a lifetime (de Beauvoir, 1972). Early developmental psychologists also proposed that memory plays a crucial role in identity formation in young adulthood and in maintaining identity in later life (Erikson, 1959). Jung (1933) suggested that, especially in the second half of life, reviewing one's past was not only central to identity but to self-growth. Similarly, reflection on, and evaluation of, one's personal past in relation to the present was proposed by Freud (1914) as necessary for mental health. Some psychiatrists argued that memory played a role in adjustment in later life or at any age when facing life transitions (Butler, 1963). Sociologists have also considered remembering one's personal past as serving adaptive functions: reviewing one's past is seen as vital for engaging in social comparisons that allow one to make progress in achieving social goals and meeting societal expectations (Neugarten et al., 1965). As such, various scholars across disciplines and across time have turned their attention to the functions of autobiographical remembering, to why humans remember their personal past (for a review see, Bluck et al., 2014).

The recent history of the functional approach

Though individual scholars have addressed memory's function across time, the functional approach to autobiographical memory gained particular prominence as part of the ecological perspective on cognition in the 1970s and 1980s. Researchers began suggesting that we ask not only how memory is organized but *why* humans remember their personal past (e.g., Baddeley, 1988; Bruce, 1989; Neisser, 1978). These two questions are, of course, inextricably linked. Form follows function: memory is organized to allow humans to, at the macro level, navigate through time and space. Beyond that general function, researchers also began asking what specific functions autobiographical memories serve in human life (Baddeley, 1988; Bruce, 1989; Bluck et al., 2010). They set about identifying the broad psychosocial functions that autobiographical remembering might serve (e.g., Bluck, 2003; Cohen, 1998; Pillemer, 1992). Pillemer (1992), for example, proposed three functions of autobiographical memory: psychodynamic, communicative, and directive. These later transitioned into the theorized self, social, and directive functions (Cohen, 1998; Bluck, 2003). Hyman and Faries (1992) conducted the first empirical work identifying self-reported functions of autobiographical remembering. In that early work, results provided support for self and social functions but less so for the directive function. Since then, empirical work has supported the existence of the three broad classes of self, social, and directive functions of remembering (Bluck, 2009; Bluck & Alea, 2002; Pillemer, 1992). These have formed the basis for empirical research, moving the field forward.

In brief, the *self* function is the use of autobiographical memory to enhance self-evaluation (Baddeley, 1988; Neisser, 1988a), develop a sense of self (Conway, 1996), or to feel that one is a continuous person over time (Barclay, 1996). The *social* function

(Alea & Bluck, 2003) involves using autobiographical memory to initiate and maintain relationships (Alea & Bluck, 2007; Neisser, 1978, 1988a), to empathize with others (Bluck et al., 2013; Cohen, 1998), or to teach and inform others (Pillemer, 1992). The *directive* function involves using memories to guide behavior (Baddeley, 1988; Schank, 1981), develop current opinions (Cohen, 1998), and to predict and plan for the future (Baddeley, 1988; Pillemer, 2003). Recent research continues to provide new potential categorizations (Harris et al., 2014; Rasmussen & Habermas, 2011).

In sum, across both distant and more recent history, the functional approach has championed the idea that autobiographical memory cannot be divorced from the environment in which individuals operate (Bluck & Alea, 2002). The form that memory takes will be guided by the functions it serves in helping humans navigate their world. Grounded in the ecological perspective to cognition (Gibson, 1966), the approach has encouraged researchers to study real-world phenomena (e.g., flashbulb memories: Brown & Kulik, 1977) in everyday context (Baddeley, 1988). The form memory takes is seen as guided by individuals' goals (Conway & Pleydell-Pearce, 2000) as those play out in the person–environment context (Berntsen, 2007; Bluck et al., 2010). As such, the functional approach to autobiographical memory allows researchers to coherently link the person to their lived environment, not just in the present, but over time (e.g., *life story schema*, Bluck & Habermas, 2000; Bluck & Liao, 2013).

Form follows function: Current issues and controversies

Having provided the reader with a brief reminder of the functional perspective, the remainder of this chapter focuses on current issues and controversies that have arisen in memory research that embraces this approach. Baddeley (1988) argued that one's approach as a scientist (e.g., functionalist versus mechanistic or reductionistic) significantly shapes the type of research questions one considers worth asking. As Neisser (1978) suggested many years ago, the functional approach to memory has intuitive, maybe even populist, appeal. It allows memory researchers to ask and answer the important questions not only of our colleagues, but that our sister, father, or neighbor might ask about how memory works in daily life.

Note, however, that whereas functionalist thinking is a touchstone to which memory researchers return from time to time, it never seems to fully catch on. That is, the functional perspective has never been the dominant paradigm in the study of human memory. Its most recent heyday was in the 1970s and 1980s. Since that time, some related areas of enquiry have emerged, potentially staged by those decades of relatively functionalist thinking. These include the growing body of research on a variety of aspects of applied cognition, everyday memory, autobiographical memory, narrative identity and life stories. Though these empirical areas have flourished over the last two decades, the functional approach to autobiographical memory has still not fully taken hold. The current boom in neuroscience following the *decade of the brain* from 1990 to 1999 (Jones & Mendell, 1999) has again left functionalism on the outskirts while biological reductionism takes center stage in the study of memory (Breckler, 2006). From a philosophy of science perspective (L'Abate, 2012), it appears that the functional perspective will likely stay on the scene but always as an alternative paradigm.

That said, many memory researchers have made great progress using a functional perspective. Both theory and empirical research have come a long way (e.g., Bluck et al., 2005; Harris et al., 2014; Pillemer, 2009). Given the current level of scholarly development, we are now able to start asking more searching questions about the functions of autobiographical memory. If form truly does follow function, what can we glean about the form, the structure, of autobiographical memory from a review of current issues in this field? In the remainder of this chapter, we address three areas of concern. These include: (i) defining basic functions versus reasons for, or uses of, remembering, (ii) considering whether there is a fundamental function, and, in contrast, (iii) identifying possible candidate functions above and beyond the three broad functions commonly seen in the literature.

Functions versus uses and reasons for remembering: Tackling adaptation

One thorny issue is that the term function implies that something is functional, that is, that it works. A tea cup serves the function of holding tea. A tea cup with a hole in the bottom cannot be called functional. Function therefore connotes utility or adaptiveness. This reference to adaptation immediately begs the question of the evolutionary history of the autobiographical memory, or self-memory, system (Conway & Pleydell-Pearce, 2000). There are, of course, great challenges in the field of evolutionary psychology. Trying to ascertain the operation of evolutionary forces on the human memory system has been described by philosophers of science as a deeply flawed enterprise (Downes, 2014). Evolutionary functional analyses of psychological processes, including memory processes, have long been considered *just-so stories* (Gould & Lewontin, 1979). Despite amazing advances in population genetics since Gould and Lewontin's (1979) work, we must still be careful to separate discussion of the current functions of autobiographical memory in the twenty-first century from claims about its adaptive origins (Nelson, 2009). We want to clarify, therefore, that our suggestion that form follows function does not refer to the idea that all aspects of the current structure of the human memory system can be traced back, specifically, to evolutionary adaptations made through natural selection. We simply do not and cannot know that (Kihlstrom, 2009). What we do argue is that the current form of autobiographical memory, how it is conceptually structured, and the forms in which it manifests in human activity are guided by basic psychosocial functions that it serves in the here-and-now of individuals' everyday life.

We believe this delimited view of the functions of autobiographical memory is central to moving the area forward. Specifically, evolutionary considerations aside, it is crucial to distinguish between functions of autobiographical memory and what might be considered uses of, or reasons for, remembering one's past. Previous researchers have similarly cautioned psychologists to differentiate between functions that are *primary* versus *possible* (Hyman & Faries, 1992). Not differentiating primary functions from other possible uses of memory invites a circular logic. Even without reference to evolutionary adaptation, it implies that, because individuals report using their memory for a certain reason, it must be functional (i.e., a new version of a just-so story). We therefore define the functions of autobiographical memory as being uses of memory that fulfill all three of the following criteria: (i) directly related to basic human needs to survive and thrive, (ii) responsive to fundamental socio-ecological demands of one's context, and (iii) adaptive in the sense of facilitating activities that positively benefit the organism.

Two lines of very interesting research have greatly contributed to the empirical literature but have also, in our opinion, inadvertently blurred the definition of the function of autobiographical memory. Examining these can help us to more precisely map out the definition of function. One well-developed line of research is on the functions of reminiscence (e.g., O'Rourke et al., 2011; Webster, 1997). The other is on the functions of autobiographical memory but, building on work from the reminiscence literature, includes maladaptive uses of memory (Harris et al., 2014). Each is discussed here in terms of their match with our proposed criteria for what might be considered a basic function of human autobiographical remembering.

Research on the functions of reminiscence has a strong grounding in lifespan developmental psychology and gerontology (Butler, 1963). Construction and validation of the Reminiscence Functions Scale (RFS; Webster, 1993, 1997) has been a great boon to reminiscence research over the last several decades. It has provided an excellent measurement tool for examining how individuals' reasons for reminiscing are meaningfully related to a variety of factors (e.g., gender, age, personality) including charting important relations between reminiscence and mental health outcomes (O'Rourke et al., 2011; Westerhof et al., 2010).

One strength of the Reminiscence Functions Scale is that it was empirically derived. Participants were asked to provide their reasons for reminiscing (i.e., reasons for looking back at their personal past through autobiographical remembering). The scale was developed based on a strong, age-and-gender-diverse sample and shows good reliability and validity. In terms of the construct being assessed, however, it reflects individuals' own reasons for remembering their personal past. The author is quite clear on this, but the name of the scale implies the measurement of functions. Webster's (1997) pioneering psychometric work indeed resulted in a valuable scale but one that assesses reasons for, but maybe not basic functions of, autobiographical remembering (Bluck & Alea, 2002). This can be seen in the resultant subscales: Boredom Reduction, Death Preparation, Intimacy Maintenance, and Bitterness Revival, as well as Identity, Problem-Solving, Conversation, and Teach/Inform Others. The first four of these do not appear to serve functions in the sense of being related to basic human needs, responding to fundamental environmental demands, and being of positive benefit to the organism.

Remembering the past because the current situation is boring, to ponder existential issues such as death, to connect with lost loved ones, or to recall past injustices are certainly all reasons people might have—and good ones at that—for thinking about the past. However, they do not seem to serve basic human functions, even in today's society. The latter four, however, do show clear functional characteristics. Maintaining a sense of identity, solving the problems that the environment presents, social conversation that maintains intimate bonds with others, and sharing information with others are all relevant to the ability to thrive as social animals navigating a complex world. These four factors also fit into the three broad classes of self, directive, and social functions of autobiographical memory (see Bluck et al., 2005; Bluck & Alea, 2011) originally postulated by Pillemer (1992; see also Cohen, 1998).

This research on reminiscence and work on autobiographical memory definitely shows overlap even though theory in these two areas arises from quite different traditions. Several authors have called for greater synthesis across these literatures (Bluck & Alea, 2002; Webster & Cappeliez, 1993). A recent, innovative empirical paper addresses that call (Harris et al., 2014). Using measures of function from both the reminiscence (RFS; Webster, 1997) and autobiographical memory literatures (Thinking about Life Experiences, TALE; Bluck & Alea, 2011) a four-factor conceptualization of personal remembering was developed. The factors include Reflective, Ruminative, Social, and Generative. The authors define function as "reasons for remembering or uses of autobiographical memory or motivations for remembering…" (pp. 559–560) to make clear that these factors do not all represent adaptive functions. Given that their factors are based partly on the RFS, with the previously discussed factors such as boredom reduction, bitterness revival, and death preparation, this definition seems prudent. As would be expected, the reflective (i.e., self-reflective) and social factors appear to fit our more stringent adaptive definition of function whereas rumination and generativity do not. This excellent research has helped researchers to think more deeply about what is a reason versus a function of remembering. It also elucidates the many ways that memory manifests in relation to basic adaptive functions as well as in relation to more sophisticated mental health and existential concerns. Moving forward, differentiating functions from uses, reasons, or motivations for remembering is important for those who aim to follow the ecological tradition to explore how form follows function.

Is there just one? Arguments for a primary function of autobiographical remembering

The idea that autobiographical memory serves three broad functions was introduced several decades ago (Cohen, 1998; Pillemer, 1992). Since that time, further theoretical and empirical work has charted the various functions of remembering (Bluck & Alea, 2003; Harris et al., 2014; Webster, 1997). Several authors have, however, proposed that there may be just one primary or fundamental function of autobiographical memory. Fitting with the idea that form follows function, such authors (e.g., Neisser, 1988b;

Nelson, 1993) suggested that the early development of the human ability to remember the personal past was driven by our adaptation, as social animals (Schellenberg & Aronson, 1973), to the social group context. The need to communicate past events within social groups and to create social bonds with others was seen as environmental presses that guided the early development, and thereby the structure, of autobiographical memory. That is, the earliest form of human autobiographical memory was seen as following the function of allowing social groups to thrive: memory allowed individuals to remember their personal and shared past and to communicate it to other members of their social group. Neisser (1988b) directly stated that the social function of autobiographical memory may be "the most important adaptive function" (p. 396). Sharing memories in social settings has been theorized as the basis of social relations, allowing the highly social human animal to create bonds and maintain group solidarity. Whereas animals can interpret both verbal and non-verbal communication within their group in a variety of complex ways, only humans can verbalize personal memories that help others to share their sophisticated thoughts and emotions (Neisser, 1988a). Nelson (1993) also suggested that the social function may be primary, based on her work in child development. Beginning in the preschool years, children represent themselves outside of the present moment (i.e., remember the self in the past) and begin sharing memories of events with others. Indeed, children first learn how to use autobiographical memory by talking about past events with others (Hudson, 1990: Social Interaction Model of Development), including their parents (Nelson & Fivush, 2004). Thus, autobiographical memory begins serving a social function very early in life. In short, theorists have suggested that autobiographical memory may have first emerged to serve a social function. Over time, this has aided in the high level of social interaction that has been instrumental in rapid species development, enabling humans to dominate the earth (Wilson, 1975).

Of course, no definitive evidence can be sourced on the evolutionary primacy of one or another of the functions of autobiographical memory. Though Nelson and Neisser both made reasonable arguments for the primacy of the social function, the tripartite (i.e., self, social, directive) model of the functions of autobiographical memory is still most widely cited in the literature. As such, it seemed that the discussion over one function being primary or more fundamental had abated several decades ago. Of late, however, neurological evidence has provided a new basis for us to speculate on whether there is one primary function of autobiographical remembering. This time our attention is turned to the directive function, the use of the past to envision and plan for the future. Recent neuroscience research has focused on mapping the areas responsible for remembering and thinking about the past as well as imagining and planning for the future (Schacter et al., 2012). This work has been part of a resurgence of interest in the extended self (Neisser, 1988a), now studied under the term *mental time travel* (Tulving, 2002). The directive function of autobiographical memory, posited by Pillemer several decades ago (1992), was defined as the use of the personal past to guide and direct present and future behavior. The directive function connotes an integration of one's mental time travel to the past and to the future, allowing individuals to use their own recalled past experiences to envision and plan for future eventualities. This ability to think ahead and organize future behavior has of course been a huge asset to human functioning and species development (Corballis, 2014). Whereas Pillemer and others theoretically postulated this function of remembering our personal past, the overlap between the two timeframes has now been demonstrated in the brain. Areas of brain activation are highly similar when one remembers the past and considers the future (for a review, see Klein, 2013). This basic link between thinking about our past and future raises the question of whether this is indeed the earliest, most primary, function served by remembering the past events of our lives.

However, firm evidence may never be supplied as to whether the directive or social function is primary. Others might also argue that the self function is primary. After all, it allows individuals the sense of "being me" over time (Bluck & Liao, 2013; Conway & Pleydell-Pearce, 2000) that is so crucial to navigating everyday life (Greenwald, 1980). It is certainly an interesting endeavor to speculate about whether one function of autobiographical memory is primary or was the first to develop in evolutionary time. In today's complex world, however, it is clear that autobiographical remembering serves several highly adaptive functions. As such, the research agenda of today, and likely of tomorrow, is to chart the ways that diverse individuals use the personal past to orient and adapt to daily life (Bluck et al., 2014). Though form may have originally followed a single function of human autobiographical remembering, the current structure of memory allows it to serve multiple functions.

Did we miss one? Searching in ecological context, ökologischen Kontext, 生态环境

As illustrated in our opening quote (Sullivan, 1896), the eagle's wing is formed to allow his sweeping flight. That is, an organism's ecological niche is important in determining its form. This idea that form follows function, including the form of autobiographical memory, embraces the notion that memory operates in relation to specific socio-ecological demands of the organism. Memory is thus theorized to be organized so that we can "get what we need" (Bluck et al., 2010) from memory, at the time it is needed. Needs change, however, as human contexts change. The environments in which humans remember their personal past vary tremendously. As shown in this section's heading, even the words for ecological context change depending on where we live (English, German, Chinese)! Is the tripartite framework of self, social, and directive functions conceptually sufficient to explain the forms that memory takes across contexts? We are not the first to ask whether we have missed a function of autobiographical memory (e.g., Harris et al., 2014; Pillemer, 2009). Might the form of autobiographical memory, its structure, also be guided by an as-yet-unnamed function?

There are clearly different sub-categories of the self, social and directive functions but these do not constitute new functions. For example, remembering the personal past for self-enhancement (e.g., D'Argembeau & Van der Linden, 2008; Demiray & Janssen,

2015; Pillemer et al., 2007; Wilson & Ross, 2003) has been considered in some research whereas other studies have examined the use of memory to maintain self-continuity (e.g., Bluck & Alea, 2009; Liao et al., 2015; McLean, 2008). Both are, however, self functions. Similarly, Rasmussen and Habermas (2011) argue for two distinct aspects of the social function: one used to initiate new relationships and a separate one to maintain existing relationships (for that distinction, see also Bluck et al., 2005). There are also numerous studies examining different aspects of the directive function in terms of various domains in which people recall life lessons based on remembered life events (e.g., Bluck & Glück, 2004; McLean & Thorne, 2003). These studies help to empirically elucidate the three existing functions, but they do not constitute new distinct psychosocial functions of autobiographical memory.

So where might we look to examine whether we have missed a function? The tenets of the functional approach suggest that if we have missed one, perhaps it is because we have not looked closely enough at the variety of contexts in which human remembering occurs in daily life. Thus, we now briefly outline some contexts in which the functions of autobiographical memory have been studied (e.g., life phase), but our emphasis is on the overarching context, that is, the press of the cultural context in which one lives (Ross & Wang, 2010; Wang, this volume, chapter 5).

Human contexts range from micro- to macro-level ecologies (Bronfenbrenner, 1977) and the functions of autobiographical memory have been studied in some of these: social contexts, such as comparisons between reminiscing alone versus with others (e.g., Kulkofsky et al., 2010; O'Rourke et al., 2017); developmental contexts, such as remembering in different life phases (e.g., McLean & Lilgendahl, 2008; Wolf & Zimprich, 2015); gendered contexts, such as comparing the functional uses of autobiographical memories in men and women (e.g., Maki et al., 2015; McLean & Breen, 2009); and examination of how remembering serves functions in various cultural contexts (Alea & Wang, 2015). As would be expected, there are definite differences in how often and to what extent memories are used to serve self, social, and directive functions across these contexts. For example, social functions of autobiographical memory are favored when sharing with other people (Kulkofsky et al., 2010). Self functions such as identity formation are, consistent with their developmental life phase (Erikson, 1959), used more by young adults as compared to older-aged adults (Bluck & Alea, 2009). Higher use of memories to form and maintain social bonds (e.g., Maki et al., 2015) and feel closer to others (e.g., Alea & Bluck, 2007) are reported by women as compared to men, likely because of early socialization experiences (see Grysman & Hudson, 2013 for a review). Recent work has focused, however, on how one's cultural context affects the functional use of memory. We therefore turn our attention to that research in order to hunt for a potential fourth function of remembering.

The press of culture on autobiographical memory is broad (Wang & Ross, 2007) and clearly relates to the functions that autobiographical remembering serves (Alea & Wang, 2015). Cross-cultural research has shown that the way individuals use memory fits with their cultural values, traditions, and daily demands. For example, in the Euro-American context, using autobiographical memory to understand one's self is especially salient (e.g., Maki et al., 2015; Wang et al., 2015) because of the need to define a self that is distinct and separate from others (Markus & Kitayama, 1991). On the other hand, cultures that value collectivism (e.g., Asian, Caribbean) compared to individualism (e.g., Euro-American) less frequently use the social function of autobiographical memory (e.g., Alea et al., 2015; Wang et al., 2015). In collectivist cultures the preservation of social ties is maintained via other cultural presses (e.g., respecting group harmony and kinship ties). This reduces reliance on autobiographical memories to keep others close (Wang, 2004). Even within a single nation, cultural differences have been related to functional memory use. Indigenous Australians have a culture that strongly values oral traditions (i.e., compared to non-Indigenous Australians). These cultural values translate into Indigenous people's greater use of autobiographical memories to serve the social function of teaching and informing others (Nile & Van Bergen, 2015).

Beyond cultural values and traditions, the daily conditions of life in WEIRD (Western, Educated, Industrialized, Rich, Democratic; Henrich et al., 2010) compared to non-WEIRD societies may also encourage using memories for specific functions that match environmental demands. For example, those in developing countries rely on the directive function of autobiographical memory more than those in developed countries (Alea & Bluck, 2013). They may be constantly pressed to use autobiographical memories to make decisions and solve problems regarding daily struggles that are common in parts of the developing world (e.g., crime, economic conditions; Alea & Bluck, 2013; Alea et al., 2015).

Taken together, it is clear that cross-cultural research to date demonstrates variation in the relative frequency with which individuals use memory to serve different functions. Cultural context does matter in how memory is used. Our goal, though, was to go beyond those findings: to examine cross-cultural research in order to gather any available clues about whether autobiographical memory may serve any as-yet-undocumented functions.

Studies using methodologies that allow unique autobiographical memory functions to emerge from the data (i.e., autobiographical narratives, open-ended questions) in diverse samples may help in identifying new autobiographical memory functions (Alea & Wang, 2015). Only a few studies have taken this approach, however (e.g., Hyman & Faries, 1992; Kulkofsky et al., 2009, 2010). Interestingly, when they do, the three basic functions, or slight variants of these, are spontaneously reported. For example, Kulkofsy and colleagues asked Euro-American and Chinese mothers why they share memories with their children (Kulkofsy, et al., 2009). They also asked adults from these two cultural groups why they think and talk about the past (Kulkofsky et al., 2010). In this open-ended format, variations of the three functions of autobiographical memory were spontaneously mentioned (self: self-defining; social: relationship maintenance; directive: teaching children how to behave, how to remember, problem-solving). In open-ended formats, however, the question presented to participants is usually "why" do you think or talk about the past? Given that they are not experts on the functional approach, and that adaptiveness is not highlighted, laypersons thus also spontaneously report using memories for non-functional reasons (e.g., daydreaming; for something to talk about; Hyman & Faries, 1992; Webster, 1993). Of greater interest, however, is that individuals do sometimes report reasons that appear, at least at face value, to fit the criteria for being functional but that are not part of the tripartite model.

One possibility is the use of memory for emotion regulation, which focuses on downregulating negative emotions to create a better (i.e., happier, less anxiety-provoking, less socially awkward) personal state (Gross & Thompson, 2007). Thus, we consider emotion regulation here as the most probable candidate for a fourth function of autobiographical memory (Pillemer, 2009). Individuals do report using reflection on their personal past to repair negative moods (Pasupathi, 2003). Even young children know that memories are used to help regulate emotions (Wang et al., 2015), and mothers use memories in joint reminiscences to help children understand their emotions and to feel better (Kulkofsky & Koh, 2009). Pasupathi (2003) found that when American adults talk about a memory to feel better there is indeed a corresponding reduction in negative emotion associated with the event, suggesting an emotion regulatory function of autobiographical memory sharing (see also Pasupathi et al., 2016).

Thus, people *use* autobiographical memory to regulate emotions. However, our question is whether emotion regulation meets our criteria, or definition, for an actual function of autobiographical memory. Does using autobiographical memory to downregulate negative emotions directly enable humans to survive and thrive, show change with socio-ecological demands, and positively benefit the organism by enabling it to adapt? Coinciding with our definition of function, regulating one's negative emotions to be more positive can, at times, allow humans to survive (e.g., Nesse, 1990) and thrive (e.g., Charles, 2010). Also, consistent with our definition of function, negative emotions are regulated in response to socio-ecological demands, particularly the demands of the immediate context (e.g., I am mad at my boss but need to suppress my anger so as not to get fired; Gross & Thompson, 2007) but also in response to macro-level cultural contexts (Tweed et al., 2004). However, we question whether regulating negative emotions so as to achieve a more positive affective state is always appropriate or adaptive.

Each specific human emotion helps to direct behavior. Thus sometimes negative affective states are necessary (e.g., fear initiates the fight or flight response; e.g., Nesse, 1990). Regulating emotion so as to simply be happier by remembering the personal past may not be universally adaptive, or a human imperative, in the same way that using autobiographical memory to maintain a sense of self, build relationships, or direct behavior is. The pursuit of happiness seems to be both culturally and historically bound (e.g., Oishi et al., 2013; Uchida et al., 2004) and is a part of the master-narrative of American culture (i.e., finding redemption; McLean & Syed, 2015). For example, the American definition of happiness involves active pursuit of heightened positive affect as a goal in itself, whereas in many other Western (e.g., Germany, France) and non-Western countries (e.g., China, Indonesia) happiness is also thought to be related to good fortune and peace of mind (Oishi et al., 2013). Note also that in societies that value collectivism (e.g., China) compared to more individualistic societies (e.g., USA), negative emotions are not re-evaluated in an effort to make them feel more positive but are instead felt and socially suppressed (Matsumoto et al., 2008). As such, whereas happiness is one of the universally expressed emotions (Ekman, 1992), emotion regulation to constantly maintain a positive state is not clearly universal and is not adaptive across situations. This makes it an unlikely candidate for a basic function of autobiographical memory.

Instead, it seems likely that emotions are affected, and sometimes regulated, as a by-product of remembering autobiographical events to serve one of the other three basic functions of memory (e.g., Cappelieze & O'Rourke, 2006; Harris et al., 2014). That is, that "feeling better" occurs not because that was the direct goal but as the result of satisfying another functional end such as, for example, social bonding (Pasupathi, 2003). Thus, though emotion regulation seemed a good candidate for a fourth function of autobiographical remembering at face value, it appears it is not likely a basic function as per our criteria. In sum, even across cultural contexts the three-function model seems—until we find a new candidate for consideration—sufficient.

Conclusion

The goal of the chapter was to apply the well-known axiom, *form follows function*, to the form of autobiographical memory. We consider the structure of autobiographical memory as reflective of its function in the same way as form ever follows function in the design of a skyscraper, an eagle in flight, a winding stream, or a tea cup. Can we better understand autobiographical memory by asking what functions it serves in human life? We believe so.

To answer this question more fully, however, we must first have clarity on the functions of autobiographical memory. How should we define function? Is there a single fundamental function of remembering? Are there three basic functions, or more? We have worked toward clarifying some of these issues, providing a more stringent definition and criteria than seen in the autobiographical memory literature to date. Function connotes adaptiveness. It goes beyond simple uses or reasons for remembering the personal past (e.g., daydreaming; Hyman & Faries, 1992), and allows humans to survive and thrive (e.g., does not include maladaptive uses such as bitterness revival; Webster, 1997). With this definition, and by keeping the tenets of the classical functional approach to cognition in mind, we are better situated to develop models of the structure of autobiographical memory (e.g., Conway et al., 2004).

The functional approach has made great strides since its inception in cognitive psychology in the 1970s (Neisser, 1978). Today, however, the zeitgeist propels scientists away from the study of persons in situ to a focus on the neurological bases of human behavior, including human remembering. Note that the most current model of the autobiographical memory system is as a flexible, reconstructive system that operates in response to the goals of the working self in everyday context (Bluck et al., 2010; Conway & Pleydell-Pierce, 2000). Though much will be learned about the structure of autobiographical memory by using multiple methods (e.g., from functional magnetic resonance imaging to narrative analysis), it behooves us to remember Baddeley's (1988) query. He urged us to take a functional approach to autobiographical memory, to keep our research grounded in the real world by asking *But what the hell is it for?* If form follows function, then that is the important question (Neisser, 1978).

References

Alea, N. & Bluck, S. (2003). Why are you telling me that? A conceptual model of the social function of autobiographical memory. *Memory, 11*, 165–178.

Alea, N. & Bluck, S. (2007). I'll keep you in mind: The intimacy function of autobiographical memory. *Applied Cognitive Psychology, 21*, 1091–1111.

Alea, N. & Bluck, S. (2013). When does meaning making predict subjective well-being? Examining young and older adults in two cultures. *Memory, 21*, 44–63.

Alea, N., Bluck, S., & Ali, S. (2015). Function in context: Why American and Trinidadian young and older adults remember the personal past. *Memory, 23*, 55–68.

Alea, N. & Wang, Q. (2015). Going global: The functions of autobiographical memory in cultural context. *Memory, 23*, 1–10.

Baddeley, A. (1988). But what the hell is it for? In: M. M. Gruneberg, P. E. Morris, & R. N. Skyes (Eds.), *Practical aspect of memory: Current research and issues* (pp. 3–18). Chichester, UK: Wiley.

Barclay, C. R. (1996). Autobiographical remembering: Narrative constraints on objectified selves. In Rubin, D. C. (ed.), *Remembering our past: Studies in autobiographical memory* (pp. 94–125). New York: Cambridge University Press.

Bartlett, F. C. (1932). *Remembering: An experimental and social study*. Cambridge: Cambridge University.

Bergson, H. (1911). Of the recognition of images. Memory and the brain. In Bergson, H. (ed.), *Matter and memory* (pp. 86–169). London: George Allen & Unwin.

Berntsen, D. (2007). Involuntary autobiographical memories: Speculations, findings, and an attempt to integrate them. In J. H. Mace (Ed.), *Involuntary memory* (pp. 20–49). Malden, MA, US: Blackwell.

Bluck, S. (2003). Autobiographical memory: Exploring its functions in everyday life. *Memory, 11*, 113–123.

Bluck, S. (2009). Baddeley revisited: The functional approach to autobiographical memory. *Applied Cognitive Psychology, 23*, 1050–1058.

Bluck, S. & Alea, N. (2002). Exploring the functions of autobiographical memory: Why do I remember the autumn? In J. D. Webster & B. K. Haight (eds.). *Critical advances in reminiscence: From theory to application* (pp. 61–75). New York: Springer.

Bluck, S. & Alea, N. (2009). Thinking and talking about the past: Why remember? *Applied Cognitive Psychology, 23*, 1089–1104.

Bluck, S. & Alea, N. (2011). Crafting the TALE: Construction of a measure to assess the functions of autobiographical remembering. *Memory, 19*, 470–486.

Bluck, S. & Glück, J. (2004) Making things better and learning a lesson: "Wisdom of experience" narratives across the lifespan. *Journal of Personality, 72*, 543–572.

Bluck, S. & Habermas, T. (2000). The life story schema. *Motivation and Emotion, 24*, 121–147.

Bluck, S. & Liao, H.-W. (2013). I was therefore I am: Creating self-continuity through remembering our personal past. *International Journal of Reminiscence and Life Review, 1*, 7–12.

Bluck, S., Alea, N., & Ali, S. (2014). Remembering the historical roots of remembering the personal past. *Applied Cognitive Psychology, 28*, 290–300.

Bluck, S., Alea, N., & Demiray, B. (2010). You get what you need: the psychosocial functions of remembering. In J. Mace (ed.), *The act of remembering: Toward an understanding of how we recall the past*. Hoboken, NJ: Wiley–Blackwell.

Bluck, S., Alea, N., Habermas, T., & Rubin, D. C. (2005). A tale of three functions: The selfreported uses of autobiographical memory. *Social Cognition, 23*, 91–117.

Bluck, S., Baron, J. M., Ainsworth, S. A., Gesselman, A. N., & Gold, K. L. (2013). Eliciting empathy for adults in chronic pain through autobiographical memory-sharing. *Applied Cognitive Psychology*, *27*, 81–90.

Breckler, S. J. (2006). The newest age of reductionism. *Monitor on Psychology*, *37*, 23.

Bronfenbrenner, U. (1977). Toward an experimental ecology of human development. *American Psychologist*, *32*, 513–531.

Brown, R. & Kulik, J. (1977). Flashbulb memories. *Cognition*, *5*, 73–99.

Bruce, D. (1989). Functional explanations of memory. In L. W. Poon, D. C. Rubin, & B. A. Wilson (eds.), *Everyday cognition in adulthood and late life* (pp. 44–58). Cambridge: Cambridge University Press.

Butler, R. N. (1963). The life review: an interpretation of reminiscence in old age. *Psychiatry, Journal for the Study of Inter-personal Processes*, *26*, 65–76.

Cappeliez, P. & O'Rourke, N. (2006). Empirical validation of a model of reminiscence and health in later life. *Journals of Gerontology Series B: Psychological Sciences and Social Sciences*, *61*, P237–P244.

Charles, S. T. (2010). Strength and vulnerability integration: A model of emotional well-being across adulthood. *Psychological Bulletin*, *136*, 1068–1091.

Cohen, G. (1998). The effects of aging on autobiographical memory. In C. P. Thompson, D. J. Herrmann, D. Bruce, D. J. Read, D. G. Payne, & M. P. Toglia (eds.), *Autobiographical memory: Theoretical and applied perspectives* (pp. 105–123). Hillsdale, NJ: Erlbaum.

Conway, M. A. (1996). Autobiographical knowledge and autobiographical memories. In: D. C. Rubin (ed.), *Remembering our past: Studies in autobiographical memory* (pp. 67–93). New York: Cambridge University Press.

Conway, M. A. & Pleydell-Pearce, C. W. (2000). The construction of autobiographical memories in the self-memory system. *Psychological Review*, *107*, 261–288.

Conway, M. A., Singer, J. A., & Tagini, A. (2004). The self and autobiographical memory: Correspondence and coherence. *Social Cognition*, *22*, 491–529.

Corballis, M. C. (2014). *The recursive mind: The origins of human language, thought, and civilization*. Princeton University Press.

D'Argembeau, A. & Van der Linden, M. (2008). Remembering pride and shame: Selfenhancement and the phenomenology of autobiographical memory. *Memory*, *16*, 538–547.

de Beauvoir, S. (1972). *The coming of age*. New York: G. P. Putnam & Sons.

Demiray, B. & Janssen, S. M. (2015). The self-enhancement function of autobiographical memory. *Applied Cognitive Psychology*, *29*, 49–60.

Downes, S. M. (2014). Evolutionary psychology, adaptation and design. In T. Heams et al. (eds.), *Handbook of Evolutionary Thinking in the Sciences* (pp. 659–673). Dordrecht: Springer.

Ekman, P. (1992). An argument for basic emotions. *Cognition and Emotion*, *6*, 169–200.

Erikson, E. H. (1959). Identity and the life cycle. *Psychological Issues*, *1*, 1–171.

Freud, S. (1914). *Remembering, repeating and working-through (Further recommendations on the technique of psycho-analysis II)*. Standard edition, 12. London: Hogarth Press.

Gibson, J. J. (1966). *The senses considered as perceptual systems*. Boston, MA: Houghton Mifflin.

Gould, S. J. & R. Lewontin, R. (1979). The spandrels of San Marco and the Panglossian Paradigm: A critique of the adaptationist programme. *Proceedings of the Royal Society London B*, *205*, 581–598.

Greenwald, A. G. (1980). The totalitarian ego: Fabrication and revision of personal history. *American Psychologist*, *35*, 603–618.

Gross, J. J. & Thompson, R. A. (2007). Emotion regulation: Conceptual foundations. In J. J. Gross (Ed.), *Handbook of emotion regulation* (pp. 3–24). New York: Guilford Press.

Grysman, A. & Hudson, J.A. (2013). Gender differences in autobiographical memory: Developmental and methodological considerations. *Developmental Review*, *33*, 239–272.

Harris, C. B., Rasmussen, A. S., & Berntsen, D. (2014). The functions of autobiographical memory: An integrative approach. *Memory*, *22*, 559–581.

Henrich, J., Heine, S. J., & Norenzayan, A. (2010). The weirdest people in the world? *Behavioral and Brain Sciences*, *33*, 61–135.

Hudson, J. A. (1990). Constructive processing in children's event memory. *Developmental Psychology*, *26*, 180–187.

Hyman Jr, I. E. & Faries, J. M. (1992). The functions of autobiographical memory. In M. A. Conway, D. C. Rubin, H. Spinnler, & W. A. Wagenaar (Eds.), *Theoretical perspectives on autobiographical memory* (pp. 207–221). Amsterdam: Springer.

James, W. (1890). *The principles of psychology (Vol. 1)*. New York: Henry Holt.

Jones, E. G. & Mendell, L. M. (1999). Assessing the decade of the brain. *Science, 284,* 739.

Jung, C. G. (1933). The stages of life. In *Modern man in search of a soul* (pp. 95–114). Orlando, FL: Harcourt Brace.

Kihlstrom, J. F. (2009). 'So that we might have roses in December': The functions of autobiographical memory. *Applied Cognitive Psychology, 23,* 1179–1192.

Klein S. B. (2013) The complex act of projecting oneself into the future. *Wiley Interdisciplinary Reviews: Cognitive Science, 4,* 63–79.

Kuhlmann, F. (1907). Problems in the analysis of the memory consciousness. *The Journal of Philosophy, Psychology and Scientific Methods, 4,* 5–14.

Kulkofsky, S. & Koh, J. B. K. (2009). Why they reminisce: Caregiver reports of the functions of joint reminiscence in early childhood. *Memory, 17,* 458–470.

Kulkofsky, S., Wang, Q., & Hou, Y. (2010). Why I remember that: The influence of contextual factors on beliefs about everyday memory. *Memory & Cognition, 38,* 461–473.

Kulkofsky, S., Wang, Q., & Koh, J. B. K. (2009). Functions of memory sharing and mother-child reminiscing behaviors: Individual and cultural variations. *Journal of Cognition and Development, 10,* 92–114.

L'Abate, L. (Ed.) (2012). *Paradigms in theory construction*. New York: Springer.

Liao, H.W., Bluck, S., Alea, N. & Cheng, C. L. (2015). Functions of autobiographical memory in Taiwanese and American emerging adults. *Memory, 4,* 1–14.

Mace, J. H. (2007). Involuntary memory: Concept and theory. In J. H. Mace (Ed.), *Involuntary memory* (pp. 1–19). Malden, MA: Blackwell.

Maki, Y., Kawasaki, Y., Demiray, B., & Janssen, S. M. (2015). Autobiographical memory functions in young Japanese men and women. *Memory, 23,* 11–24.

Markus, H. R. & Kitayama, S. (1991). Culture and the self: Implications for cognition, emotion, and motivation. *Psychological Review, 98,* 224–253.

McLean, K. C. (2008). Stories of the young and the old: Personal continuity and narrative identity. *Developmental Psychology, 44,* 254–264.

McLean, K. C. & Breen, A. V. (2009). Processes and content of narrative identity development in adolescence: Gender and well-being. *Developmental Psychology, 45,* 702–710.

McLean, K. C. & Lilgendahl, J. P. (2008). Why recall our highs and lows: Relations between memory functions, age, and well-being. *Memory, 16,* 751–762.

McLean, K. C. & Syed, M. (2015). Personal, master, and alternative narratives: An integrative framework for understanding identity development in context. *Human Development, 58,* 318–349.

McLean, K. C. & Thorne, A. (2003). Adolescents' self-defining memories about relationships. *Developmental Psychology, 39,* 635–645.

Matsumoto, D., Yoo, S. H., Nakagawa, S.; 37 members of the Multinational Study of Cultural Display Rules (2008). Culture, emotion regulation, and adjustment. *Journal of Personality and Social Psychology, 94,* 925–937.

Neisser, U. (1978). Memory: What are the important questions? In M. M. Gruneberg, P. Morris, & R. H. Sykes (eds.), *Practical aspects of memory* (pp. 3–24). New York: Academic Press.

Neisser, U. (1986). Nested structure in autobiographical memory. In D. C. Rubin (ed.), *Autobiographical memory* (pp.71–81). New York: Cambridge University Press.

Neisser, U. (1988a). Five kinds of self-knowledge. *Philosophical Psychology, 1,* 35–59.

Neisser, U. (1988b). What is ordinary memory the memory of? In U. Neisser & E. Winograd (eds.), *Remembering reconsidered: Ecological and traditional approaches to the study of memory.* (pp. 356–373). New York: Cambridge University Press.

Nelson, K. (1993). The psychological and social origins of autobiographical memory. *Psychological Science, 4,* 7–14.

Nelson, K. (2009). Narrative practices and folk psychology: A perspective from developmental psychology. *Journal of Consciousness Studies, 16,* 69–93.

Nelson, K. & Fivush, R. (2004). The emergence of autobiographical memory: A social cultural developmental theory. *Psychological Review*, *111*, 486–511.

Nesse, R. M. (1990). Evolutionary explanations of emotions. *Human Nature*, *1*, 261–289.

Neugarten, B. L., Moore, J.W., & Lowe, J. C. (1965). Age norms, age constraints, and adult socialization. *American Journal of Sociology*, *70*, 710–717.

Newman, E. J. & Lindsay, D. S. (2009). False memories: What the hell are they for?. *Applied Cognitive Psychology*, *23*, 1105–1121.

Nile, E. & Van Bergen, P. (2015). Not all semantics: Similarities and differences in reminiscing function and content between Indigenous and non-Indigenous Australians. *Memory*, *23*, 83–98.

O'Rourke, N., Cappeliez, P., & Claxton, A. (2011). Functions of reminiscence and the psychological well-being of young-old and older adults over time. *Aging & Mental Health*, *15*, 272–281.

O'Rourke, N., King, D. B., & Cappeliez, P. (2017). Reminiscence functions over time: Consistency of self functions and variation of prosocial functions. *Memory*, *25*, 403–411.

Oishi, S., Graham, J., Kesebir, S., & Galinha, I. C. (2013). Concepts of happiness across time and cultures. *Personality and Social Psychology Bulletin*, *39*, 559–577.

Pasupathi, M. (2003). Emotion regulation during social remembering: Differences between emotions elicited during an event and emotions elicited when talking about it. *Memory*, *11*, 151–163.

Pasupathi, M., Wainryb, C., Mansfield, C. D., & Bourne, S. (2016). The feeling of the story: Narrating to regulate anger and sadness. *Cognition and Emotion*, *3*, 1–18.

Pillemer, D. B. (1992). Remembering personal circumstances: A functional analysis. In Winograd E., Neisser U. (eds.), *Affect and accuracy in recall: Studies of "flashbulb" memories* (Vol. 4, pp. 236–264). New York: Cambridge University Press.

Pillemer, D. B. (2003). Directive functions of autobiographical memory: The guiding power of the specific episode. *Memory*, *11*, 193–202.

Pillemer, D. B. (2009). Twenty years after Baddeley (1988): Is the study of autobiographical memory fully functional? *Applied Cognitive Psychology*, *23*, 1193–1208.

Pillemer, D. B., Ivcevic, Z., Gooze, R. A., & Collins, K. A. (2007). Self-esteem memories: Feeling good about achievement success, feeling bad about relationship distress. *Personality and Social Psychology Bulletin*, *33*, 1292–1305.

Rasmussen, A. S. & Habermas, T. (2011). Factor structure of overall autobiographical memory usage: The directive, self and social functions revisited. *Memory*, *19*, 597–605.

Robinson, J. A. & Swanson, K. L. (1990). Autobiographical memory: The next phase. *Applied Cognitive Psychology*, *4*, 321–335.

Roediger, H. L. & Karpicke, J. D. (2006). The power of testing memory: Basic research and implications for educational practice. *Perspectives on Psychological Science*, *1*, 181–210.

Ross, M. & Wang, Q. (2010). Why we remember and what we remember: Culture and autobiographical memory. *Perspectives on Psychological Science*, *5*, 401–409.

Schacter, D. L., Addis, D. R., Hassabis, D., Martin, V. C., Spreng, R. N., & Szpunar, K. K. (2012). The future of memory: Remembering, imagining, and the brain. *Neuron*, *76*, 677–694.

Schank, R. C. (1981). Failure-driven memory. *Cognition and Brain Theory*, *4*, 41–60.

Schellenberg, J. A. & Aronson, E. (1973). The social animal. *Contemporary Sociology*, *2*, 397.

Sullivan, L. H. (1896). The tall office building artistically considered. *Lippincott's Magazine, March*, 403–409.

Tulving, E. (2002). Chronesthesia: Conscious awareness of subjective time. In D. T. Stuss & R. C. Knight (eds.), *Principles of frontal lobe function* (pp. 311–325). Oxford: Oxford University Press.

Tweed, R. G., White, K., & Lehman, D. R. (2004). Culture, stress, and coping: Internally- and externally-targeted control strategies of European Canadians, East Asian Canadians, and Japanese. *Journal of Cross-Cultural Psychology*, *35*, 652–668.

Uchida, Y., Norasakkunkit, V., & Kitayama, S (2004). Cultural constructions of happiness: Theory and empirical evidence. *Journal of Happiness Studies*, *5*, 223–239.

Wang (2004). The cultural context of parent-child reminiscing: A functional analysis. In M. W. Pratt & B. Fiese (eds.), *Family stories and the life course: Across time and generations* (pp. 279–301). Mahwah, NJ: Earlbaum.

Wang, Q. & Ross, M. (2007). Culture and memory. In Kitayama, S. & Cohen, D. (eds.), *Handbook of cultural psychology* (pp. 645–667). New York: Guilford Press.

Wang, Q., Koh, J. B. K., Song, Q., & Hou, Y. (2015). Knowledge of memory functions in European and Asian American adults and children: The relation to autobiographical memory. *Memory, 23*, 25–38.

Webster, J. D. (1993). Construction and validation of the Reminiscence Functions Scale. *Journal of Gerontology, 48*, 256–262.

Webster, J. D. (1997). The reminiscence functions scale: A replication. *The International Journal of Aging and Human Development, 44*, 137–148.

Webster, J. D. & Cappeliez, P. (1993). Reminiscence and autobiographical memory: Complementary contexts for cognitive aging research. *Developmental Review, 13*, 54–91.

Wells, G. L. & Quinlivan, D. S. (2009). The eyewitness post-identification feedback effect: What is the function of flexible confidence estimates for autobiographical events? *Applied Cognitive Psychology, 23*, 1153–1163.

Westerhof, G. J., Bohlmeijer, E., & Webster, J. D. (2010). Reminiscence and mental health: A review of recent progress in theory, research and interventions. *Ageing and Society, 30*, 697–721.

Wilson, A. & Ross, M. (2003). The identity function of autobiographical memory: Time is on our side. *Memory, 11*, 137–149.

Wilson, E. O. (1975). *Sociobiology: The new synthesis*. Cambridge: Belknap.

Wolf, T. & Zimprich, D. (2015). Differences in the use of autobiographical memory across the adult lifespan. *Memory, 23*, 1238–1254.

7

The Neural Basis of Autobiographical Memory

Heather Iriye and Peggy L. St. Jacques

Introduction

Considerable progress has been made in linking retrieval of our personal memories, or autobiographical memories (AMs), to the inner workings of the brain through advances in functional neuroimaging and the development of creative paradigms to investigate naturalistic stimuli in the scanning environment (for review see St. Jacques, 2012; St. Jacques & De Brigard, 2012). Understanding how such complex, emotionally intense, highly vivid, and potentially very remote memories are instantiated in the brain may provide insight into aspects of memory that are challenging to study with events formed within the confines of the laboratory (for review see Cabeza & St. Jacques, 2007; St. Jacques & Cabeza, 2012). The neural basis of AM has been demonstrated primarily by using functional magnetic resonance imaging (fMRI), and less frequently positron emission tomography and electroencephalography. These modern neuroimaging techniques have allowed researchers to gain insight into the dynamic online processes underlying AM retrieval. In the current chapter we focus on how functional neuroimaging studies have developed our understanding of the self in AM.

A distinguishing feature of AM is its relation to the self, and several theoretical accounts have been proposed to account for the relationship between AM and the self (Conway, Justice, & D'Argembeau, this volume; Conway, 2005; Conway & Pleydell-Pearce, 2000; Prebble et al., 2013; Tulving, 1985; Wheeler et al., 1997). Brewer (1986) even claims that one can "define AM as memory for information related to the self" (p. 26). Unlike most events encoded in the laboratory, AMs are by definition memories from one's own personal past, which include both spatiotemporally specific events (i.e. episodic memory) and knowledge (i.e. semantic memory). Self-referential processes in AMs support the awareness of the self in time, or autonoetic consciousness (Tulving, 1985; Wheeler et al., 1997). Remembering AMs also relies on adopting an egocentric perspective (i.e. self-referential frame of reference; Rubin & Umanath, 2015), which provides a window from which to view mental images arising from memories.

The importance of the self in AM is reflected in its neural basis. Early neuroimaging studies of AM highlighted that self-relevant aspects of AM can distinguish it from other memory tasks (Maguire & Mummery, 1999), and suggested that aspects of the self may importantly contribute to the construction of AMs (Conway et al., 1999, 2003). The first neuroimaging study of AM by Andreasen et al. (1995) revealed how self-related aspects of AM retrieval recruited similar neural correlates to those involved in internally directed cognitive states occurring during passive rest (i.e. absence of an explicit task). Later investigations linked this overlap between AM retrieval and passive resting states to the *default network* (Spreng & Grady, 2010; Spreng et al., 2009), a pattern of interconnected brain regions that has been suggested to support self-related and internally driven processes (Andrews-Hanna et al., 2014; Buckner et al., 2008; Buckner & Carroll, 2006; Gusnard et al., 2001). In the current chapter we address how the brain supports self-referential information, the neural mechanisms that enable autonoetic consciousness, and the neural basis of egocentric perspective during AM retrieval. The chapter closes with a brief discussion and avenues for future research. Before turning to the important role of the self in AM, we first provide an overview of the neural correlates of AM.

Overview of the neural correlates of autobiographical memory

A wealth of neuroimaging evidence has shown consensus in the key neural correlates of AM, which include lateral prefrontal cortex (PFC) and medial PFC (mPFC), lateral temporal and medial temporal lobes (MTL; including hippocampus and posterior parahippocampal cortex), lateral posterior parietal cortices, and posterior midline regions (retrosplenial, posterior cingulate, and precuneus; for reviews see Cabeza & St. Jacques, 2007; Gilboa, 2004; McDermott et al., 2009; Maguire, 2001, 2002; Rice & Rubin, 2009; Svoboda et al., 2006). AM retrieval is typically characterized by left-lateralized neural recruitment during its early retrieval, due to a reliance on semantic processing and strategic search. However, as details of an event are elaborated on and vividly re-experienced, activity shifts towards the right hemisphere of the brain (Conway & Pleydell-Pearce, 2000; Tulving et al., 1994; but see Daselaar et al., 2008). AM retrieval roughly follows an anterior–posterior gradient, whereby left-lateralized anterior frontotemporal regions subserve strategic search and semantic retrieval processes whereas posterior regions contribute to the recollection of sensory and perceptual details present at the time of memory encoding (Fossati, 2013). Semantic information including autobiographical knowledge is stored in lateral temporal cortex, especially in the right hemisphere, and is considered a core region of AM (Svoboda et al., 2006).

MTL structures play a crucial role in AM, a point first shown by the landmark case study of patient H.M., who underwent widespread resection of the anterior two thirds of his hippocampus, parahippocampal cortex, entorhinal cortex, piriform cortex, and amygdala for epilepsy treatment (Annese et al., 2014; Corkin, 2002). H.M.'s inability to form new episodic memories combined with the relative sparing of early childhood experiences contributed to theories of memory consolidation regarding the critical role of the MTL (Squire, 2009). Researchers hypothesized memories to be initially stored in the hippocampus, explaining H.M.'s inability to create new ones in the absence of this critical structure. Over time the memory trace, or engram, is transferred to neocortical sites through a process of consolidation. Additionally, recent theories have suggested that reactivation of memories can support additional reconsolidation processes that enable memories to be updated and reconstructed over time (e.g. Winocur & Moscovitch, 2011), with evidence that such effects extend to AM retrieval (St. Jacques et al., 2013). Whether retrieval eventually occurs independently of the hippocampus (e.g. Squire, 1992) or is continually dependent on its functioning regardless of memory age (e.g. Nadel & Moscovitch, 1997; Winocur & Moscovitch, 2011; Hassabis & Maguire, 2009; Hassabis et al., 2007) is still a topic of debate. Current evidence lends weight to the latter point of view, as patterns of activation in the posterior hippocampus have been found to represent temporally remote memories (i.e. 10 years old), whereas recent memory retrieval recruits both posterior and anterior aspects of the hippocampus (Bonnici et al., 2012; Bonnici & Maguire, 2017). This work is consistent with converging lines of evidence supporting the existence of functional segregation of the hippocampus along its anterior–posterior axis (for reviews see Poppenk & Moscovitch, 2013; Sheldon & Levine, 2016; Zeidman & Maguire, 2016), in contrast to earlier research that outlined a lateralized account of hippocampal functioning, implicating the left hippocampus in the retrieval of contextual details from memory and the right hippocampus in spatial memory and navigation (Spiers et al., 2001; Svoboda et al., 2006). The anterior portions of the hippocampus coordinate with other regions belonging to the AM retrieval network to effectively bind elements of a mental scene in a unified spatial representation to create an "internal global scene model" of a specific event (Zeidman & Maguire, 2016, p. 178). In support of this theory, anterior medial sub-regions of the hippocampus are activated during scene recall, both real and imagined (Addis et al., 2007), and only during the initial construction phase of memory retrieval (McCormick et al., 2013). Posterior regions of the hippocampus are thought to play a role in visuospatial processing as it has been shown to be uniquely engaged by visual scene perception (Chadwick et al., 2013) and during memory elaboration, when specific contextual details of the event are fleshed out (McCormick et al., 2013). Further evidence stems from the existence of direct, reciprocal connections between the posterior hippocampus and other regions involved in visuospatial processing such as parahippocampal and retrosplenial cortices (for review see Poppenk & Moscovitch, 2013).

A growing number of functional neuroimaging studies have shown that AM retrieval is supported by the interaction between brain regions. Specifically, AM retrieval is supported by enhanced effective connectivity between parahippocampal cortex and the hippocampus as well as between parahippocampal cortex and the temporal pole, reflecting a reliance on reconstructing the spatiotemporal characteristics of an event when compared to other types of memory (i.e. for general knowledge, public events, and autobiographical facts; Maguire et al., 2000; also see Maguire et al., 2001). The importance of the interaction between frontal and temporal regions during AM retrieval is highlighted by the finding of increased functional connectivity between the amygdala, hippocampus, and inferior frontal gyrus relative to the retrieval of semantic information (Greenberg et al., 2005).

By outlining the overarching involvement of the neural correlates associated with AM retrieval, we are better able to discuss how the self serves as its organizing force. However natural the notion of selfhood may seem, it is in fact a multifaceted, complex concept whose definition requires clarification. Thus, first we address what the term *self* really means.

The self in autobiographical memory

The self, although intuitive, remains a difficult concept to capture. For general purposes, we define selfhood as encompassing the "mental processes that provide one with the feelings of singularity, coherence, individuality, and unity that define one as a unique and particular human being" (Prebble et al., 2013, p. 816). Theoretical links between the self and AM have deep roots and for good reason. Their connection speaks to the idea that a core function of AM is to resolve the psychological paradox posed by the task of creating a coherent, stable self-concept from fragmented, inconstant stores of information spanning a lifetime. By drawing on a rich array of past experiences, one can build a foundation of conceptual self-knowledge that creates a sense of unified selfhood. This conceptual base can then be used to interpret the present and inform future behavior, though precisely how the brain accomplishes this feat is an ongoing area of research (Martinelli, 2013).

Conway and colleagues (Conway, 2005; Conway, Justice, & D'Argembeau, this volume, chapter 3; Conway & Pleydell-Pearce, 2000: Conway et al., 2004) proposed an influential theory of the dynamic interplay between self and AM known as the self-memory system model. Their account of AM posits tight theoretical links between self-related and memory processes by linking the current goals and motivations of the individual with a distributed knowledge base regarding that individual's personal experiences. The ultimate aim of this self-memory system is to provide a coherent narrative account of the self, based on the reciprocal interaction between an individual's goals and autobiographical knowledge. Goals are instantiated and maintained by "the working self," which serves to regulate an individual's behavior such that (s)he attains desired states and avoids undesirable states. The working self may trigger AMs stored in the underlying knowledge base congruent with personal goals or it may inhibit AMs that do not align with those goals that pose a threat to the self's structural coherence. The relationship is reversible such that autobiographical knowledge delimits which aims become incorporated into the working self, negating the possibility of adopting unrealistic or random goals. The authors argue that a key feature of autobiographical knowledge is indeed to "ground the self" (p. 271).

A more recent theory espoused by Prebble et al. (2013) conceptualizes the role of the self in AM as a 2×2 matrix. The first dimension of this matrix refers to level of selfhood (i.e. "I" versus "me"); the second addresses its temporal characteristics (i.e. present versus temporally extended). With regards to the former, the authors split the self into two widely recognized components originally formally recognized by James (1890/

1950): an "I," the subject of experience, and a "me," the object of reflective thought. This "experiencing I" is comprised of a series of bottom-up processes that provide a moment-to-moment record of an event replete with highly detailed perceptual information. As a trade-off, it is a fleeting construction lacking an overarching conceptual structure. In such ways this level of selfhood is intuitively connected with the ability to vividly recreate a past personal event from a specific place and time based on sensory details (Tulving, 1984, 1985, 2002, 2005; Wheeler et al., 1997). A hallmark of episodic AM is autonoetic consciousness, or the sense of vivid reliving that accompanies projection of the self throughout time (Tulving, 1984, 1985, 2002, 2005). The "I" is important for AM because it lays a foundation for autonoetic recollection, built from a combination of pre-reflective self-experience and self-awareness (Prebble et al., 2013). The pre-reflective self is a low level of selfhood based on a sense of connected embodiment and ownership of one's physical form that not only delineates self from the external world, but also provides a constant update of the internal state of the body (Prebble et al., 2013—also referred to as *protoself* in Damasio, 2012). It is not capable of self-reflexive thought, but rather is what self-reflexive thought acts on as moments are strung together and summarized by episodic memory. This process is dependent upon self-awareness, or the metacognitive ability to take a primary representation of an individual's conscious experience and use it in a flexible, meaningful way to perform the wide array of cognitive functions including "remembering, knowing, thinking, predicting, believing, feeling, doubting, pretending" (Prebble et al., 2013; p. 823). The topic of autonoetic consciousness and its relation to an "experiencing I" will be expanded upon later in the chapter.

The second level of selfhood described by Prebble et al.'s (2013) theory is the "me," which views the self as an object comprised of abstract qualities that span over time. The "me" represents the distillation of episodic AMs into conceptualized knowledge of personal traits and characteristics that form the basis of life stories, chapters, and general events. Over time, a core foundation of self-knowledge expands to cover an increasingly wide array of one's thoughts, feelings, and behaviors under a variety of circumstances, which then serves to reinforce a stable, grounded understanding of conceptual selfhood (Conway, 2005; Conway et al., 2004). In line with its abstract, conceptual nature, this high level of selfhood is associated with a unique form of semantic memory largely independent from episodic memory (Klein & Lax, 2010; Prebble et al., 2013). Thus, rather than being tied to an isolated moment in time centered on a first-person perspective of the world like the "I," the "me" contains a well-developed conceptual structure capable of extracting global patterns and connecting broad themes in one's life. The semanticization of personal experiences into self-knowledge enables an individual to consider him/herself as an object amenable to investigation, which in turn enables the adoption of a third-person egocentric perspective (i.e. an individual visualizes him/herself in the mental scene as an object in the external environment) during AM retrieval. The second dimension of Prebble et al.'s (2013) matrix for defining the role of the self in AM refers to temporal considerations and aims to explain how a sense of self-continuity, or the strongly held belief that one is and will continue to be the same person that one has been in the past in the face of drastic change, arises over time.

In sum, whereas Conway and colleagues emphasize how the overriding goals held by an individual influence what is retrieved from AM based on an expansive autobiographical knowledge base, the theory proposed by Prebble et al. (2013) suggests that the self in AM should be considered according to the level of selfhood affected (i.e. either the "experiencing I" or the "conceptual me") and whether retrieval influences a present or temporally extended self. Now that a common theoretical ground for conceptualizing the role of the self in AM has been established, we turn to the question of how the brain processes self-related information.

Self-related information

Processing of self-related information during AM retrieval is associated with involvement of the mPFC (for review see Denny et al., 2012; Gilbert et al., 2006; Northoff et al., 2006), which is one of the brain regions most reliably reported in functional neuroimaging studies of AM (Svoboda et al., 2006). Manipulating the degree of self-referential processing within AM modulates the involvement of the mPFC (Levine et al., 2004; Maguire et al., 2001; Muscatell et al., 2010). For example, dynamic connections between the mPFC and left hippocampus operate in-sync with the right amygdala–hippocampal complex during retrieval of events with high levels of self-involvement, but are less in-sync for low-self involvement events (Muscatell et al., 2010).

The mPFC is a large and heterogeneous region, and different sub-regions have been linked to different functions (for review see de la Vega et al., 2016). Ventral and dorsal portions of the mPFC have been linked to self versus other related processes, respectively (for review see Denny et al., 2012). For example, St. Jacques et al. (2011) found that ventral portions of the mPFC were recruited to a greater extent when participants were asked to retrieve AMs cued from photos from their own life, whereas dorsal portions of the mPFC were recruited more when making inferences about photos from another person's life. Similarly, Rissman et al. (2016) used multivoxel pattern analysis to demonstrate that distributed patterns of neural activity, including the ventral mPFC, could accurately decode whether participants had strongly recollected AMs cued by personal photos or had correctly rejected photos of novel events taken from another person's life. However, a separate study that asked participants to rate the degree to which they identified with a set of self-views found that both ventral and dorsal regions of the mPFC responded to the self-evaluation (D'Argembeau et al., 2012). Ventral mPFC was associated with the degree of "emotive investment," or the level of personal significance attached to a given self-view, whereas dorsal mPFC tracked "epistemic investment," or the level of certainty with which a self-view is endorsed. These latter results support the theory that regional differentiation of the mPFC may be organized according to level of certainty with which a given stimulus is processed (Legrand & Ruby, 2009). According to this view, ventral portions of the mPFC respond strongly to self-related cues simply because there is more information related to the self (i.e. episodic AM, semantic AM, information related to the conceptual self) upon which to draw, and, thus, a high degree of certainty. In contrast, dorsal mPFC may be preferentially recruited when decisions are based on less available information, as is the case when trying to decipher the mind of another person or when making ambiguous judgments about the self. A recent meta-analysis showed that whereas mPFC was involved more generally in tasks requiring evaluations concerning conceptual selfhood, rostral sub-regions were specific to episodic components of AM retrieval and caudal sub-regions to semantic components of AM (Martinelli et al., 2013).

In addition to self-referential processing, ventral portions of the mPFC have also been linked to emotion (Roy et al., 2012), decision-making (Euston et al., 2012), social cognition (Michell et al., 2005; Murray et al., 2012), and schemas (Ghosh & Gilboa, 2014; Ghosh et al., 2014). Reconciling these different viewpoints, it has been suggested that a core function of the ventral mPFC is to attach a sense of subjective value to a given stimulus (Delgado et al., 2016). With specific respect to AM, the ventral mPFC has been argued to endow memories with subjective value by incorporating personal significance and emotional intensity (D'Argembeau et al., 2012; Lin et al., 2015; Summerfield et al., 2009). For example, Lin et al. (2015) showed that recruitment of the ventral mPFC during AM retrieval modulates the personal significance and emotional intensity of memories. Critically, they showed that recruitment of the ventral mPFC during AM retrieval was correlated with ratings on the likability of isolated components of each memory. Taken together, these results suggest that the ventral mPFC adds a subjective sense of value informed by the emotional self-relevance of the individual components of memories.

In accordance with the viewpoint that mPFC contributes more broadly to evaluative aspects related to the self, Legrand and Ruby (2009) identified the mPFC as a member of the E-network, a connected set of brain regions that have been traditionally linked to self-referential processing but are argued to respond more strongly to evaluative processing in general including the self, others, or objects in the world. The authors emphasize that self-referential information is not self-specific, as regions within the E-network can be adapted to perform a host of functions that all require inferential processing of information retrieved from memory (e.g., theory-of-mind judgments; Legrand & Ruby, 2009). AM is a prime example of inferential processing, which is why regions of the E-network are commonly recruited during functional neuroimaging studies of AM retrieval. Besides the mPFC, the E-network comprises the precuneus, posterior cingulate, and right temporal parietal junction (TPJ), and the temporal poles.

Although cortical midline structures of the E-network may not be self-specific, they do play a large role in supporting self-specific processes. Summerfield et al. (2009) observed activation of the precuneus, posterior cingulate, and right TPJ in response to authentic AMs as opposed to imagined events involving the self. Moreover, a recent study that tracked the brain activity of highly trained meditators as they dissolved their sense of selfhood by loosening the lines separating self from external world found pronounced deactivations of the TPJ, as well as in medial structures including the precuneus and portions of the posterior cingulate (Dor-Ziderman et al., 2016). The authors reasoned that these areas play a large role in creating a fundamental sense of selfhood by delineating boundaries between internal and external environments. Early intuitions on the function of the TPJ proposed that this region manipulates the visuo-spatial representation of the body schema (Gerstmann, 1957). More recent evidence has supported this viewpoint. For example, the TPJ responds to mental imagery of one's own body (Blanke et al., 2005), and has been linked to the site of multisensory and vestibular integration responsible for creating a sense of embodiment (i.e. the feeling of being centrally located within one's own body; see Lenggenhager et al., 2006 for review). The posterior cingulate has also been associated with processes underlying a fundamental sense of selfhood based on bodily centered processes. Guterstam et al. (2015) demonstrated that activation patterns of the posterior cingulate correspond to perceived bodily location and to the visual perspective from which an event is experienced. They suggested that the posterior cingulate plays a role in the "perceptual representation of the bodily self in space" (p. 1416) by combining feelings of embodiment, decoded from activity in the hippocampus, posterior cingulate, retrosplenial cortex, and intraparietal cortex, with bodily self-location, decoded from activity within premotor and intraparietal cortex. The finding that the posterior cingulate is more responsive to real versus imagined events (Summerfield et al., 2009) may well be because authentic life events entail higher degrees of embodiment compared to their imagined counterparts.

More generally the posterior cingulate has been proposed as a "central hub system that integrates self-referential processing with ... episodic retrieval, emotional processing, visual imagery, and awareness" (Kim, 2012, p. 973). This region shows consistent preference for manipulations involving high degrees of self-relatedness (Kim, 2012). It is functionally divided according to hemisphere; the right posterior cingulate displays a preference for real as opposed to imagined events involving the self, whereas the left posterior cingulate is sensitive to more general modulation by real events regardless of whether the self is involved (Summerfield et al., 2009). Portions of the posterior cingulate are additionally known to be involved in decoding the familiarity associated with specific, personally meaningful locations (Horn et al., 2016; Qin et al., 2012; Montalidi et al., 2006; Rissman et al., 2016; Sugiura et al., 2005). Rissman and colleagues (2016) also decoded the strength of familiarity accompanying a given memory based on activity within the posterior cingulate and retrosplenial cortex. During AM retrieval, sub-regions of the posterior cingulate sensitive to self-processing and familiarity are thought to operate in conjunction with additional areas such as the precuneus and mPFC to tease apart real from imagined mental simulations (Hassabis & Maguire, 2007; Hassabis et al., 2007).

Taken together, these findings indicate that the brain co-opts neural circuits and regions used for general evaluation based on inferential processing in order to process self-related information during AM retrieval. The mPFC is highly involved in tasks that require inductive and deductive reasoning, both of which are recruited during AM retrieval as several disparate traces of information are combined to form a coherent, detailed mental representation of a past personal event (Legrand & Ruby, 2009; Wicker et al., 2003). Dorsal sub-regions tend to respond more to other relative to self-related processing whereas ventral regions tend to show the opposite preference. However, these distinctions are not clear-cut and further research is necessary to properly classify the individual sub-regions of the mPFC. The TPJ, especially in the right hemisphere, plays a significant role in establishing a fundamental sense of selfhood based on creating boundaries between self and world by enabling visuospatial representations of the body schema to be manipulated and establishing a sense of embodiment. Supporting this idea, abnormal functioning of the TPJ has been linked to out-of-body experiences (Blanke & Arzy, 2005). The posterior cingulate also plays a role in combining embodiment and bodily self-location (Guterstam et al., 2015). More generally this region has been proposed to integrate several cognitive functions (e.g. episodic, affective, and visual processes) with self-referential information (Kim, 2012).

While the self is the organizing force of AM, AM is not solely comprised of self-related processes. Rather the recollection of personal past events involves a form of mental time travel accompanied by a vivid sense of reliving that enables an individual to reflect on previous experiences known as autonoetic consciousness (Tulving, 1985; Wheeler et al., 1997). We now turn to the neural correlates of this unique phenomenon before addressing how another key factor, namely the egocentric perspective adopted at retrieval, influences AM.

Autonoetic consciousness

Autobiographical memory retrieval typically involves the awareness of the self in time (i.e. subjective sense of time) or autonoetic consciousness—the capacity that enables us to mentally travel back in time to re-experience events from the personal past (Tulving, 1983; Wheeler et al., 1997). Traditional viewpoints on autonoetic consciousness have tended to focus on its cognitive aspects, but more recent accounts suggest that it arises from an embodied pre-reflective sense of selfhood alongside the capacity for self-awareness (Prebble et al., 2013). Thus, aforementioned regions responsible for coding bodily aspects of selfhood such as the TPJ and posterior cingulate (Blanke & Arzy, 2005; Guterstam et al., 2015) may also contribute to a pre-reflective sense of selfhood. Additionally, the insular cortex is associated with interoceptive aspects of the body that contribute to subjective awareness (for review see Craig, 2002). In particular, the posterior extent of the insular cortex has been shown to monitor the internal state of the body based on interoceptive information, whereas its anterior extent is linked to the generation of conscious awareness of these bodily states (Craig & Craig 2009; Seth, 2013; Seth & Friston, 2016).

Self-awareness in autonoetic consciousness is thought to arise from sites within the frontal cortex that coordinate the retrieval of self-related information. Indeed, in an early review Wheeler et al. (1997) linked autonoetic consciousness to the involvement of the frontal cortex during episodic memory retrieval. Moreover, frontal cortex impairment in frontotemporal dementia, a neurodegenerative disorder that progressively destroys neurons within the frontal and temporal lobes in addition to their connections to other brain regions, has been linked to impaired autonoetic consciousness (Piolino et al., 2003). Some studies have also shown that medial portions of the frontal cortex are recruited to a greater extent during AM retrieval when memory involves episodic versus semantic information, likely due to increased autonoetic consciousness in episodic memories (Levine et al., 2004; Maguire & Mummery, 1999—although see Martinelli et al., 2013).

Autonoetic consciousness during AM retrieval is typically tested with subjective reports of reliving, recollection, or re-experience (Rubin et al., 2003). Reliving depends upon structures within the MTL that encode the conscious awareness that accompanies encoding and retrieval (Moscovitch, 1995). Supporting this idea, patients with transient global amnesia resulting in damage to the CA1 sub-region of the hippocampus are impaired on autonoetic recollection during AM retrieval, as shown by reduced frequency of remember responses as opposed to know judgments during recognition memory (Bartsch et al., 2011). The hippocampus is especially sensitive to the phenomenological characteristics that tend to correlate with reliving, such as level of memory detail, emotional intensity, and degree of personal significance (Addis et al., 2004). However, rather than being the source of these phenomenological characteristics, the hippocampus acts more like an index that enables the retrieval of stored contextual information in neocortical structures outside of the hippocampus, which then enables the rich recollection that contributes to autonoetic consciousness.

Posterior parietal cortices have also been associated with recollective qualities of AM retrieval supporting autonoetic consciousness. Evidence from patients with lesions to the posterior parietal cortex are impaired on free recall of some aspects of AM (Berryhill, 2012; Berryhill et al., 2007). For example, Berryhill et al. (2007) tested two patients with bilateral lesions of the posterior parietal cortex and found that they were unable to spontaneously recall specific episodic details associated with AM retrieval compared to healthy controls. However, when explicitly questioned the patients were able to retrieve additional episodic details in memories, suggesting that posterior parietal cortex is integral for mediating attention to recovered memory details. In line with this theory, the attention-to-memory hypothesis of parietal function suggests that dorsal parietal cortex is sensitive to top-down, goal-directed attention during memory retrieval, whereas activity in ventral parietal cortex is cued by salient aspects of retrieved memory contents in a bottom-up fashion (Cabeza et al., 2008). Taking into account these findings, Berryhill (2012) proposed that lesions of the posterior parietal cortex generally prevent access to the rich details available in memory, which results in a diminished sense of recollection during retrieval. In support of this idea, the same voxels in ventral parietal cortex (i.e. angular gyrus) sensitive to subjectively reported vividness during retrieval also carry specific visual information about the retrieved event (Kuhl & Chun, 2014). Loss of access to the stored details of AM may also be due to disrupted coordination between posterior parietal cortex and frontal regions (Moscovitch et al., 2016).

Together, several lines of converging evidence imply a role for posterior parietal cortex in establishing the recollective qualities of remembering, a hallmark of autonoetic consciousness, by directing attentional resources to content-specific memory representations in a goal-directive way. This unique ability to mentally travel through time is distinctly contingent upon the concept of being a self, since "there can be no travel without a traveler" (Tulving, 2005, pp. 14–15). A key implication is that this traveler must adopt a certain visual perspective in his or her memory, which we know has significant implications for AM retrieval.

Egocentric perspective

Autobiographical memories may be retrieved from one of two egocentric perspectives (i.e., self-centered frame of reference): (1) an own-eyes perspective, whereby one re-experiences the memory as events are typically encoded, and (2) an observer perspective, whereby one is able to see oneself in the memory as if from a bystander's point of view (Nigro & Neisser, 1983). Having an egocentric visual perspective is a necessary feature for remembering AMs (Rubin & Umanath, 2015). Moreover, the visual perspective adopted during memory retrieval can influence the phenomenology, content, and accuracy of memories, and these changes can persist over time (Berntsen & Rubin, 2006; Marcotti & St. Jacques, 2018; McIsaac & Eich, 2002; Robinson & Swanson, 1993; Sekiguchi & Nonaka, 2014).

Visual perspective in memory has been linked to mental imagery processes in the posterior parietal cortex (Aguirre & D'Esposito, 1999; Ciaramelli et al., 2010; Wilson et al., 2005), and to the precuneus (for reviews see Byrne et al., 2007; Cavanna & Trimble, 2006). The precuneus is associated with mental imagery processes during memory retrieval, as well as visuospatial imagery and self-referential processes (for review see Cavanna & Trimble, 2006), which may support the ability to navigate in space (Ghaem et al., 1997; Spiers and Maguire, 2006; for review see Boccia et al., 2014). Some researchers have argued that many of the functions attributed to the precuneus reflect the capacity to orient the internal representations of the self with the external world (Peer et al., 2015). Much less is known about how visual perspective influences the neural mechanisms of AM retrieval. One reason is that visual perspective is frequently left uncontrolled or restricted to an "own eyes" perspective in functional neuroimaging studies of AM. This may explain why the precuneus is not considered to be a core region during AM (for review see Svoboda et al., 2006), despite robust recruitment in nearby posterior cingulate regions. Those AM studies that have reported precuneus have linked neural recruitment to the ability to generate and elaborate upon vivid mental images (Daselaar et al., 2008; Fuentemilla et al., 2014; Gardini et al., 2006; Söderlund et al., 2012), as well as the construction of complex and realistic scenes (Hassabis et al., 2007; Summerfield et al., 2009).

Recently a few studies have directly investigated visual perspective during AM retrieval, but they have found inconsistent findings related to the involvement of posterior parietal cortices. Structural MRI studies have suggested that the volume of gray matter in the precuneus is positively related to the spontaneous retrieval of AMs from an own eyes perspective (Freton et al., 2014; Hebscher et al., 2018). However, fMRI studies have reported greater recruitment of the precuneus for observer perspectives (Grol et al., 2017) or common involvement (Eich et al., 2009). In a recent fMRI study, Iriye and St. Jacques (2018) found that the involvement of posterior parietal cortices depended upon how and when these regions interact with the hippocampus. During early phases of retrieval, when a particular memory was searched for and constructed, observer perspectives were associated with stronger hippocampal functional connectivity with posterior parietal regions (i.e., precuneus, angular gyrus), and subsequently led to less recruitment of posterior parietal and other core AM regions during later phases of retrieval when memory details were elaborated upon.

The inconsistent findings regarding the involvement of posterior parietal cortices when adopting a particular egocentric perspective during memory retrieval could be explained by differing demands related to shifting visual perspective. Supporting this idea, St. Jacques et al. (2017) recently demonstrated involvement of the posterior parietal cortex (i.e., precuneus and angular gyrus) when participants were asked to actively shift their visual perspective during AM retrieval from a dominant own eyes perspective to an observer perspective. Moreover, they found that the degree of precuneus involvement when shifting visual perspective also predicted the degree of online reductions in emotional intensity during retrieval, as well as subsequent changes in the dominant visual perspective of AMs. Subsequent research has replicated this finding, demonstrating increased involvement of the precuneus when shifting visual perspective—regardless of the direction of the shift in perspective (St. Jacques et al., 2018). These findings dovetail with theories of memory and imagination suggesting that egocentric frameworks generated during retrieval from long term memory within the precuneus can be manipulated and updated when people imagine the possible movements they can make within the remembered scene (Byrne et al., 2007). Such processes may be recruited more when people adopt an observer perspective during retrieval, which is more likely to require updating of internal representations of the world in order to retrieve memories from a novel self-location in space. Interestingly, the manipulation of egocentric perspective during AM retrieval is also associated with neural recruitment in some of the same brain regions that are typically more involved in the constructive processes that support imagination (St. Jacques et al., 2018).

Visual perspective may influence not only the viewpoint from which mental imagery contributes to remembering, but also the role of the body in memory. For example, Grol et al. (2017) observed that neural recruitment of the TPJ was greater after adopting an observer perspective compared to an own eyes perspective during AM retrieval, which they suggested was related to the greater transformations required to mentally shift an egocentric perspective to an alternative location in the memory when adopting an observer perspective in line with the role of this region in mental transformations of one's own body (Arzy et al., 2006; Blanke & Arzy, 2005; Blanke et al., 2005). An additional neuroimaging study by Eich et al. (2009) found that retrieving events from observer perspectives involved reduced recruitment in brain regions associated with bodily states, namely insular, somatosensory, and motor cortices (Critchley et al., 2001, 2004). Visual perspective also influences how systems regulating memory and bodily sensations communicate with one another. Iriye & St. Jacques (2018) found that retrieving AMs from observer perspectives was associated with greater functional connectivity between the hippocampus and insula, perhaps reflecting increased effort required to restore internal bodily states when adopting a visual perspective centered outside of the body. Thus, adopting an observer perspective during memory retrieval is linked to increased activation of areas that mediate mental imagery of one's own body (i.e. TPJ; Grol et al., 2017), alongside decreased recruitment of regions associated with bodily sensations (i.e. insular and somatomotor cortices; Eich et al., 2009) in spite of increased functional connectivity between critical hubs of memory and bodily representation (Iriye & St. Jacques, 2018).

Discussion

In the current chapter we have reviewed evidence regarding the neural basis of the self in AM. The evidence has shown that the neural basis of AM is largely devoted to the processing of self-referential information in a network of regions known as the E-network (Legrand & Ruby, 2009). Medial PFC is ubiquitously activated by functional neuroimaging studies of AM (Svoboda et al., 2007), with separate sub-regions sensitive to episodic, semantic, and conceptual self-components of AM (Martinelli et al., 2013). Aspects of bodily selfhood activated by AM retrieval have been associated with activity of the right TPJ and posterior cingulate, whereas the precuneus has been linked to visuospatial processing of mental images. Autonoetic consciousness, which allows the projection of the self in time, thereby permitting an individual to reflect on his/her experience, is linked to coordination of MTL and posterior parietal cortices that mediate the vivid re-experiencing of the event with frontal sites that have been associated with self-awareness and reality monitoring processes (Greenberg & Rubin, 2003; Prebble et al., 2013). The egocentric perspective of memories is the least understood, but likely relies on precuneus and other posterior parietal cortices that interact with medial temporal regions to modulate the types of information recalled in AM, thereby fundamentally altering how an event is re-experienced. Much progress has been made in understanding how self-referential information, autonoetic consciousness, and egocentric perspective are instantiated by the brain. However, many questions remain. Below we discuss some of the exciting future directions of this research.

How visual perspective and embodiment (i.e. sense of bodily selfhood) interact to support AM at both encoding and retrieval stages is an important but underdeveloped field of research. During AM retrieval, the current position of the body has been shown to cue memories associated with similar body postures when they were originally encoded (Dijkstra et al., 2007). Visual perspective and the sense of embodiment during memory encoding may also contribute to how memories are later retrieved.

Supporting this viewpoint, anecdotal clinical reports have linked out-of-body experiences during dissociative episodes to impaired memory (e.g., Cardena & Spiegel, 1993; Ozer & Weiss, 2004). Dissociative symptoms are reported in several mental illnesses, including post-traumatic stress disorder, anxiety (Nicholson et al., 2015), and schizophrenia (de Haan & Fuchs, 2010; Stanghellini, 2009). Moreover, these individuals adopt observer perspectives more often compared to healthy controls during mental imagery (posttraumatic stress disorder: McIsaac & Eich, 2004; St. Jacques et al., 2013; social anxiety: Hackmann et al., 1998; Wells et al., 1998; schizophrenia: Parnas & Handest, 2003; Potheegadoo et al., 2013).

Recent advances in immersive virtual reality techniques now provide the means to manipulate visual perspective and the level of embodiment during memory encoding. For example, Bergouignan et al. (2014) investigated, for the first time, how encoding realistic events from a first-person perspective centered within the body versus outside of the body influenced how memories were later remembered. Participants experienced a realistic social interaction while wearing a virtual reality headset live-linked to a 360° camera positioned to create a first-person perspective within or outside of the body, and the sense of embodiment was manipulated using a standard approach involving synchronous or asynchronous visuo-tactile feedback. They found that memories encoded from an out-of-body perspective were associated with a decrease in recollection and changes in recruitment of the posterior hippocampus, when compared to memories encoded from within the body. This preliminary study provides an initial glimpse into how embodiment influences the interaction between visual perspective and AM. Better understanding the influence of embodiment on visual perspective in AM will be an exciting area for future development.

The simple sense of having a body and being able to separate its physical boundaries from the external world makes it clear that something rather nebulous we refer to as a self must exist. Yet, attempts to identify the neural underpinnings of self-specific processes have largely failed since neural circuits devoted to self-specific processes are also engaged by a number of other cognitive functions, including theory-of-mind judgments (Buckner & Carroll, 2007: Hassabis & Maguire, 2007; Rabin et al., 2010) and the evaluation of objects (Legrand & Ruby, 2009). Such evidence leads to the somewhat disturbing thought that there may not actually be a self, according to the brain.

However, egocentric perspective is a prime example of a purely self-specific process and, consequently, a robust target for future research into the neural correlates of selfhood. Egocentric perspective is inextricably linked to the perceiving subject and no-one else, thereby drawing a distinction between self and non-self (Legrand & Ruby, 2009). Moreover, adopting another person's egocentric perspective is impossible, even in the case of social perspective taking or visualizing mental scenes from an observer's perspective, because these shifts would always remain one's own "self-specific perspective on the world" (Legrand & Ruby, 2009; p. 276). Thus, the handful of neuroimaging studies investigating the neural correlates of visual perspective in AM must be expanded in future research in order to elucidate the mechanisms of self-specific processing. This research should be embedded within an empirically testable theory of how humans are able to experience a sense of self-continuity, both phenomeno-logical and narrative, from disparate, degraded, and dynamic information found in the contents of AM (Prebble et al., 2013). Investigating aberrant cognitive processes that underlie disorders characterized by a fragmented sense of selfhood will likely provide additional insights into the nature of the self.

One such disorder involving a fractured sense of self is schizophrenia (Sass & Parnass, 2003; Sass et al., 2018; Zandersen & Parnas, 2018). Further study of this dis-order offers a unique opportunity to understand how fundamental layers of selfhood based in the physical body interact with higher levels, such as the narrative-self con-structed from personal past experiences. One of the earliest symptoms of schizo-phrenia is a disordered sense of embodiment, wherein one feels disconnected from the physical self (e.g. the body feels the wrong size or alien altogether) and/or a loss of bodily coherence (e.g. individual body parts feel detached from one another; Fuchs & Schlimme, 2009; Parnas & Handest, 2003). In addition to clinical reports detailing disordered bodily selfhood, experimental evidence demonstrates that schizophrenic patients do not show an advantage for processing of bodily self, versus non-self, re-lated information, which characterizes behavior of control subjects (Ferri et al., 2012). Narrative selfhood, a high-level form of selfhood derived from AM, is also impaired in schizophrenia; patients exhibit a disordered connection between the self and auto-biographical memory (Berna et al., 2015), including deficits in conscious recollection during AM retrieval linked to executive dysfunction (Danion et al., 2007) and auto-biographical reasoning (i.e. the process of extracting meaning from AM; Berna et al., 2011). A comprehensive understanding of the disordered relationship between high (e.g. narrative) and low (e.g. bodily) levels of selfhood in the context of schizophrenia not only stands to point towards improved treatment options, but ultimately elucidate how a unitary, stable concept of selfhood is created in healthy individuals.

Whereas this chapter has focused on the relationship between self and AM, selfhood is also an essential component of other cognitive processes involving internal mental simulation, such as those governed by the default network, which show a high degree of overlap with the neural correlates of AM (e.g., imagination, future episodic simula-tion, counterfactual thinking; e.g. Andrews-Hanna et al., 2010; Schacter et al. , 2012, 2015). For example, adopting a novel egocentric perspective in AM and constructing an episodic counterfactual simulation of how a past event could have occurred both recruit similar frontoparietal regions (St. Jacques et al., 2018). Additional research has also corroborated the similarities between memory for the past with the im-agining of future events (Schacter & Addis, 2007; Schacter et al., 2007). Consequently, by investigating the biological and self-structured basis of our autobiographical past, one is also investigating the brain's most valuable ability, namely the creation of mental models based on prior experiences of the surrounding world both real and imagined, capable of orienting to past, present, or future. Further investigation into the similar-ities and differences between how sense of self plays into the variety of cognitive func-tions requiring the creation of mental scenes will do much to build a broader, more comprehensive understanding of how a stable, unified, yet flexible self-concept is constructed and maintained throughout time.

Conclusion

The wealth of neuroimaging studies to date has revealed how the neural correlates of AM are structured according to self-related processes in three key areas: the processing of self-related information, autonoetic consciousness, and egocentric visual perspective. Future research should make use of rapid advances in affordable virtual reality technology to explore previously side-swept topics such as the influence of embodiment on visual perspective in AM, and similarities and differences underlying additional cognitive processes strongly linked to selfhood such as imagination, future episodic thinking, and memory.

References

Addis, D. R., Knapp, K., Roberts, R. P., & Schacter, D. L. (2012). Routes to the past: neural substrates of direct and generative autobiographical memory retrieval. *Neuroimage*, *59*, 2908–2922.

Addis, D. R., Moscovitch, M., & McAndrews, M. P. (2007). Consequences of hippocampal damage across the autobiographical memory network in left temporal lobe epilepsy. *Brain*, *130*, 2327–2342.

Addis, D. R., Wong, A. T., & Schacter, D. L. (2007). Remembering the past and imagining the future: Common and distinct neural substrates during event construction and elaboration. *Neuropsychologia*, *45*, 1363–1377.

Addis, D. R., McIntosh, A. R., Moscovitch, M., Crawley, A. P., & McAndrews, M. P. (2004). Characterizing spatial and temporal features of autobiographical memory retrieval networks: A partial least squares approach. *Neuroimage*, *23*, 1460–1471.

Addis, D. R., Moscovitch, M., Crawley, A. P., & McAndrews, M. P. (2004). Recollective qualities modulate hippocampal activation during autobiographical memory retrieval. *Hippocampus*, *14*, 752–762.

Aguirre, G. K., & D'Esposito, M. (1999). Topographical disorientation: a synthesis and taxonomy. *Brain*, *122*, 1613–1628.

Andreasen, N. C., O'Leary, D. S., Cizadlo, T., Arndt, S., Rezai, K., Watkins, G. L., et al. (1995). Remembering the past: two facets of episodic memory explored with positron emission tomography. *American Journal of Psychiatry*, *152*, 1576–1585.

Andrews-Hanna, J. R., Smallwood, J., & Spreng, N.R. (2014). The default network and self-generated thought: component processes, dynamic control, and clinical relevance. *Annals of the New York Academy of Sciences*, *1316*, 29–52.

Andrews-Hanna, J. R., Reidler, J. S., Sepulcre, J., Poulin, R., & Buckner, R. L. (2010). Functional–anatomic fractionation of the brain's default network. *Neuron*, *65*, 550–562.

Annese, J., Schenker-Ahmed, N. M., Bartsch, H., Maechler, P., Sheh, C., Thomas, N., et al. (2014). Postmortem examination of patient HM's brain based on histological sectioning and digital 3D reconstruction. *Nature Communications*, *5*, 3122.

Arzy, S., Thut, G., Mohr, C., Michel, C. M., & Blanke, O. (2006). Neural basis of embodiment: distinct contributions of temporoparietal junction and extrastriate body area. *Journal of Neuroscience*, *26*, 8074–8081.

Bartsch, T., Döhring, J., Rohr, A., Jansen, O., & Deuschl, G. (2011). CA1 neurons in the human hippocampus are critical for autobiographical memory, mental time travel, and autonoetic consciousness. *Proceedings of the National Academy of Sciences of the USA*, *108*, 17562–17567.

Benoit, R. G., & Schacter, D. L. (2015). Specifying the core network supporting episodic simulation and episodic memory by activation likelihood estimation. *Neuropsychologia, 75*, 450–457.

Bergouignan, L., Nyberg, L., & Ehrsson, H. H. (2014). Out-of-body-induced hippocampal amnesia. *Proceedings of the National Academy of Sciences of the USA, 111*, 4421–4426.

Berna, F., Bennouna-Greene, M., Potheegadoo, J., Verry, P., Conway, M. A., & Danion, J. M. (2011). Self-defining memories related to illness and their integration into the self in patients with schizophrenia. *Psychiatry Research, 189*, 49–54.

Berna, F., Potheegadoo, J., Aouadi, I., Ricarte, J. J., Allé, M. C., Coutelle, R., et al. (2015). A meta-analysis of autobiographical memory studies in schizophrenia spectrum disorder. *Schizophrenia Bulletin, 42*, 56–66.

Berntsen, D., & Rubin, D. C. (2006). Emotion and vantage point in autobiographical. *Cognition and Emotion, 20*, 1193–1215.

Berryhill, M. E. (2012). Insights from neuropsychology: pinpointing the role of the posterior parietal cortex in episodic and working memory. *Frontiers in Integrative Neuroscience, 6*, 31.

Berryhill, M. E., Phuong, L., Picasso, L., Cabeza, R., & Olson, I. R. (2007). Parietal lobe and episodic memory: bilateral damage causes impaired free recall of autobiographical memory. *Journal of Neuroscience, 27*, 14415–14423.

Blanke, O., & Arzy, S. (2005). The out-of-body experience: disturbed self-processing at the temporo-parietal junction. *The Neuroscientist, 11*, 16–24.

Blanke, O., Mohr, C., Michel, C. M., Pascual-Leone, A., Brugger, P., Seeck, M., et al. (2005). Linking out-of-body experience and self processing to mental own-body imagery at the temporoparietal junction. *Journal of Neuroscience, 25*, 550–557.

Boccia, M., Nemmi, F., & Guariglia, C. (2014). Neuropsychology of environmental navigation in humans: review and meta-analysis of fMRI studies in healthy participants. *Neuropsychology Review, 24*, 236–251.

Bonnici, H. M., Chadwick, M. J., Lutti, A., Hassabis, D., Weiskopf, N., & Maguire, E. A. (2012). Detecting representations of recent and remote autobiographical memories in vmPFC and hippocampus. *Journal of Neuroscience, 32*, 16982–16991.

Bonnici, H. M., Maguire, E.A. (2017). Two years later—Revisiting autobiographical memory representations in vmPFC and hippocampus. *Neuropsychologia, 110*, 159–169.

Brewer, W. F. (1986). What is autobiographical memory? In D. C. Rubin (ed.), *Autobiographical memory* (pp. 25–49). New York: Cambridge University Press.

Buckner, R. L., Andrews-Hanna, J. R., & Schacter, D. L. (2008). The brain's default network. *Annals of the New York Academy of Sciences, 1124*, 1–38.

Buckner, R. L., & Carroll, D. C. (2007). Self-projection and the brain. *Trends in Cognitive Sciences, 11*, 49–57.

Byrne, P., Becker, S., & Burgess, N. (2007). Remembering the past and imagining the future: a neural model of spatial memory and imagery. *Psychological Review, 114*, 340.

Cabeza, R., Ciaramelli, E., Olson, I. R., & Moscovitch, M. (2008). The parietal cortex and episodic memory: an attentional account. *Nature Reviews Neuroscience, 9*, 613–625.

Cabeza, R., & St Jacques, P. (2007). Functional neuroimaging of autobiographical memory. *Trends in Cognitive Sciences, 11*, 219–227.

Cardena, E., Spiegel, D. (1993). Dissociative reactions to the San-Francisco Bay Area earthquake of 1989. *American Journal of Psychiatry, 150*, 474–478.

Cavanna, A. E., & Trimble, M. R. (2006). The precuneus: a review of its functional anatomy and behavioural correlates. *Brain, 129*, 564–583.

Chadwick, M. J., Mullally, S. L., & Maguire, E. A. (2013). The hippocampus extrapolates beyond the view in scenes: an fMRI study of boundary extension. *Cortex, 49*, 2067–2079.

Ciaramelli, E., Rosenbaum, R. S., Solcz, S., Levine, B., & Moscovitch, M. (2010). Mental space travel: damage to posterior parietal cortex prevents egocentric navigation and reexperiencing of remote spatial memories. *Journal of Experimental Psychology: Learning, Memory, and Cognition, 36*, 619.

Conway, M. A., & Holmes, E. (2005). Autobiographical memory and the working self. In N. Braisby & A. Gellatly (eds.), *Cognitive psychology* (pp. 507–43). Oxford: Oxford University Press.

Conway, M. A., & Pleydell-Pearce, C. W. (2000). The construction of autobiographical memories in the self-memory system. *Psychological Review, 107,* 261.

Conway, M. A., Turk, D. J., Miller, S. L., Logan, J., Nebes, R. D., Meltzer, C. C., & Becker, J. T. (1999). A positron emission tomography (PET) study of autobiographical memory retrieval. *Memory, 7,* 679–703.

Conway, M. A., Singer, J. A., & Tagini, A. (2004). The self and autobiographical memory: Correspondence and coherence. *Social Cognition, 22,* 491.

Corkin, S. (2002). What's new with the amnesic patient HM? *Nature Reviews Neuroscience, 3,* 153–160.

Craig, A. D. (2002). How do you feel? Interoception: the sense of the physiological condition of the body. *Nature Reviews Neuroscience, 3,* 655.

Craig, A. D., & Craig, A. D. (2009). How do you feel—now? The anterior insula and human awareness. *Nature Reviews Neuroscience, 10,* 59–70.

Critchley, H. D., Wiens, S., Rotshtein, P., Öhman, A., & Dolan, R. J. (2004). Neural systems supporting interoceptive awareness. *Nature Neuroscience, 7,* 189–195.

Critchley, H. D., Mathias, C. J., & Dolan, R. J. (2001). Neuroanatomical basis for first-and second-order representations of bodily states. *Nature Neuroscience, 4,* 207–212.

Daltrozzo, J., Kotchoubey, B., Gueler, F., & Karim, A. A. (2016). Effects of transcranial magnetic stimulation on body perception: no evidence for specificity of the right temporo-parietal junction. *Brain Topography, 29,* 704–715.

Damasio, A. (2012). *Self comes to mind: Constructing the conscious brain.* New York: Vintage.

Danion, J. M., Huron, C., Vidailhet, P., & Berna, F. (2007). Functional mechanisms of episodic memory impairment in schizophrenia. *Canadian Journal of Psychiatry, 52,* 693–701.

D'Argembeau, A., Jedidi, H., Balteau, E., Bahri, M., Phillips, C., & Salmon, E. (2012). Valuing one's self: medial prefrontal involvement in epistemic and emotive investments in self-views. *Cerebral Cortex, 22,* 659–667.

Daselaar, S. M., Rice, H. J., Greenberg, D. L., Cabeza, R., LaBar, K. S., & Rubin, D. C. (2008). The spatiotemporal dynamics of autobiographical memory: neural correlates of recall, emotional intensity, and reliving. *Cerebral Cortex, 18,* 217–229.

Daselaar, S. M., Fleck, M. S., & Cabeza, R. (2006). Triple dissociation in the medial temporal lobes: recollection, familiarity, and novelty. *Journal of Neurophysiology, 96,* 1902–1911.

de Haan, S., & Fuchs, T. (2010). The ghost in the machine: disembodiment in schizophrenia—two case studies. *Psychopathology, 43,* 327–333.

de la Vega, A., Chang, L. J., Banich, M. T., Wager, T. D., & Yarkoni, T. (2016). Large-scale meta-analysis of human medial frontal cortex reveals tripartite functional organization. *Journal of Neuroscience, 36,* 6553–6562.

Delgado, M. R., Beer, J. S., Fellows, L. K., Huettel, S. A., Platt, M. L., Quirk, G. J., & Schiller, D. (2016). Viewpoints: Dialogues on the functional role of the ventromedial prefrontal cortex. *Nature Neuroscience, 19,* 1545–1552.

Denny, B. T., Kober, H., Wager, T. D., & Ochsner, K. N. (2012). A meta-analysis of functional neuroimaging studies of self-and other judgments reveals a spatial gradient for mentalizing in medial prefrontal cortex. *Journal of Cognitive Neuroscience, 24,* 1742–1752.

Dhindsa, K., Drobinin, V., King, J., Hall, G.B., Burgess, N., Becker, S. (2014). Examining the role of the temporo-parietal network in memory, imagery, and viewpoint transformations. *Frontiers in Human Neuroscience, 8,* 709.

Dijkstra, K., Kaschak, M. P., & Zwaan, R. A. (2007). Body posture facilitates retrieval of autobiographical memories. *Cognition, 102,* 139–149.

Dor-Ziderman, Y., Ataria, Y., Fulder, S., Goldstein, A., & Berkovich-Ohana, A. (2016). Self-specific processing in the meditating brain: a MEG neurophenomenology study. *Neuroscience of Consciousness, 2016,* niw019.

Eich, E., Nelson, A. L., Leghari, M. A., & Handy, T. C. (2009). Neural systems mediating field and observer memories. *Neuropsychologia, 47,* 2239–2251.

Euston, D. R., Gruber, A. J., & McNaughton, B. L. (2012). The role of medial prefrontal cortex in memory and decision making. *Neuron, 76,* 1057–1070.

Ferri, F., Frassinetti, F., Mastrangelo, F., Salone, A., Ferro, F. M., & Gallese, V. (2012). Bodily self and schizophrenia: the loss of implicit self-body knowledge. *Consciousness and Cognition, 21,* 1365–1374.

Fossati, P. (2013). Imaging autobiographical memory. *Dialogues in Clinical Neuroscience, 15,* 487.

Freton, M., Lemogne, C., Bergouignan, L., Delaveau, P., Lehéricy, S., & Fossati, P. (2014). The eye of the self: precuneus volume and visual perspective during autobiographical memory retrieval. *Brain Structure and Function, 219,* 959–968.

Fuchs, T., & Schlimme, J. E. (2009). Embodiment and psychopathology: a phenomenological perspective. *Current Opinion in Psychiatry, 22,* 570–575.

Fuentemilla, L., Barnes, G.R., Düzel, E., Levine, B. (2014). Theta oscillations orchestrate medial temporal lobe and neocortex in remembering autobiographical memories. *Neuroimage, 85,* Part 2, 730–737.

Gardini, S., Cornoldi, C., De Beni, R., Venneri, A. (2006). Left mediotemporal structures mediate the retrieval of episodic autobiographical mental images. *Neuroimage, 30,* 645–655.

Gerstmann, J. (1957). Some notes on the Gerstmann syndrome. *Neurology, 7,* 866–866.

Ghaem, O., Mellet, E., Crivello, F., Tzourio, N., Mazoyer, B., Berthoz, A., & Denis, M. (1997). Mental navigation along memorized routes activates the hippocampus, precuneus, and insula. *Neuroreport, 8,* 739–744.

Ghosh, V. E., & Gilboa, A. (2014). What is a memory schema? A historical perspective on current neuroscience literature. *Neuropsychologia, 53,* 104–114.

Ghosh, V. E., Moscovitch, M., Colella, B. M., & Gilboa, A. (2014). Schema representation in patients with ventromedial PFC lesions. *Journal of Neuroscience, 34,* 12057–12070.

Gilbert, S. J., Spengler, S., Simons, J. S., Steele, J. D., Lawrie, S. M., Frith, C. D., & Burgess, P. W. (2006). Functional specialization within rostral prefrontal cortex (area 10): a meta-analysis. *Journal of Cognitive Neuroscience, 18,* 932–948.

Gilboa, A. (2004). Autobiographical and episodic memory—one and the same?: Evidence from prefrontal activation in neuroimaging studies. *Neuropsychologia, 42,* 1336–1349.

Gilboa, A., Winocur, G., Grady, C. L., Hevenor, S. J., & Moscovitch, M. (2004). Remembering our past: functional neuroanatomy of recollection of recent and very remote personal events. *Cerebral Cortex, 14,* 1214–1225.

Graham, K. S., Lee, A. C., Brett, M., & Patterson, K. (2003). The neural basis of autobiographical and semantic memory: new evidence from three PET studies. *Cognitive, Affective, & Behavioral Neuroscience, 3,* 234–254.

Greenberg, D. L., Rice, H. J., Cooper, J. J., Cabeza, R., Rubin, D. C., & LaBar, K. S. (2005). Co-activation of the amygdala, hippocampus and inferior frontal gyrus during autobiographical memory retrieval. *Neuropsychologia, 43,* 659–674.

Greenberg, D. L., & Rubin, D. C. (2003). The neuropsychology of autobiographical memory. *Cortex, 39,* 687–728.

Greicius, M. D., Krasnow, B., Reiss, A. L., & Menon, V. (2003). Functional connectivity in the resting brain: a network analysis of the default mode hypothesis. *Proceedings of the National Academy of Sciences of the USA, 100,* 253–258.

Grol, M., Vingerhoets, G., & De Raedt, R. (2017). Mental imagery of positive and neutral memories: A fMRI study comparing field perspective imagery to observer perspective imagery. *Brain and Cognition, 111,* 13–24.

Gusnard, D. A., Akbudak, E., Shulman, G. L., & Raichle, M. E. (2001). Medial prefrontal cortex and self-referential mental activity: relation to a default mode of brain function. *Proceedings of the National Academy of Sciences of the USA, 98,* 4259–4264.

Guterstam, A., Björnsdotter, M., Gentile, G., & Ehrsson, H. H. (2015). Posterior cingulate cortex integrates the senses of self-location and body ownership. *Current Biology, 25,* 1416–1425.

Hackmann, A., Surawy, C., & Clark, D. M. (1998). Seeing yourself through others' eyes: A study of spontaneously occurring images in social phobia. *Behavioural and Cognitive Psychotherapy, 26,* 3–12.

Hassabis, D., & Maguire, E. A. (2007). Deconstructing episodic memory with construction. *Trends in Cognitive Sciences, 11,* 299–306.

Hassabis, D., Kumaran, D., & Maguire, E. A. (2007). Using imagination to understand the neural basis of episodic memory. *Journal of Neuroscience, 27,* 14365–14374.

Hebscher, M., Levine, B., & Gilboa, A. (2018). The precuneus and hippocampus contribute to individual differences in the unfolding of spatial representations during episodic autobiographical memory. *Neuropsychologia, 110,* 123–133.

Horn, M., Jardri, R., D'Hondt, F., Vaiva, G., Thomas, P., & Pins, D. (2016). The multiple neural networks of familiarity: A meta-analysis of functional imaging studies. *Cognitive, Affective, and Behavioral Neuroscience, 16,* 176–190.

Iriye, H., & St. Jacques, P. L. (2018). Construction and elaboration of autobiographical memories from multiple visual perspectives. *bioRχiv.* doi: https://doi.org/10.1101/317594

James, W. (1890/1950). *The principles of psychology* (Vol. 1). New York: Dover.

Kim, H. (2012). A dual-subsystem model of the brain's default network: self-referential processing, memory retrieval processes, and autobiographical memory retrieval. *Neuroimage, 61,* 966–977.

Klein, S. B. & Lax, M. L. (2010). The unanticipated resilience of trait self-knowledge in the face of neural damage. *Memory, 18,* 918–948.

Kuhl, B. A., & Chun, M. M. (2014). Successful remembering elicits event-specific activity patterns in lateral parietal cortex. *Journal of Neuroscience, 34,* 8051–8060.

Legrand, D., & Ruby, P. (2009). What is self-specific? Theoretical investigation and critical review of neuroimaging results. *Psychological Review, 116,* 252.

Lenggenhager, B., Smith, S. T., & Blanke, O. (2006). Functional and neural mechanisms of embodiment: importance of the vestibular system and the temporal parietal junction. *Reviews in the Neurosciences, 17,* 643–657.

Levine, B., Turner, G. R., Tisserand, D., Hevenor, S. J., Graham, S. J., & McIntosh, A. R. (2004). The functional neuroanatomy of episodic and semantic autobiographical remembering: A prospective functional MRI study. *Journal of Cognitive Neuroscience, 16,* 1633–1646.

Lin, W. J., Horner, A. J., & Burgess, N. (2016). Ventromedial prefrontal cortex, adding value to autobiographical memories. *Scientific Reports, 6,* 28630.

Maguire, E. A. (2001). Neuroimaging studies of autobiographical event memory. *Philosophical Transactions of the Royal Society B: Biological Sciences, 356,* 1441–1451.

Maguire, E. A., Henson, R. N., Mummery, C. J., & Frith, C. D. (2001). Activity in prefrontal cortex, not hippocampus, varies parametrically with the increasing remoteness of memories. *Neuroreport, 12,* 441–444.

Maguire, E. A., & Mummery, C. J. (1999). Differential modulation of a common memory retrieval network revealed by positron emission tomography. *Hippocampus, 9,* 54–61.

Maguire, E. A., Mummery, C. J., & Büchel, C. (2000). Patterns of hippocampal-cortical interaction dissociate temporal lobe memory subsystems. *Hippocampus, 10,* 475–482.

Maguire, E. A., Vargha-Khadem, F., & Mishkin, M. (2001). The effects of bilateral hippocampal damage on fMRI regional activations and interactions during memory retrieval. *Brain, 124,* 1156–1170.

Marcotti, P., & St. Jacques, P. L. (2018). Shifting visual perspective during memory retrieval reduces the accuracy of subsequent memories. *Memory, 26,* 330–341.

Martinelli, P., Sperduti, M., & Piolino, P. (2013). Neural substrates of the self-memory system: New insights from a meta-analysis. *Human Brain Mapping, 34,* 1515–1529.

McCormick, C., St-Laurent, M., Ty, A., Valiante, T. A., & McAndrews, M. P. (2013). Functional and effective hippocampal–neocortical connectivity during construction and elaboration of autobiographical memory retrieval. *Cerebral Cortex, 25,* 1297–1305.

McDermott, K. B., Szpunar, K. K., & Christ, S. E. (2009). Laboratory-based and autobiographical retrieval tasks differ substantially in their neural substrates. *Neuropsychologia, 47,* 2290–2298.

McIsaac, H. K., & Eich, E. (2002). Vantage point in episodic memory. *Psychonomic Bulletin and Review, 9,* 146–150.

McIsaac, H. K., & Eich, E. (2004). Vantage point in traumatic memory. *Psychological Science, 15,* 248–253.

Mitchell, J. P., Banaji, M. R., & MacRae, C. N. (2005). The link between social cognition and self-referential thought in the medial prefrontal cortex. *Journal of Cognitive Neuroscience, 17,* 1306–1315.

Montaldi, D., Spencer, T. J., Roberts, N., & Mayes, A. R. (2006). The neural system that mediates familiarity memory. *Hippocampus, 16,* 504–520.

Moscovitch, M., Cabeza, R., Winocur, G., & Nadel, L. (2016). Episodic memory and beyond: the hippocampus and neocortex in transformation. *Annual Review of Psychology, 67,* 105–134.

Moscovitch, M. (1995). Recovered consciousness: A hypothesis concerning modularity and episodic memory. *Journal of Clinical and Experimental Neuropsychology, 17,* 276–290.

Murray, R. J., Schaer, M., & Debbané, M. (2012). Degrees of separation: a quantitative neuroimaging meta-analysis investigating self-specificity and shared neural activation between self-and other-reflection. *Neuroscience and Biobehavioral Reviews, 36,* 1043–1059.

Muscatell, K. A., Addis, D. R., & Kensinger, E. A. (2010). Self-involvement modulates the effective connectivity of the autobiographical memory network. *Social Cognitive and Affective Neuroscience, 5,* 68–76.

Nadel, L., & Moscovitch, M. (1997). Memory consolidation, retrograde amnesia and the hippocampal complex. *Current Opinion in Neurobiology, 7,* 217–227.

Nigro, G., & Neisser, U. (1983). Point of view in personal memories. *Cognitive Psychology, 15,* 467–482.

Nicholson, A. A., Densmore, M., Frewen, P. A., Théberge, J., Neufeld, R. W., McKinnon, M. C., & Lanius, R. A. (2015). The dissociative subtype of posttraumatic stress disorder: Unique resting-state functional connectivity of basolateral and centromedial amygdala complexes. *Neuropsychopharmacology, 40,* 2317–2326.

Northoff, G., Heinzel, A., De Greck, M., Bermpohl, F., Dobrowolny, H., & Panksepp, J. (2006). Self-referential processing in our brain—a meta-analysis of imaging studies on the self. *Neuroimage, 31,* 440–457.

Ozer, E.J., Weiss, D.S. (2004). Who develops posttraumatic stress disorder? *Current Directions in Psychological Science, 13,* 169–172.

Parnas, J., & Handest, P. (2003). Phenomenology of anomalous self-experience in early schizophrenia. *Comprehensive Psychiatry, 44,* 121–134.

Potheegadoo, J., Berna, F., Cuervo-Lombard, C., & Danion, J. M. (2013). Field visual perspective during autobiographical memory recall is less frequent among patients with schizophrenia. *Schizophrenia Research, 150,* 88–92.

Peer, M., Salomon, R., Goldberg, I., Blanke, O., & Arzy, S. (2015). Brain system for mental orientation in space, time, and person. *Proceedings of the National Academy of Sciences of the USA, 112,* 11072–11077.

Piolino, P., Desgranges, B., Belliard, S., Matuszewski, V., Lalevée, C., De La Sayette, V., & Eustache, F. (2003). Autobiographical memory and autonoetic consciousness: triple dissociation in neurodegenerative diseases. *Brain, 126,* 2203–2219.

Poppenk, J., Evensmoen, H. R., Moscovitch, M., & Nadel, L. (2013). Long-axis specialization of the human hippocampus. *Trends in Cognitive Sciences, 17,* 230–240.

Prebble, S. C., Addis, D. R., & Tippett, L. J. (2013). Autobiographical memory and sense of self. *Psychological Bulletin, 139,* 815–40.

Qin, P., Liu, Y., Shi, J., Wang, Y., Duncan, N., Gong, Q., et al. (2012). Dissociation between anterior and posterior cortical regions during self-specificity and familiarity: A combined fMRI–meta-analytic study. *Human Brain Mapping, 33,* 154–164.

Rabin, J. S., Gilboa, A., Stuss, D. T., Mar, R. A., & Rosenbaum, R. S. (2010). Common and unique neural correlates of autobiographical memory and theory of mind. *Journal of Cognitive Neuroscience, 22,* 1095–1111.

Rice, H. J., & Rubin, D. C. (2009). I can see it both ways: First-and third-person visual perspectives at retrieval. *Consciousness and Cognition, 18,* 877–890.

Rissman, J., Chow, T. E., Reggente, N., & Wagner, A. D. (2016). Decoding fMRI signatures of real-world autobiographical memory retrieval. *Journal of Cognitive Neuroscience, 28,* 604–620.

Robinson, J. A., & Swanson, K. L. (1993). Field and observer modes of remembering. *Memory, 1,* 169–184.

Roy, M., Shohamy, D., & Wager, T. D. (2012). Ventromedial prefrontal–subcortical systems and the generation of affective meaning. *Trends in Cognitive Sciences, 16,* 147–156.

Rubin, D. C., Schrauf, R. W., & Greenberg, D. L. (2003). Belief and recollection of autobiographical memories. *Memory & Cognition, 31,* 887–901.

Rubin, D. C., & Umanath, S. (2015). Event memory: A theory of memory for laboratory, autobiographical, and fictional events. *Psychological Review, 122,* 1.

Sass, L., Borda, J. P., Madeira, L., Pienkos, E., & Nelson, B. (2018). Varieties of self disorder: A bio-pheno-social model of schizophrenia. *Schizophrenia Bulletin, 44,* 720–727.

Sass, L. A., & Parnas, J. (2003). Schizophrenia, consciousness, and the self. *Schizophrenia Bulletin, 29,* 427–444.

Schacter, D. L., Benoit, R. G., De Brigard, F., & Szpunar, K. K. (2015). Episodic future thinking and episodic counterfactual thinking: Intersections between memory and decisions. *Neurobiology of Learning and Memory, 117,* 14–21.

Schacter, D. L., Addis, D. R., Hassabis, D., Martin, V. C., Spreng, R. N., & Szpunar, K. K. (2012). The future of memory: remembering, imagining, and the brain. *Neuron, 76,* 677–694.

Schacter, D. L., & Addis, D. R. (2007). The cognitive neuroscience of constructive memory: remembering the past and imagining the future. *Philosophical Transactions of the Royal Society B: Biological Sciences, 362,* 773–786.

Schacter, D. L., Addis, D. R., & Buckner, R. L. (2007). Remembering the past to imagine the future: the prospective brain. *Nature Reviews Neuroscience, 8,* 657–661.

Sekiguchi, T., & Nonaka, S. (2014). The long-term effect of perspective change on the emotional intensity of autobiographical memories. *Cognition & Emotion, 28,* 375–383.

Seth, A. K. (2013). Interoceptive inference, emotion, and the embodied self. *Trends in Cognitive Sciences, 17,* 565–573.

Seth, A. K., & Friston, K. J. (2016). Active interoceptive inference and the emotional brain. *Philosophical Transactions of the Royal Society B: Biological Sciences, 371*(1708).

Sheldon, S., & Levine, B. (2016). The role of the hippocampus in memory and mental construction. *Annals of the New York Academy of Sciences, 1369,* 76–92.

Simons, J. S., Gilbert, S. J., Owen, A. M., Fletcher, P. C., & Burgess, P. W. (2005). Distinct roles for lateral and medial anterior prefrontal cortex in contextual recollection. *Journal of Neurophysiology, 94,* 813–820.

Söderlund, H., Moscovitch, M., Kumar, N., Mandic, M., & Levine, B. (2012). As time goes by: Hippocampal connectivity changes with remoteness of autobiographical memory retrieval. *Hippocampus, 22,* 670–679.

Summerfield, J. J., Hassabis, D., & Maguire, E. A. (2009). Cortical midline involvement in autobiographical memory. *Neuroimage, 44,* 1188–1200.

Squire, L. R. (2009). Memory and brain systems: 1969–2009. *Journal of Neuroscience, 29,* 12711–12716.

Spiers, H. J., & Maguire, E. A. (2006). Thoughts, behaviour, and brain dynamics during navigation in the real world. *Neuroimage, 31,* 1826–1840.

Spiers, H. J., Maguire, E. A., & Burgess, N. (2001). Hippocampal amnesia. *Neurocase, 7,* 357–382.

Spreng, R. N., & Grady, C. L. (2010). Patterns of brain activity supporting autobiographical memory, prospection, and theory of mind, and their relationship to the default mode network. *Journal of Cognitive Neuroscience, 22,* 1112–1123.

Spreng, R. N., Mar, R. A., & Kim, A. S. (2009). The common neural basis of autobiographical memory, prospection, navigation, theory of mind, and the default mode: a quantitative meta-analysis. *Journal of Cognitive Neuroscience, 21,* 489–510.

Stanghellini, G. (2009). Embodiment and schizophrenia. *World Psychiatry, 8,* 56–59.

St. Jacques, P. L., Carpenter, A. C., Szpunar, K. K., & Schacter, D. L. (2018). Remembering and imagining alternative versions of the personal past. *Neuropsychologia, 110,* 170–179.

St. Jacques, P.L., Szpunar, K. K., & Schacter, D. L. (2017). Shifting visual perspective during retrieval shapes autobiographical memories. *Neuroimage, 148,* 103–114.

Hupbach, A. (2018). The Ever-Changing Engram: Towards an Integrated Understanding of Long-Term Memory Dynamics. *Memory, 26*(3), 330–341.

St. Jacques, P.L., Kragel, P. A., & Rubin, D. C. (2013). Neural networks supporting autobiographical memory retrieval in posttraumatic stress disorder. *Cognitive, Affective, & Behavioral Neuroscience*, *13*, 554–566.

St. Jacques P.L. (2012). Functional neuroimaging of autobiographical memory. In D. Bernsten & D. C. Rubin (eds.), *Understanding autobiographical memory: Theories and approaches* (pp. 114–138). Cambridge: Cambridge University Press.

St. Jacques, P. L., Cabeza, R. (2012) Neural correlates of autobiographical memory. In S. Ghetti & P. J. Bauer (eds.), Origins and development of recollection (pp. 188–218). New York: Oxford University Press.

St. Jacques, P.L., & De Brigard, F. (2012). Neural correlates of autobiographical memory. *The Wiley handbook on the cognitive neuroscience of memory* (pp. 265–286). New York: Wiley.

St. Jacques, P. L., Conway, M. A., Lowder, M. W., & Cabeza, R. (2011). Watching my mind unfold versus yours: An fMRI study using a novel camera technology to examine neural differences in self-projection of self versus other perspectives. *Journal of Cognitive Neuroscience, 23*, 1275–1284.

St. Jacques, P. L., Kragel, P. A., & Rubin, D. C. (2011). Dynamic neural networks supporting memory retrieval. *Neuroimage, 57*, 608–616.

Squire, L. R. (1992). Memory and the hippocampus: a synthesis from findings with rats, monkeys, and humans. *Psychological Review, 99*, 195.

Sugiura, M., Shah, N. J., Zilles, K., & Fink, G. R. (2005). Cortical representations of personally familiar objects and places: functional organization of the human posterior cingulate cortex. *Journal of Cognitive Neuroscience, 17*, 183–198.

Sulpizio, V., Committeri, G., Lambrey, S., Berthoz, A., & Galati, G. (2016). Role of the human retrosplenial cortex/parieto-occipital sulcus in perspective priming. *Neuroimage 125*, 108–119.

Summerfield, J. J., Hassabis, D., & Maguire, E. A. (2009). Cortical midline involvement in autobiographical memory. *Neuroimage, 44*, 1188–1200.

Svoboda, E., McKinnon, M. C., & Levine, B. (2006). The functional neuroanatomy of autobiographical memory: a meta-analysis. *Neuropsychologia, 44*, 2189–2208.

Szpunar, K. K., Watson, J. M., & McDermott, K. B. (2007). Neural substrates of envisioning the future. *Proceedings of the National Academy of Sciences of the USA, 104*, 642–647.

Tulving, E. (1984). Precis of elements of episodic memory. *Behavioral and Brain Sciences, 7*, 223–238.

Tulving, E. (1985). Memory and consciousness. *Canadian Psychology/Psychologie canadienne, 26*, 1.

Tulving, E. (2002). Episodic memory: From mind to brain. *Annual Review of Psychology, 53*, 1–25.

Tulving, E. (2005). Episodic memory and autonoesis: Uniquely human. In H. S. Terrace, & J. Metcalfe (eds.), *The missing link in cognition: Origins of self-reflective consciousness* (pp. 3–56). New York: Oxford University Press.

Tulving, E., Kapur, S., Craik, F. I., Moscovitch, M., & Houle, S. (1994). Hemispheric encoding/retrieval asymmetry in episodic memory: positron emission tomography findings. *Proceedings of the National Academy of Sciences of the USA, 91*, 2016–2020.

Wells, A., Clark, D. M., & Ahmad, S. (1998). How do I look with my minds eye: Perspective taking in social phobic imagery. *Behaviour Research and Therapy, 36*, 631–634.

Wicker, B., Ruby, P., Royet, J. P., & Fonlupt, P. (2003). A relation between rest and the self in the brain? *Brain Research Reviews, 43*, 224–230.

Wilson, B. A., Berry, E., Gracey, F., Harrison, C., Stow, I., Macniven, J., et al. (2005). Egocentric disorientation following bilateral parietal lobe damage. *Cortex, 41*, 547–554.

Winocur, G., & Moscovitch, M. (2011). Memory transformation and systems consolidation. *Journal of the International Neuropsychological Society, 17*, 766–780.

Wheeler, M. A., Stuss, D. T., & Tulving, E. (1997). Toward a theory of episodic memory: the frontal lobes and autonoetic consciousness. *Psychological Bulletin, 121*, 331.

Zandersen, M., & Parnas, J. (2018). Identity disturbance, feelings of emptiness, and the boundaries of the schizophrenia spectrum. *Schizophrenia Bulletin, 45*, 106–113.

Zeidman, P., & Maguire, E. A. (2016). Anterior hippocampus: the anatomy of perception, imagination and episodic memory. *Nature Reviews Neuroscience, 17*, 173–182.

8

The Role of the Self in the Organization of Memories and Imagined Future Events

Alexandra Ernst and Clare J. Rathbone

Introduction

The idea that the self and autobiographical memory (AM) share a close relationship was put forward by early psychologists such as William James (1890). Since this conceptualization, debates have emerged about the definition and the theoretical models of the self, which represent a complex and multifaceted concept (Klein, 2012; Klein & Gangi, 2010; Prebble et al., 2013). With the rise of cognitive sciences, there has been a recent upsurge of interest in the relationship between the self and AM, using scientific methods from experimental psychology, cognitive neuropsychology, or neuro-imaging to address this issue. This new era has provided theoretical frameworks to develop operationalized definitions of the self and to build empirical research, which aims to better understand the complex and subtle interactions between AM and the self (Prebble et al., 2013).

Nevertheless, according to Klein (2010, 2012), most of the studies conducted to date only explore a subset of the cognitive and neural underpinnings of the self. In fact, the self encompasses a broad range of aspects, from implicit processes (e.g. low-level bodily perception) to declarative forms of self-knowledge (e.g. self-images, personality traits, values). Providing a complete picture of the different definitions and approaches used is beyond the scope of this chapter (but see Klein, 2012, for a discussion on this issue), in which we thus focus on the declarative aspects of the self—that is, the content of the self, or more specifically, knowledge that people have about themselves. Indeed, in the same way that people have conceptual knowledge about the world (e.g. Paris is the capital of France), they also possess a series of self-concepts about who they are, including abstract representations or facts about themselves (e.g. I am an independent person; I am optimistic; I like contemporary art).

Based on this conceptualization of the self, the self-memory system (SMS; Conway, 2005; see also Conway, Justice, & D'Argembeau, this volume, chapter 3) offers a prolific theoretical model to explore the relationship between AM and the self. The SMS model relies on the distinction of different memory sub-systems, hierarchically organized, which entails AM conceptual knowledge (including life-story schemas or themes, life periods, generic or extended events) and episodic memories (a unique and specific episode, generally no longer than one day). Within this model, two sub-components of the self are also distinguished. First, the *conceptual self* is a sub-component of semantic AM, which encompasses all the attributes, traits, physical characteristics, values, or social roles that we attribute to ourselves. Broadly speaking, the conceptual self enables people to describe who they are and the different aspects of their identity. Second, the *working self* is a dynamic control structure that combines episodic memories with AM conceptual knowledge. The working self consists of self-concepts, goals, and other forms of self-knowledge and may function to exercise inhibitory control over the knowledge base. In other words, based on current personal goals, the working self controls AM encoding and retrieval.

With respect to the relationship between AM and the self, the SMS model postulates that this connection is bidirectional. As such, the self has an organizing role in memory, and, in return, identity formation is supported by a set of memories important for the self. The conceptual self is linked to AM conceptual knowledge and episodic memories to ground, illustrate, and contextualize self-concepts (Conway et al., 2004).

Parallel to these theoretical developments on AM, a key issue that has sparked the interest of memory researchers is the close link between AM and future thinking. Suddendorf and Busby (2005) suggested that our ability to revisit the past may be a feature of our ability to conceive the future and that memories provide the "ingredients" for future simulations. This idea was developed with the constructive episodic simulation hypothesis (Schacter & Addis, 2007), which postulates that past and future events rely on similar information stored in episodic memory, which are flexibly (re) combined into a coherent event, involving similar cognitive mechanisms and neural underpinnings. In addition to the idea that shared mechanisms are involved in the generation of personal past and future events, the existence of future self-concepts has been proposed. Marcus and Nurius (1986, p. 954) defined "possible selves" as individuals' representations of what they "might become, what they would like to become, and what they are afraid of becoming." Whereas the existence of future selves has been postulated for several decades, research on their relationship with future thinking is in its infancy.

In summary, the current chapter attempts to provide an overview of studies from experimental psychology, cognitive neuropsychology, and neuroimaging that focus on how the self organizes the way we think about the past and future. To this end, the first section covers the key methods and results from memory studies conducted in healthy participants, before extending these findings to future thinking in the second section. The third section will explore the neural correlates of the self. The final section will be devoted to investigations in people with brain damage and neuropsychiatric populations, and their particular contribution to improving our understanding of the relationships between AM, future thinking, and the self, before concluding with future directions in the field.

Organization of memory and the self

The self-reference effect

The self-reference effect (SRE) refers to the tendency for people to better remember information that is encoded with reference to the self (Rogers et al., 1977). The general idea behind this line of research is to explore whether knowledge about the self is represented and organized differently to knowledge about others or the world. The self is viewed as a powerful and rich cognitive structure that encourages the organization and elaboration of knowledge in memory, at both encoding and retrieval (Symons & Johnson, 1997). As such, new information will be assimilated with reference to the self, which provides knowledge about previous personal experiences that have the potential to enrich new incoming information. On this basis, Lalanne et al. (2010) suggested that the working self is involved in the SRE.

According to Klein (2012), the SRE is the most widely used method to explore the role of the self in memory. Paradigms exploring the SRE consist of comparing its relative benefit to other encoding strategies, with varying depths of processing (e.g., semantic, phonemic, etc.) on the recall of the material. For example, Rogers et al. (1977) compared participants' memory performance for adjectives across four conditions in which they were asked to judge: the size of the letters from the word (i.e., structural encoding), whether the word rhymed with another word (i.e., phonemic encoding), whether the item is a synonym for another word (i.e., semantic encoding), or whether the word describes oneself (i.e., self-reference condition). Participants retrieved a higher number of words from the self-reference condition.

Although the SRE is generally described as a robust finding, conflicting results have been reported in the literature (Symons & Johnson, 1997). Indeed, as raised by Klein et al. (1989), contradictory results obtained in the initial SRE experiments might have been due to a failure to distinguish between two different self-reference processes which were used interchangeably in the literature. To avoid such confusion, Klein et al. (1989) suggested a distinction between the descriptive variant (i.e., describe whether an item is self-descriptive) and the autobiographical variant of the SRE task (i.e., retrieve an autobiographical memory associated with an item). More than just a methodological matter, these two variants of the SRE task rely on different cognitive mechanisms. Specifically, the descriptive form involves the semantic aspects of AM, whereas the autobiographical variant implies access to information stored in episodic AM (Klein et al., 1989; Klein, 2012).

In parallel, debates also focused on cognitive mechanisms underlying the SRE. To date, two main hypotheses have been put forward to account for the role of the self in memory: the elaborative processing hypothesis and the organizational processing hypothesis (see Klein, 2012; Symons & Johnson, 1997). Historically, the elaborative processing hypothesis was the first to be developed and relates to models of memory facilitation (Craik & Tulving, 1975). Here, the basic assumption is that during encoding, a stimulus will be elaborated by means of the formation of multiple associations between it and external information (that is, information not provided as items to-be-remembered). For instance, with the word "cat," one could elaborate on this word by thinking about "the cat I had during my childhood," or "the day my cat ran away." By doing this, the item will be encoded with a high depth of encoding processing, since multiple routes for retrieval could be created. Thus, the more participants elaborate the item during encoding, the more it increases the probability of successful later retrieval. With respect to the organizational processing hypothesis (Klein & Kihlstrom, 1986), the assumption is that associations will be created among stimuli, but also by associating items to a more general category. For example, the items "luggage" and "map" could benefit from inter-item associations, but could also be associated to a general common category relating to "my last holiday." This organization of items in memory is then reflected by the presence of clustering during further recall.

Nevertheless, some studies raised concerns about the uniqueness of the SRE. In other words, when similar organization of items is encouraged with different types of association (such as semantic information, or relating the information to a close family member or friend, instead of to oneself), the SRE per se did not consistently lead to superior performance (see, for instance, Bower & Gilligan, 1979; Klein & Kihlstrom, 1986). In his review, Klein (2012) concludes that the SRE cannot be accounted for by a single type of processing, but instead that both elaborative and organizational processes are at play, of which the level of involvement depends on the task used. On this basis, a more fruitful approach would be to consider an explanatory hypothesis which combines elaborative and organizational processing.

As stated earlier, despite these limitations, the SRE remains a robust finding in the literature. The SRE has been replicated in young adults (see Symons & Johnson, 1997 for a review) and in healthy older adults (Glisky & Marquine, 2009; Gutchess et al., 2007). Regarding the latter, previous findings even suggested that the negative effect of aging on episodic memory could be alleviated by the SRE (Dulas et al., 2011; Hamami et al., 2011). In support of this claim, neuroimaging studies have shown that the neural correlates of the SRE are mostly the same in young and older adults (Gutchess et al., 2007, 2010). Beyond the number of items recalled, the SRE seems to influence the state of consciousness at retrieval. To illustrate that, D'Argembeau et al. (2005) reported a higher degree of recollection when items were processed in relation to the self than with a celebrity. In the same study, D'Argembeau and colleagues also found a differential effect of the emotional valence, showing that higher memory performance was only observed for positive adjectives related to the self (versus related to a celebrity), but no significant difference was reported between the two conditions for negative adjectives.

In addition to the findings obtained with the classical SRE paradigm, Rathbone and Moulin (2010) documented that the SRE is also present when retrieving everyday information stored in long-term memory that was not explicitly related to the self, such as birthday dates of friends. Indeed, they found that participants tended to recall more birthdays from on or around the date of their own birthday compared to around the date of completing the task (i.e., recency effect), salient calendar events (e.g., Christmas day, Halloween), or the date of a close friend's birthday.

Self-defining memories

A central assumption of Conway's SMS model is the key role of the self in the encoding and retrieval of memories. Thus, memories that are not or no longer related to the self and to current goals are quickly forgotten or become inaccessible because they are not integrated in long-term knowledge structures. Taking the opposite argument, memories which are highly relevant for the self and reflect personal long-term goals might benefit from a privileged accessibility. This specific type of memory, namely self-defining memories (Blagov & Singer, 2004; Singer & Salovey, 1993), corresponds to highly significant and vivid memories that are accompanied by strong emotion at the time of recollection, are frequently rehearsed, and share strong links with other memories involving similar narrative themes or enduring concerns. Typically, self-defining memories contribute to the generation and attainment of sets of long-term goals and thus remain highly accessible because of their strong association with the working self (Conway & Pleydell-Pearce, 2000). Endorsing this function, self-defining memories have an organizational role in AM knowledge and represent references or turning points in one's life. For instance, the memory of a car accident during which someone helped an injured person before the paramedics arrived may have contributed to the goal of becoming a doctor. This long-term goal of "being a doctor" is then associated to AM knowledge and other related memories, such as "studying medicine," "staff meetings with colleagues," or "the first patient."

Thus, self-defining memories could be conceived as powerful personal scripts, which are linked to the conceptual self and AM knowledge (Conway et al., 2004). In this sense, self-defining memories have a directive function and are critical to psychological well-being and mood regulation. Indeed, when long-term goals are challenged by changes in their status, self-defining memories are crucial to resolve these mental discrepancies, since they provide guidance to the working self, based on goal-directed, affective, and self-relevant knowledge (Conway et al., 2004). The goal-challenging event is thus reinterpreted through the lens of the personal script conveyed by the self-defining memory, which then determines the encoding of this new memory in accord with the structure imposed by the self-defining memory.

Usually, self-defining protocols consist of asking participants to retrieve memories that fit the aforementioned criteria (i.e., emotional intensity, vividness, frequently rehearsed, connection to similar memories, and focus on enduring concerns). Depending on the study purpose, several dimensions or measures associated with these memories could be gathered (e.g., vividness, importance, etc.). However, in order to provide a common theoretical and interpretation framework, Singer and Blagov (2000) have developed a comprehensive scoring procedure, which covers the following dimensions: (i) Memory specificity, which refers to the SMS model and the fact that autobiographical memories are retrieved through different stages, going from abstract representations (life period, generic event) to specific detailed events. (ii) Integrative meaning, that is the process by which a meaning (i.e., insights, lessons, explanations, evaluations, or interpretations) is attributed to a memory. This has in turn a positive influence on motivation, emotion, goal attainment, or well-being (Singer & Blagov, 2004). (iii) Content, which corresponds to the main theme or concern emphasized in the memory. Seven mutually exclusive categories have been isolated, which include life-threatening event, leisure/exploration, relationship, achievement/mastery, guilt/shame, drug/alcohol/tobacco, or non-classifiable event (Thorne & McLean, 2001). (iv) Affect at the time of memory recall, which is assessed for both valence and intensity.

Studies exploring self-defining memories in healthy participants have shown that these memories are mostly specific and frequently concern relationships, life-threatening events, achievement, and leisure (Blagov & Singer, 2004; Lardi et al., 2010; Moffitt & Singer, 1994; Thorne et al., 2004). In addition, the great majority of self-defining memories are also related to positive affect (Moffitt & Singer, 1994). Of interest, self-defining memories and their characteristic features appear relatively stable across cultures (Lardi et al., 2010). From a lifespan perspective, it has been demonstrated that self-defining memories are generally better preserved in older adults than more mundane and less self-relevant memories (Martinelli et al., 2013) and that they are rated as more positive, less specific, but more likely containing integrative meaning compared to young adults (Singer et al., 2007).

Overall, self-defining memories represent a specific class of memories, which make a direct connection between the self and AM knowledge. Thus, self-defining memories have inspired several lines of research addressing the link between AM and the self, as discussed in the next section.

The organization of memories around self-images

An intuitive idea about how we keep track of our memories is that we do not equally remember events that occur at different moments in life. Indeed, AM studies demonstrate that the distribution of memories differs across the lifespan. Three main components have been identified: (i) childhood amnesia, which is the inability to retrieve episodic memories from events that occurred before the age of 3–4 years; (ii) the reminiscence bump, which corresponds to the lifetime period between 10 and 30 years, that is associated with a disproportionately higher recall of memories; (iii) the recency effect, which extends from the present and declines back to the reminiscence bump.

Various explanations have been suggested to account for the reminiscence bump (see Rubin et al., 1998; see also Koppel & Berntsen, this volume, chapter 9), one of which places the self as a key factor. In relation to the idea that the self plays a role in the reminiscence bump, many memories from the period of the reminiscence bump are described as "self-defining" experiences (Singer & Salovey, 1993), occurring at a time of important life changes and development (Erikson, 1950) and are thus critical for the construction and maintenance of a stable self. As such, these memories remain intricately linked to the self over the lifespan and serve as the foundation of AM conceptual knowledge (Conway et al., 2005). In addition, since identity consists of a narration of important aspects of one's life (Fitzgerald, 1988), a prerequisite of a coherent overall life story is that memories are organized and related to the self (Rubin et al., 1998).

The reminiscence bump has been robustly observed under a variety of procedures consisting of plotting memories in terms of age at encoding of the remembered experiences. However, an important methodological aspect of these procedures is that they generally do not tap into memories that are very important for the self (Jansari & Parkin, 1996). To directly address this point, the IAM task (Rathbone et al., 2008) was developed to explore more specifically the distribution of self-cued memories across lifespan. Here, the assumption was that any relevant aspect of the self would be accompanied by a series of self-defining memories that would cluster around the time of identity formation.

Based on the Twenty Statements Test (TST; Kuhn & McPartland, 1954), the first step of the IAM task involves the collection of "I" statements that represent enduring and important facets of the self, including physical (e.g., I am dark-haired), psychological (e.g., I am a funny person), or social aspects (e.g., I am a mother). Each self-image is then used as a cue to elicit the retrieval of associated memories (e.g., to "I am a funny person": Having a laughing fit with Julie during a lecture). Finally, participants are asked to date each memory and to provide the age at which they felt that each self-image became a part of their identity. This final step enables exploration of the distribution of memories around the time of self-image formation. To that aim, a cluster score is calculated, by looking at the difference (in years) between the age of memories and of self-images. In this way, the cluster score could be zero (i.e., the memory occurred in the same year that the self-image emerged), negative (i.e., the memory occurred before the self-image emerged), or positive (i.e., the memory occurred after the self-image emerged).

As expected, Rathbone et al. (2008)—who developed the IAM task, found a temporal clustering of memories around the time of self-emergence. An example of distribution of memories typically found in studies using the IAM task is shown in figure 8.1—most of the memories clustered around zero. In relation to the SMS model (Conway, 2005), this finding was interpreted as reflecting the activation of a set of highly accessible memories associated with each self-image through the working self. In the same study, a similar distribution of memories was reproduced for concrete aspects of the self (i.e., non-ambiguous statements whose conditions of membership are common knowledge, such as "I am a wife," "I am a sister") as well as more abstract self-images (i.e., statements without consensual group meaning, corresponding for instance to an attribute or trait, such as "I am ambitious," "I am honest").

This distribution of memories around the time that identity emerges has consistently been observed across studies, showing a similar pattern in both young and older adults (Chessell et al., 2014; Rathbone et al., 2011), and for both positive and negative self-images (Rathbone & Steel, 2015). Furthermore, experimental work has shown that self-images generated earlier in lists are more salient for identity and associated with larger networks of memories (Rathbone & Moulin, 2014).

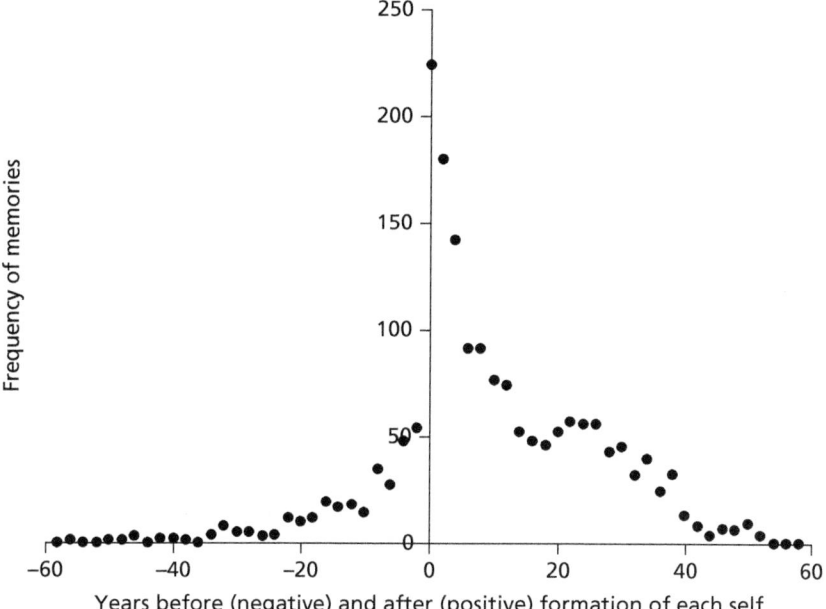

Figure 8.1 Number of memories generated by age of self-image.

Reproduced with permission from Rathbone, C. J., Moulin, C. J. A., & Conway, M. A. 'Self-centered memories: the reminiscence bump and the self.' *Memory & Cognition*, 36(8), 1403–1414, Figure 2, Copyright © 2008 Psychonomic Society, Inc.

Finally, and turning back to the reminiscence bump, a robust finding across studies using the IAM task is that the formation of self-images occurs primarily during adolescence and early adulthood (Erikson, 1950). As such, the reminiscence bump observed for memories is possibly due to the clustering of these memories around self-images that are critical for the self. This finding supports the idea that the reminiscence bump is associated with the formation of adult identity (Conway, 1996).

Organization of future events and the self

When it comes to future selves and their relationship with personal events that might occur in one's life, this is a domain that remains largely underexplored to date (but see Manning, 2016, for an overview). Yet, the idea that people can represent themselves in the future is not new. In his early conceptualization of the self, James (1890) introduced the notion of "potential selves," which was then developed by Marcus and Nurius (1986) as "possible selves." Whereas future selves often derive from and are connected to past or current self-concepts, they represent distinct entities, which might be related to enduring goals, motives, hopes, fears, or threats (Marcus & Nurius, 1986). In this context, future events associated with future selves might be seen as mental representations that motivate the development of goals for achieving or avoiding these possible selves. In addition, future selves might also promote self-regulation (Hoyle & Sherrill, 2006) or the formation of adult identity during adolescence (Dunkel & Anthis, 2001).

Based on the close relationship between AM and future thinking, most the methodologies used to examine future selves and their links with future events stem from those developed for the past. Mirroring the first part of this chapter, the next section provides an overview of the main findings obtained in research tackling this issue.

Self-defining future projections

As previously discussed in "Self-defining memories," self-defining memories consist of a specific class of memories that are particularly relevant in the study of the relationship between AM and the self. Recently, D'Argembeau et al. (2012) introduced the term of self-defining future projections as the future counterpart of self-defining memories. Behind this term, there is the idea that some future events are more relevant to the self than others, since they provide critical information to support or exemplify future selves. Reflecting the SMS (Conway, 2005), the relationship between self-defining future projections and the self is assumed to be bidirectional, and self-defining future projections are defined based on the same criteria as self-defining memories (e.g. vivid, frequently rehearsed, etc.).

Consistent with the literature on the phenomenological properties of past and future events, the comparison between self-defining memories and self-defining future projections revealed a profile that includes both commonalities and differences (D'Argembeau et al., 2012). Self-defining future projections referred mostly to themes of achievement, relationship, leisure, or life-threatening events, and were less specific and integrative than their past counterparts. Conversely, self-defining future projections were rated as more positive. However, the structures of self-defining memories and future projections were highly correlated for specificity and integrative meaning, and a negative correlation was found between specificity and integrative meaning for both temporal directions. To our knowledge, D'Argembeau et al.'s study was the only one that has explored self-defining future projections and, although more research is necessary to further our understanding of this construct, it offers a valuable framework for studying the concept of personal continuity across time.

The organization of future events around future selves

As previously discussed in "The organization of memories around self-images," there is evidence that self-images play an organizational role within AM. The extent to which future events follow a similar pattern was explored by Rathbone et al., (2011), using the I Will Be task as a future counterpart to the IAM task. This task follows the same procedure as the IAM task, with the exception that participants are asked to generate "I will be" statements, which describe new selves that they might become in the future (e.g., "I will be a traveler"). Then, participants provide associated future events (e.g., with "I will be a traveler": "Visiting the Sydney Opera House") before dating these events, as well as the age at which they think these self-images will become a defining part of their identity. A cluster score is then calculated to examine whether the events occurred at the same time, before, or after identity formation.

Using the IAM and the I Will Be tasks in a sample of young adults, Rathbone et al. (2011) reported a very similar clustering effect around the time of identity emergence for both current and future selves. Future self-images appeared to have an organizational function within future thinking. A more direct comparison between the past and the future also revealed that this self-centered clustering effect was even more pronounced for future events than for memories. The nascent interest in this topic has encouraged the replication of these findings in older adults (Chessell et al., 2014). Just as in young adults, memories and future events clustered temporally around times of self-image formation in older adults. However, whereas most of the self-images and associated personal events generated by younger adults pertained to the typical period of identity formation (adolescence and early adulthood), older adults' future self-images were closer to the present and their current self-images were formed longer ago relative to younger adults.

Taken together, these results indicate that the self plays an important role in future thinking. The symmetry observed between the past and the future might be a key factor contributing to the maintenance of a sense of continuity and stability across time (Conway, 2009).

Organization in event networks

Having discussed the role of self-defining past and future events in the construction and maintenance of self-images, a striking observation is that less is known about the organization within sets of these self-defining events and the role of the self in this organization. Indeed, whereas a hallmark of self-defining events is their connection to other events sharing similar concerns, the extent to which the organization of self-defining events differs from that of less personally significant events lacks empirical support.

To address this knowledge gap, Demblon and D'Argembeau (2016) explored the presence of "event networks" or "event clusters"—that is, structures that organize sets of causally and thematically related events (Brown & Schopflocher, 1998)—in past and future events with varying degrees of personal significance. Specifically, participants were first asked to provide four personal events fitting the following categories: a self-defining memory, a self-defining future event, a mundane word-cued memory (e.g., to the word "bag"), and a mundane word-cued future event (e.g., to the word "tool"). Then, for each event category, participants generated associated events that came spontaneously to mind, before assessing the type of link (i.e., direct versus indirect) and the relational dimensions shared by these events (i.e., surface, causal, pertaining to the same general event, to the same goal, or to a common theme). In addition to the greater number of events produced in association with self-defining events, the latter were also more organized in meaningful event networks than more mundane events triggered by word-cues. In parallel, these networks of self-defining events were found to play a greater role in identity, especially since their organization was notably driven by identity motives (i.e., motivational pressures toward particular ways of seeing oneself, including self-esteem, distinctiveness, continuity, meaning, belonging, and efficacy; see Vignoles, 2011, for a review). Notably, event network organization appeared similar for past and future self-defining events, supporting the idea that the formation and integration of coherent event networks plays a critical role in fostering a sense of personal continuity across time.

The self and the brain

With the rise of cognitive neurosciences, neuroimaging studies have enabled deeper understanding of cognitive and affective processes through exploration of their neural correlates. In the domain of AM and future thinking, neuroimaging techniques have played a major role in disentangling the key features, similarities, and differences between the two temporal directions (for a review see Schacter et al., 2012).

With respect to the self, without denying the potential of neuroimaging techniques in this field, one should acknowledge that the success of attempts to "locate" the self in the brain depends on the ability to define the self. However, rather than seeing this issue as a barrier to research, this merely emphasizes the critical need to base empirical research on fine-grained definitions of the self—a complex and multifaceted set of processes. As raised by Klein (2013), a primary distinction must be made between the more implicit, subjective aspects ("the self of first-person subjectivity") that could not be an object of scientific inquiry and the declarative aspects of the self, which are capable of investigation through descriptive analysis. As in the preceding parts of this chapter, we continue to follow this primary distinction and thus focus on neuroimaging studies that explore the declarative aspects of self-knowledge. As such, we do not claim to provide an exhaustive review of the literature on the neural substrates of the self, but instead, we present a summary of studies directly related to the concept of self-knowledge (we refer readers to more complete reviews such as Gillihan & Farah, 2005; Klein, 2013; Martinelli et al., 2013; Northoff et al., 2006; Ruby & Legrand, 2007).

One of the earliest studies that attempted to explore the neural underpinnings of the self was based on the SRE paradigm. Craik et al. (1999) showed that self-relevant encoding was highly associated with brain activity in both the bilateral prefrontal regions. Findings from this inaugural study have been widely replicated and have pinpointed the involvement of cortical midline structures in the SRE, including the medial prefrontal cortex and extending to the anterior cingulate cortex (Gutchess et al., 2010; Kelley et al., 2002; Macrae et al., 2004; Morel et al., 2014; Zhu et al., 2012). A recent clinical study echoed these results by showing that focal brain damage in the medial prefrontal region abolished the self-reference effect, suggesting that this brain structure is critical for this process (Philippi et al., 2012).

Not only involved in the SRE, the medial prefrontal cortex is also associated with self-descriptiveness judgments—that is, judging to what extent some personality traits, self-images, physical descriptions, values, attitudes, etc., describe oneself or not (for recent reviews see Murray et al., 2012; van der Meer et al., 2010). Of interest, advances in AM and future thinking research have also broadened the perspectives on different classes of self-representations. Indeed, exploring the neural correlates of future selves naturally calls on the inclusion of personal goals as one type of self-representation. Accordingly, the medial prefrontal cortex was found to be responsive to thinking about one's hopes, aspirations, or personal goals (D'Argembeau et al., 2010; Johnson et al., 2006; Mitchell et al., 2009; Packer & Cunningham, 2009; Stawarczyk & D'Argembeau, 2015).

As stated earlier, most of the studies dealing with AM and the self are grounded in the SMS model (Conway, 2005). Recently, Martinelli et al. (2013) provided a comprehensive picture of the neural correlates of the SMS components, including episodic autobiographical memory, semantic autobiographical memory (e.g., generic events, autobiographical facts), and the conceptual self (figure 8.2). Focusing on the two last components (which are more directly related to the self), this meta-analysis revealed that (i) semantic autobiographical memory engages the medial and the left ventrolateral prefrontal regions, the anterior and posterior cingulate gyri, as well as some left temporal regions (superior and middle temporal gyri, fusiform gyrus and parahippocampus) and the left thalamus, whereas (ii) the conceptual self is more specifically associated with brain activations in the medial prefrontal cortex and the anterior cingulate cortex. In keeping with previous studies, a noticeable finding is the involvement of the medial prefrontal region irrespective of the SMS components.

Through this brief review of the literature, a striking observation is the consistent engagement of the medial prefrontal cortex in self-processing, with robust evidence across studies using different research approaches. As such, one obvious question is about the specific function of this brain region during self-processing. In this regard, D'Argembeau (2013) put forward the valuation hypothesis, the basic assumption of which is that the medial prefrontal cortex is associated with the appraisal of the subjective value and personal significance of information from multiple sources. Thus, medial prefrontal activation might act as an indicator of personal significance. As reviewed by D'Argembeau (2013), the valuation hypothesis is supported by evidence showing (i) greater neural response of the medial prefrontal cortex when thinking about the present self (versus the past self or the future self, which were judged as less relevant for current self-representations due to being more temporally distant; D'Argembeau et al., 2008, 2010); (ii) involvement of this brain region in psychological investment in self-representations—that is, the level of certainty and of importance attached to self-representations (D'Argembeau et al., 2012); or (iii) increased activity in the medial prefrontal region during autobiographical reasoning (i.e., reflecting on the meaning of personal experiences), especially in people with high self-reflection aptitudes (D'Argembeau et al., 2013). Although this hypothesis calls for more empirical

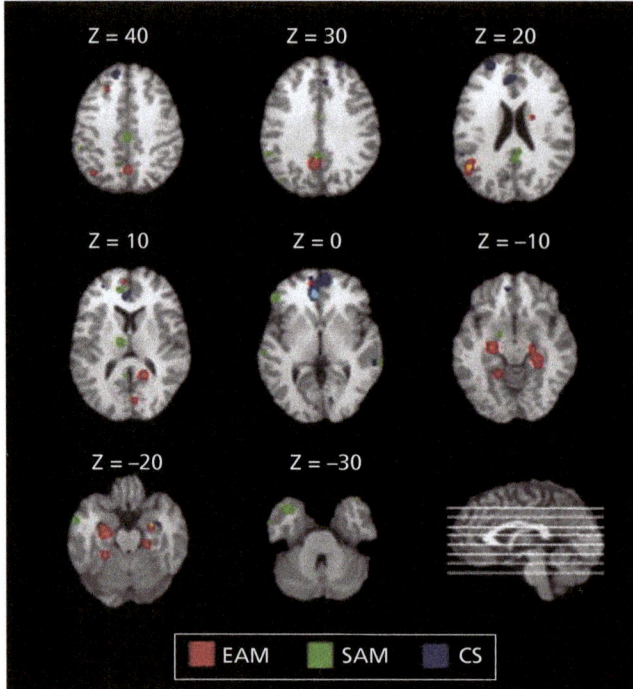

Figure 8.2 Neural correlates of the self-memory system (SMS) components (Conway, 2005), including episodic autobiographical memory (EAM), semantic autobiographical memory (SAM) and the conceptual self (CS). All activations are significant at $P < 0.05$ corrected for multiple comparisons (false discovery rate).

Reproduced with permission from Martinelli, P., Sperduti, M., & Piolino, P. 'Neural substrates of the self-memory system: New insights from a meta-analysis.' *Human Brain Mapping*, Volume 34, Issue 7. Copyright © (2013) John Wiley and Sons.

support, it offers an interesting framework to relate evidence from different lines of research and elucidate the specific contribution of the medial prefrontal region to self-referential processing.

The self, memory, and future thoughts in clinical groups

Through discussion of theoretical and empirical research, the previous sections of this chapter have emphasized the close relationships shared by the self, AM, and future thinking. As postulated in the SMS model (Conway, 2005; Conway, Justice, & D'Argembeau, this volume, chapter 3), this relationship is bidirectional. Thus, a direct implication of this assumption is that this link might be disrupted in a situation where one of these components fails. In this context, neuropsychological studies in patients suffering from memory and future thinking impairments represent a unique opportunity to further our understanding of this complex relationship. Importantly, this line of research is also highly clinically relevant. Indeed, the experience of cognitive impairment provokes major disruptions in many domains of everyday life and leads, more often than not, to significant changes in how people perceive and interpret themselves and the world (Gracey et al., 2008). In the event of memory and/or future thinking impairment, people would be, to some degree, unable to remember how they used to be or what they wanted to become. Thus, the inability to adjust and integrate self-images may be part of the changes provoked by cognitive impairment (Coetzer, 2008).

In the following sections, we attempt to outline the main findings of research that has explored the self, AM, and future thinking in clinical conditions. To that end, we distinguish the contribution of neurological and neuropsychiatric clinical groups with a focus on studies that have used the methods described in the previous sections.

Neurological populations

In terms of main scientific progress in our understanding of human memory, neuropsychological research in people with memory impairment has made an outstanding contribution and the relationship between memory, future thinking and the self is no exception. Specifically, neuropsychological groups give the opportunity to examine which components of AM and future thinking are essential for self-concepts.

Single-case studies in amnesic patients
Single-case studies in amnesic patients have been illuminating here. Klein and Gangi (2010) reviewed the findings obtained in several patients. A notable feature of patients with amnesia is that, in most of the cases, they show episodic memory impairment together with a relative preservation of semantic memory. With respect to the self, the main conclusion drawn by Klein and Gangi was the apparent preservation of the self despite severe episodic amnesia. As this result appears to contradict theoretical predictions, deeper investigation of those memories that support the self in amnesia appears valuable.

This research question was the basis for the study of P.J.M.—a 38-year-old woman, who developed focal retrograde amnesia after a bicycle accident (Rathbone et al., 2009). Focal retrograde amnesia is an organic-based memory loss, restricted to the period of time prior to trauma. A characteristic of this condition is that semantic memory is relatively spared, whereas profound episodic memory loss is generally observed. P.J.M.'s neuropsychological examination showed an isolated memory deficit, with tests exploring AM (i.e., the Autobiographical Memory Interview, AMI; Kopelman et al., 1989; and the Crovitz test; Crovitz & Schiffman, 1974) revealing a clear impairment of episodic AM and borderline score for semantic AM. When asked to retrieve specific episodic events, P.J.M. instead provided semantic facts (i.e. general knowledge about her life, such as "I used to write to Kristin after I moved"). Vital for our argument, P.J.M. also underwent the IAM and the TST; she was able to list self-statements that defined her identity in the same way as healthy controls. Interestingly, in the IAM task, memories cued by self-images tended to be semantic facts rather than specific episodic events. However, this did not influence the temporal distribution of her memories since the pattern was consistent with that previously found: memories clustered around age of self-emergence. In light of the SMS model, these findings suggest that when episodic memories are inaccessible, AM conceptual knowledge may serve to organize and structure knowledge about the self and may ultimately support the self and sense of personal continuity across time.

The case of J.H., a 60-year-old male diagnosed with psychogenic amnesia, addressed the role of the self in AM and future thinking (Rathbone et al., 2015). Psychogenic amnesia is rare and generally the consequence of psychological trauma or emotional stress. Personal identity loss is a hallmark of psychogenic amnesia and is conceived as a memory retrieval failure of pre-onset memories, which are no longer accessible but still stored (Staniloiu et al., 2010). In the case of J.H., his psychogenic amnesia spanned back from age 53 years to early childhood. After hypnotherapy, J.H. showed a remarkable recovery, giving the authors a unique opportunity to test J.H. before and after recovery. Regarding AM tests (AMI and Crovitz test), before hypnotherapy, performance was impaired for both semantic and episodic AM components for the period preceding the amnesia onset (except for the more recent period), whereas J.H. performed at control level post hypnotherapy. Deficits in imagining the future were also part of J.H.'s cognitive profile and persisted after therapy. Turning to identity measures, whereas J.H. generated as many self-images as matched controls in the IAM task before recovery, he generated far fewer memories supporting these self-images. The distribution of self-images and associated memories also followed an atypical pattern, since all of them were dated as very recent (post onset of amnesia) and showed an extreme clustering effect. When retested after hypnotherapy, marked changes were noticed in the number of memories triggered by self-images, their dating, and distribution. In fact, J.H.'s pattern of self-formation was similar to controls, with most identities dated as emerging in early adulthood, and with a wider distribution of memories across lifespan. The case of J.H. thus offers insights into the role of motivational processes in AM, especially the importance of congruency between memories and the goals of the self, which is a core feature of the SMS model (Conway, 2005). As illustrated by J.H.'s case, in the absence of such congruency, memories could be inhibited at both episodic and semantic levels.

Dementia

From a clinical standpoint, dementia has generated the greatest interest in the question of how memory loss impacts on identity. Indeed, the global and gradual cognitive changes, together with diminished awareness, and restrictions in daily functioning of individuals with dementia have certainly the potential to provoke identity changes. However, the picture is not so clear-cut, and many debates remain about the extent to which identity is impaired in dementia (see the excellent review by Caddell & Clare, 2010). This debate is probably nourished by the wide range of models and methodologies used to explore the self, especially in dementia. Providing an overview of all of these is beyond the scope of this chapter, so we focus on research examining the links between the self, AM, and future thinking in dementia.

Alzheimer's disease is the most extensively explored type of dementia on this topic. This condition is characterized by the progressive loss of neurons (relative to healthy older adults), which tends to disproportionately affect the medial temporal lobe in the early stages of the disease. Research on the self and identity change in Alzheimer's disease patients reveals a failure to update self-images, which more closely match pre-morbid personality, leading to the idea of the "petrified self" (Mograbi et al., 2009). Whereas only a few studies have explored the SRE in patients with Alzheimer's disease, all demonstrate a relative preservation of this effect, despite the fact that the SRE was not powerful enough to alleviate memory impairment in this clinical population (Kalenzaga & Clarys, 2013; Kalenzaga et al., 2013; Lalanne et al., 2013). Consistent with data reported in healthy individuals, the SRE seemed especially clear for positive aspects of the self. In a recent study (Leblond et al., 2016), the SRE has been compared in healthy older adults, in amnestic mild cognitive impairment (aMCI) patients and patients with Alzheimer's disease (although the latter were excluded from analysis due to poor task completion). Of note, the authors took into account the valence of material (positive and negative adjectives) and the global identity valence of participants. Whereas the authors documented a typical SRE in healthy older adults, a more nuanced profile was observed in aMCI patients, for whom the SRE benefit was only observed for positive adjectives. However, a correlation was found between negative identity valence and poor recognition of negative self-referential adjectives in these patients.

With respect to studies exploring the link between self-concepts and AM in patients with Alzheimer's disease, the seminal study was conducted by Addis and Tippett (2004). Combining identity questionnaires and AM measures, Addis and Tippett found a close relationship between AM loss, especially memories from childhood and early adulthood, and a weaker strength and quality of identity.

Semantic dementia is a neurodegenerative disorder characterized by the primary deterioration of the lateral temporal cortices, leading to the amodal loss of semantic knowledge, in the context of a relative preservation of general cognitive abilities, including episodic memory. Therefore, semantic dementia represents a unique pattern of impairment since AM semantic knowledge might be compromised despite relatively preserved episodic memories. Using a task similar to the IAM procedure, research has shown that patients with semantic dementia define their past and current selves without difficulty, but they exhibited impairments when imagining future selves and associating personal events to these images, regardless of whether these self-representations were episodic or semantic in nature (Duval et al., 2012). This pattern of identity change restricted to the future has important clinical implications since it has been related to suicidal behavior in a single case with semantic dementia (Hsiao et al., 2013).

Other neurological conditions

Although their neuropsychological profile is the result of two completely different etiologies, several parallels can be drawn between the cases of P.J.M. and E.B. (Illman et al., 2011). E.B., a 73-year-old man, was diagnosed with transient epileptic amnesia, which is characterized by subtle memory impairments, generally expressed by a subjective AM complaint in the context of normal performance in anterograde memory tests. When AM is formally assessed, a severe episodic AM deficit covering the entire lifespan has been found in these patients, with a milder impairment for semantic AM (Milton et al., 2010). Focusing on memories connected to E.B.'s self-images, a very similar pattern to that found with P.J.M. was observed: clustering of memories was centered on self-images but, qualitatively, these memories were more like semantic facts than specific episodic memories. Again, these findings support the idea that the self can be maintained despite episodic AM impairment, by a scaffold of semantic AMs.

AM impairments have also frequently been described in chronic focal epilepsy (see for instance Voltzenlogel et al., 2006). However, only one study to our knowledge directly explored the consequences of this deficit on the self. Allebone et al. (2015) found that patients displayed a greater number of semantic or overgeneral memories, but fewer specific episodic memories than healthy controls. Based on the Ego Identity Process Questionnaire (Balistreri et al., 1995), patients also showed an altered identity profile. Interestingly, this seemed particularly evident in patients with medial temporal lobe epilepsy (compared to epilepsy involving other epileptogenic foci) and this effect was exacerbated in those with an early seizure onset (before or during adolescence). In the same vein, a strong association between AM score and identity status was found, but—again—only in patients with medial temporal lobe epilepsy. This study provides new insights and perspectives not only on the impact of brain injury occurring at an important age of identity development, but also on the role of different brain structures in this process.

Recently, the relationship between AM and the self has been explored in a single case of chronic unilateral spatial neglect (Ernst et al., 2016). Patient D.R., a 59-year-old woman, completed the IAM task and a classical AM test, namely the Test Episodique de la Mémoire du Passé Autobiographique (TEMPau; Piolino et al., 2000). The TEMPau test consists of generating specific memories in response to generic cue-words (e.g., school, travel). D.R. successfully generated a series of self-images describing herself. However, the main finding relies on the comparison of D.R.'s performance in these two tasks: whereas her score on the TEMPau was characteristic of AM impairment, D.R. expressed memories with an episodic quality similar to those from healthy participants when memories were cued by her self-images in the IAM task. Unfortunately, the temporal distribution of memories was not explored in this case. However, D.R.'s case is informative in supporting the idea that, under some circumstances, the link existing between self-images and their associated episodic memories could be strong enough to withstand the presence of AM impairment.

Neuropsychiatric populations

Alterations in the self are intrinsically related to conditions such as schizophrenia, autism, and depression, and have been corroborated by abnormal brain activity in the medial prefrontal cortex in these populations (Holt et al., 2011; Lemogne et al., 2012; Lombardo et al., 2010).

Schizophrenia

The notion that sense of self is altered in schizophrenia is not new (Freedman, 1974). In fact, many aspects of schizophrenia symptomatology (e.g., delusions, auditory hallucinations, etc.) might be grounded in the breakdown of sense of agency and ownership of experience (Prebble et al., 2013). In parallel, evidence converges to support the presence of episodic AM impairment in this clinical condition (for a recent review see Berna et al., 2015).

To date, most studies dealing with AM and the self in schizophrenia have focused on self-defining memories (Berna et al., 2011a, 2011b; Raffard et al., 2009, 2010). Across these studies, patients with schizophrenia generated as many specific self-defining memories as matched healthy controls, with an equivalent personal significance and subjective impact, but demonstrated an impaired ability to extract meaning from these personal experiences. In the same vein, their memories contained fewer self-event connections (i.e., explicit links between some aspect of the memory and the self) and showed a lower narrative coherence. In addition, these patients also displayed an earlier reminiscence bump (aged around 15–19 years versus 20–24 years in healthy controls)—a finding that has been related to the typical age of schizophrenia onset. Qualitatively, the content of self-defining memories also differed from healthy controls, with fewer episodes related to past achievement but more about illness. Importantly, measures of self-defining memories, notably of meaning making, were significantly influenced by clinical characteristics such as disease onset, negative symptoms, or duration of illness but also executive dysfunctions.

However, connecting these identity changes to AM disturbances is not straightforward, especially since the aforementioned investigations only provided indirect evidence of this relationship. To our knowledge, Bennouna-Greene et al. (2012) were the first to directly address this issue. By means of the TST and the IAM task, they explored the qualitative properties of self-images, the memories associated with those self-images, and their organization in schizophrenic patients and matched healthy controls. With respect to identity quality, patients with schizophrenia did not differ from healthy controls. Whereas memories supporting self-images in these patients were less episodic, these self-defining events were centered around the period of identity formation, as consistently found in previous studies. Thus, it appears that the temporal organization of memories in patients with schizophrenia follows the typical pattern observed in healthy controls. Of interest, Bennouna-Greene and colleagues also examined the thematic organization of memories, that is, the strength of the link between self-images and the related events. This measure elucidated the relationship between self and memory in schizophrenia, as the thematic link between self-images and memories appeared weaker in patients.

Autism spectrum disorder

Differences in identity processes have also been described in autism spectrum disorder (ASD), which is a neurodevelopmental disorder characterized by difficulties in social interactions, verbal and non-verbal communication, and repetitive behaviors. Evidence of a disrupted link between AM and the self in ASD comes from studies showing a reduced SRE in this population (Hare et al., 2007; Lombardo et al., 2007; Millward et al., 2000). This suggests that the organization of self-related information might be different in people with ASD.

Following previous clinical reports, Tanweer et al. (2010) explored AM and the self in ASD by means of the TEMPau and the TST. Results showed that individuals with ASD generated fewer specific memories, also associated with poor recollective experience. This was accompanied by qualitative identity changes, including reduced identity complexity, fewer specific and social self-images, but more abstract and autonomous self-concepts than healthy controls. In other words, the results indicated that the ASD group tended to perceive themselves as isolated individuals, which is possibly related to difficulties in social interaction commonly described in this disorder.

Mood disorders and related clinical conditions

Negative beliefs and distortions about oneself are common in depression, as in AM impairment (Beck, 1967; Williams et al., 1996). Somewhat surprisingly, few studies have directly examined the relationship between self-distortions and AM impairment in people with depression. The SRE paradigm has been used to this effect and the studies report consistent findings related to depression: individuals with depression tended to demonstrate a higher SRE for negative adjectives, but a lower SRE for positive adjectives, which were thus more congruent with their own view of themselves (Derry & Kuiper, 1981; Dozois & Dobson, 2001; Kuiper & Derry, 1982).

This bias toward negative self-related information was also observed in patients with borderline personality disorder, for whom self-defining memories have been found to be more negative and less coherent than matched healthy controls (Jørgensen et al., 2012). In the same vein, integration of negative or traumatic experiences into personal identity might be an important process in the onset and maintenance of posttraumatic stress disorder (PTSD) symptoms (Berntsen & Rubin, 2007). Studies have shown that self-defining memories in people with PTSD were generally trauma-related and of negative valence (Sutherland & Bryant, 2005). Together, these results suggest that current mood or mental state might affect and shape the organization of self-related information.

Conclusions and future directions

In this chapter we have reviewed research exploring the self-related processes that organize the way people think about the past and the future. The methods and research paradigms used to date have been diverse, spanning experimental laboratory-based approaches (e.g. the SRE), naturalistic AM studies (e.g. reminiscence bump research and self-defining memories), and neuroimaging work (e.g. identifying parts of the brain associated with self-related memory retrieval). Participants have ranged from healthy adults to neurological and neuropsychiatric patient groups, with whom our understanding of the link between self and memory has been elucidated further.

Notwithstanding the advances made by the studies discussed, several important questions remain unanswered. First, framing the relationship between self and memory as bidirectional, as in Conway's SMS, makes it difficult to disentangle the effect of memory impairments on the self and vice versa. This is relevant when studying clinical groups for whom memory deficits may be one of several cognitive impairments. Are the changes to the self that we see in disorders such as schizophrenia and dementia a direct consequence of alterations in memory, or are they related to more global cognitive impairment? Although studies with various clinical groups have started to address these important questions, this line of enquiry is in its infancy. Finally, there is a marked discrepancy between the number of studies examining the self in relation to memories compared to imagined future events. The organizational effects of the self in memory have been shown using a wide variety of paradigms over the decades. By contrast, it is only relatively recently that the links between the self and imagined future events have been the focus of psychological enquiry.

From a clinical perspective, it is hoped that work on the relationship between the self, autobiographical memory, and future thinking will also stimulate the development of neuropsychological interventions aiming to support the self and identity in clinical populations. Thus far, studies in this domain have mainly focused on improving autobiographical memory, but the inclusion of its future counterpart, together with measures of the psychological and functional consequences of alterations in the self, are emerging as promising avenues of research.

Acknowledgments

A. Ernst is a postdoctoral researcher supported by a research funding from the Agence Nationale pour la Recherche awarded to Dr. Chris Moulin (ANR-15-CE33-0010). C. J. Rathbone was supported by the ESRC (ES/K000918/1).

References

Addis, D. R. & Tippett, L. J. (2004). Memory of myself: autobiographical memory and identity in Alzheimer's disease. *Memory*, *12*, 56–74.

Allebone, J., Rayner, G., Siveges, B., & Wilson, S. J. (2015). Altered self-identity and autobiographical memory in epilepsy. *Epilepsia*, *56*, 1982–1991.

Balistreri, E., Busch-Rossnagel, K. F., & Geisinger, N. A. (1995). Development and preliminary validation of the Ego Identity Process Questionnaire. *Journal of Adolescence*, *18*, 179–192.

Beck, A. T. (1967). *Depression: Causes and treatment*. Philadelphia: University of Pennsylvania Press.

Bennouna-Greene, M., Berna, F., Conway, M. A., Rathbone, C. J., Vidailhet, P., & Danion, J. M. (2012). Self-images and related autobiographical memories in schizophrenia. *Consciousness and Cognition*, *21*, 247–257.

Berna, F., Bennouna-Greene, M., Potheegadoo, J., Verry, P., Conway, M. A., & Danion, J. M. (2011a). Impaired ability to give a meaning to personally significant events in patients with schizophrenia. *Consciousness and Cognition*, *20*, 703–711.

Berna, F., Bennouna-Greene, M., Potheegadoo, J., Verry, P., Conway, M. A., & Danion, J. M. (2011b). Self-defining memories related to illness and their integration into the self in patients with schizophrenia. *Psychiatry Research*, *189*, 49–54.

Berna, F., Potheegadoo, J., Aouadi, I., Ricarte, J. J., Allé, M. C., Coutelle, R., et al. (2015). A meta-analysis of autobiographical memory studies in schizophrenia spectrum disorder. *Schizophrenia Bulletin*, *42*, 56–66.

Berntsen, D. & Rubin, D. C. (2007). When a trauma becomes a key to identity: Enhanced integration of trauma memories predicts posttraumatic stress disorder symptoms. *Applied Cognitive Psychology*, *21*, 417–431.

Blagov, P. S. & Singer, J. A. (2004). Four dimensions of self-defining memories (specificity, meaning, content, and affect) and their relationships to self-restraint, distress, and repressive defensiveness. *Journal of Personality*, *72*, 481–511.

Bower, G. H. & Gilligan, S. G. (1979). Remembering information related to ones-self. *Journal of Research in Personality*, *13*, 420–432.

Brown, N. R. & Schopflocher, D. (1998). Event clusters: An organization of personal events in autobiographical memory. *Psychological Science*, *9*, 470–475.

Caddell, L. S. & Clare, L. (2010). The impact of dementia on self and identity: A systematic review. *Clinical Psychology Review*, *30*, 113–126.

Chessell, Z. J., Rathbone, C. J., Souchay, C., Charlesworth, L., & Moulin, C. J. A. (2014). Autobiographical memory, past and future events, and self-images in younger and older adults. *Self and Identity*, *13*, 380–397.

Coetzer, R. (2008). Holistic neuro-rehabilitation in the community: Is identity a key issue? *Neuropsychological Rehabilitation*, *18*, 766–783.

Conway, M. A. (1996). Autobiographical knowledge and autobiographical memories. In D. C. Rubin (ed.), *Remembering our past: Studies in autobiographical memory* (pp. 67–93). Cambridge: Cambridge University Press.

Conway, M. A. (2005). Memory and the self. *Journal of Memory and Language*, *53*, 594–628.

Conway, M. A. (2009). Episodic memories. *Neuropsychologia*, *47*, 2305–2313.

Conway, M. A. & Pleydell-Pearce, C. W. (2000). The construction of autobiographical memories in the self-memory system. *Psychological Review*, *107*, 261–288.

Conway, M. A., Singer, J. A., & Tagini, A. (2004). The self and autobiographical memory: Correspondence and coherence. *Social Cognition*, *22*, 491–529.

Conway, M. A., Wang, Q., Hanyu, K., & Haque, S. (2005). A cross-cultural investigation of autobiographical memory on the universality and cultural variation of the reminiscence bump. *Journal of Cross-Cultural Psychology*, *36*, 739–749.

Craik, F. I. M., Moroz, T. M., Moscovitch, M., Stuss, D. T., Winocur, G., Tulving, E., & Kapur, S. (1999). In search of the self: A positron emission tomography study. *Psychological Science*, *10*, 26–34.

Craik, F. I. & Tulving, E. (1975). Depth of processing and the retention of words in episodic memory. *Journal of Experimental Psychology: General*, *104*, 268–294.

Crovitz, H. F. & Schiffman, H. (1974). Frequency of episodic memories as a function of their age. *Bulletin of the Psychonomic Society*, *4*, 517–518.

D'Argembeau, A. (2013). On the role of the ventromedial prefrontal cortex in self-processing: the valuation hypothesis. *Frontiers in Human Neuroscience*, *7*, 1–13.

D'Argembeau, A., Cassol, H., Phillips, C., Balteau, E., Salmon, E., & Van der Linden, M. (2013). Brains creating stories of selves: the neural basis of autobiographical reasoning. *Social Cognitive and Affective Neuroscience*, *9*, 646–652.

D'Argembeau, A., Comblain, C., & Linden, M. (2005). Affective valence and the self-reference effect: Influence of retrieval conditions. *British Journal of Psychology*, *96*, 457–466.

D'Argembeau, A., Feyers, D., Majerus, S., Collette, F., Van der Linden, M., Maquet, P., & Salmon, E. (2008). Self-reflection across time: Cortical midline structures differentiate between present and past selves. *Social Cognitive and Affective Neuroscience, 3*, 244–252.

D'Argembeau, A., Jedidi, H., Balteau, E., Bahri, M., Phillips, C., & Salmon, E. (2012). Valuing one's self: Medial prefrontal involvement in epistemic and emotive investments in self-views. *Cerebral Cortex, 22*, 659–667.

D'Argembeau, A., Lardi, C., & Van der Linden, M. (2012). Self-defining future projections: Exploring the identity function of thinking about the future. *Memory, 20*, 110–120.

D'Argembeau, A., Stawarczyk, D., Majerus, S., Collette, F., Van der Linden, M., Feyers, D., et al. (2010). The neural basis of personal goal processing when envisioning future events. *Journal of Cognitive Neuroscience, 22*, 1701–1713.

D'Argembeau, A., Stawarczyk, D., Majerus, S., Collette, F., Van der Linden, M., & Salmon, E. (2010). Modulation of medial prefrontal and inferior parietal cortices when thinking about past, present, and future selves. *Social Neuroscience, 5*, 187–200.

Demblon, J. & D'Argembeau, A. (2017). Contribution of past and future self-defining event networks to personal identity. *Memory, 25*, 656–665.

Derry, P. A. & Kuiper, N. A. (1981). Schematic processing and self-reference in clinical depression. *Journal of Abnormal Psychology, 90*, 286–297.

Dozois, D. J. & Dobson, K. S. (2001). Information processing and cognitive organization in unipolar depression: specificity and comorbidity issues. *Journal of Abnormal Psychology, 110*, 236–246.

Dulas, M. R., Newsome, R. N., & Duarte, A. (2011). The effects of aging on ERP correlates of source memory retrieval for self-referential information. *Brain Research, 1377*, 84–100.

Dunkel, C. S. & Anthis, K. S. (2001). The role of possible selves in identity formation: A short-term longitudinal study. *Journal of Adolescence, 24*, 765–776.

Duval, C., Desgranges, B., de La Sayette, V., Belliard, S., Eustache, F., & Piolino, P. (2012). What happens to personal identity when semantic knowledge degrades? A study of the self and autobiographical memory in semantic dementia. *Neuropsychologia, 50*, 254–265.

Erikson, E. H. (1950). *Childhood and society.* New York: Norton.

Ernst, A., Gourisse, L., Wauquiez, G., & Souchay, C. (2016). Autobiographical memory and the self in a single-case of chronic unilateral spatial neglect. *Neurocase, 22*, 276–280.

Fitzgerald, M. (1988). Vivid memories and the reminiscence phenomenon: The role of a self narrative. *Human Development, 31*, 261–273.

Freedman, B. J. (1974). The subjective experience of perceptual and cognitive disturbances in schizophrenia. A review of autobiographical accounts. *Archives of General Psychiatry, 30*, 333–340.

Gillihan, S. J. & Farah, M. J. (2005). Is self special? A critical review of evidence from experimental psychology and cognitive neuroscience. *Psychological Bulletin, 131*, 76–97.

Glisky, E. L. & Marquine, M. J. (2009). Semantic and self-referential processing of positive and negative trait adjectives in older adults. *Memory, 17*, 144–157.

Gracey, F., Palmer, S., Rous, B., Psaila, K., Shaw, K., O'Dell, J., et al. (2008). "Feeling part of things": personal construction of self after brain injury. *Neuropsychological Rehabilitation, 18*, 627–650.

Gutchess, A. H., Kensinger, E. A., & Schacter, D. L. (2007). Aging, self-referencing, and medial prefrontal cortex. *Social Neuroscience, 2*, 117–133.

Gutchess, A. H., Kensinger, E. A., Yoon, C., & Schacter, D. L. (2007). Ageing and the self-reference effect in memory. *Memory, 15*, 822–837.

Gutchess, A. H., Kensinger, E. A., & Schacter, D. L. (2010). Functional neuroimaging of self-referential encoding with age. *Neuropsychologia, 48*, 211–219.

Hamami, A., Serbun, S. J., & Gutchess, A. H. (2011). Self-referencing enhances memory specificity with age. *Psychology and Aging, 26*, 636–646.

Hare, D. J., Mellor, C., & Azmi, S. (2007). Episodic memory in adults with autistic spectrum disorders: Recall for self- versus other-experienced events. *Research in Developmental Disabilities, 28*, 317–329.

Holt, D. J., Cassidy, B. S., Andrews-Hanna, J. R., Lee, S. M., Coombs, G., Goff, D. C., et al. (2011). An anterior-to-posterior shift in midline cortical activity in schizophrenia during self-reflection. *Biological Psychiatry, 69*, 415–423.

Hoyle, R. H. & Sherrill, M. R. (2006). Future orientation in the self-system: Possible selves, self-regulation, and behavior. *Journal of Personality, 74*, 1673–1696.

Hsiao, J. J., Kaiser, N., Fong, S., & Mendez, M. F. (2013). Suicidal behavior and loss of the future self in semantic dementia. *Cognitive and Behavioral Neurology, 26*, 85–92.

Illman, N. A., Rathbone, C. J., Kemp, S., & Moulin, C. J. A. (2011). Autobiographical memory and the self in a case of transient epileptic amnesia. *Epilepsy and Behavior, 21*, 36–41.

James, W. (1890). *The principles of psychology* (Vol. 1). New York: Holt.

Jansari, A. & Parkin, A. J. (1996). Things that go bump in your life: Explaining the reminiscence bump in autobiographical memory. *Psychology and Aging, 11*, 85.

Johnson, M. K., Raye, C. L., Mitchell, K. J., Touryan, S. R., Greene, E. J., & Nolen-Hoeksema, S. (2006). Dissociating medial frontal and posterior cingulate activity during self-reflection. *Social Cognitive and Affective Neuroscience, 1*, 56–64.

Jørgensen, C. R., Berntsen, D., Bech, M., Kjølbye, M., Bennedsen, B. E., & Ramsgaard, S. B. (2012). Identity-related autobiographical memories and cultural life scripts in patients with Borderline Personality Disorder. *Consciousness and Cognition, 21*, 788–798.

Kalenzaga, S., Bugaïska, A., & Clarys, D. (2013). Self-reference effect and autonoetic consciousness in Alzheimer's disease: Evidence for a persistent affective self in dementia patients. *Alzheimer Disease & Associated Disorders, 27*, 116–122.

Kalenzaga, S. & Clarys, D. (2013). Self-referential processing in Alzheimer's disease: two different ways of processing self-knowledge? *Journal of Clinical and Experimental Neuropsychology, 35*, 455–71.

Kelley, W. M., Macrae, C. N., Wyland, C. L., Caglar, S., Inati, S., & Heatherton, T. F. (2002). Finding the self? An event-related fMRI study. *Journal of Cognitive Neuroscience, 14*, 785–794.

Klein, S. B. (2012). Self, memory, and the self-reference effect: An examination of conceptual and methodological issues. *Personality and Social Psychology Review, 16*, 283–300.

Klein, S. B. (2013). Images and constructs: Can the neural correlates of self be revealed through radiological analysis? *International Journal of Psychological Research, 6*, 117–132.

Klein, S. B. & Gangi, C. E. (2010). The multiplicity of self: Neuropsychological evidence and its implications for the self as a construct in psychological research. *Annals of the New York Academy of Sciences, 1191*, 1–15.

Klein, S. B. & Kihlstrom, J. F. (1986). Elaboration, organization, and the self-reference effect in memory. *Journal of Experimental Psychology: General, 115*, 26–38.

Klein, S. B., Loftus, J., & Burton, H. A. (1989). Two self-reference effects: The importance of distinguishing between self-descriptiveness judgments and autobiographical retrieval in self-referent encoding. *Journal of Personality and Social Psychology, 56*, 853–865.

Kopelman, M., Wilson, B., & Baddeley, A. (1989). The Autobiographical Memory Interview: A new assessment of autobiographical and personal semantic memory in amnesic patients. *Journal of Experimental and Clinical Neuropsychology, 11*, 724–744.

Kuhn, M. H. & McPartland, T. S. (1954). An empirical investigation of self-attitudes. *American Sociological Review, 19*, 68–76.

Kuiper, N. A. & Derry, P. A. (1982). Depressed and nondepressed content self-reference in mild depressives. *Journal of Personality, 50*, 67–80.

Lalanne, J., Grolleau, P., & Piolino, P. (2010). Self-reference effect and episodic memory in normal aging and Alzheimer's disease: myth or reality? *Psychologie & neuropsychiatrie du vieillissement, 8*, 277–294.

Lalanne, J., Rozenberg, J., Grolleau, P., & Piolino, P. (2013). The self-reference effect on episodic memory recollection in young and older adults and Alzheimer's disease. *Current Alzheimer Research, 10*, 1107–1117.

Lardi, C., D'Argembeau, A., Chanal, J., Ghisletta, P., & Van der Linden, M. (2010). Further characterisation of self-defining memories in young adults: a study of a Swiss sample. *Memory, 18*, 293–309.

Leblond, M., Laisney, M., Lamidey, V., Egret, S., de La Sayette, V., Chételat, G., et al. (2016). Self-reference effect on memory in healthy aging, mild cognitive impairment and Alzheimer's disease: Influence of identity valence. *Cortex, 74*, 177–190.

Lemogne, C., Delaveau, P., Freton, M., Guionnet, S., & Fossati, P. (2012). Medial prefrontal cortex and the self in major depression. *Journal of Affective Disorders, 136*, e1–e11.

Lombardo, M. V., Barnes, J. L., Wheelwright, S. J., & Baron-Cohen, S. (2007). Self-referential cognition and empathy in austism. *PLoS One*, 2(9).

Lombardo, M. V., Chakrabarti, B., Bullmore, E. T., Sadek, S. A., Pasco, G., Wheelwright, S. J., et al. (2010). Atypical neural self-representation in autism. *Brain*, 133, 611–624.

Macrae, C. N., Moran, J. M., Heatherton, T. F., Banfield, J. F., & Kelley, W. M. (2004). Medial prefrontal activity predicts memory for self. *Cerebral Cortex*, 14, 647–654.

Manning, L. (2016). Future mental time travel and the me-self. In K. Michaelian, S. B. Klein, & K. K. Szpunar (eds.), *Seeing the future: Theoretical perspectives on future-oriented mental time travel* (pp. 183–198). Oxford: Oxford University Press.

Marcus, H. & Nurius, P. (1986). Possible selves. *American Psychologist*, 41, 954–969.

Martinelli, P., Anssens, A., Sperduti, M., & Piolino, P. (2013). The influence of normal aging and Alzheimer's disease in autobiographical memory highly related to the self. *Neuropsychology*, 27, 69–78.

Martinelli, P., Sperduti, M., & Piolino, P. (2013). Neural substrates of the self-memory system: New insights from a meta-analysis. *Human Brain Mapping*, 34, 1515–1529.

Millward, C., Powell, S., Messer, D., & Jordan, R. (2000). Recall for self and other in autism: Children's memory for events experienced by themselves and their peers. *Journal of Autism and Developmental Disorders*, 30, 15–28.

Milton, F., Muhlert, N., Pindus, D. M., Butler, C. R., Kapur, N., Graham, K. S., & Zeman, A. Z. J. (2010). Remote memory deficits in transient epileptic amnesia. *Brain*, 133, 1368–1379.

Mitchell, K. J., Raye, C. L., Ebner, N. C., Tubridy, S. M., Frankel, H., & Johnson, M. K. (2009). Age-group differences in medial cortex activity associated with thinking about self-relevant agendas. *Psychology and Aging*, 24, 438–449.

Moffitt, K. H. & Singer, J. A. (1994). Continuity in the life story: Self-defining memories, affect, and approach/avoidance personal strivings. *Journal of Personality*, 62, 21–43.

Mograbi, D. C., Brown, R. G., & Morris, R. G. (2009). Anosognosia in Alzheimer's disease—The petrified self. *Consciousness and Cognition*, 18, 989–1003.

Morel, N., Villain, N., Rauchs, G., Gaubert, M., Piolino, P., Landeau, B., et al. (2014). Brain activity and functional coupling changes associated with self-reference effect during both encoding and retrieval. *PLoS One*, 9(3).

Murray, R. J., Schaer, M., & Debbané, M. (2012). Degrees of separation: A quantitative neuroimaging meta-analysis investigating self-specificity and shared neural activation between self- and other-reflection. *Neuroscience and Biobehavioral Reviews*, 36, 1043–1059.

Northoff, G., Heinzel, A., de Greck, M., Bermpohl, F., Dobrowolny, H., & Panksepp, J. (2006). Self-referential processing in our brain—A meta-analysis of imaging studies on the self. *NeuroImage*, 31, 440–457.

Packer, D. J. & Cunningham, W. A. (2009). Neural correlates of reflection on goal states: The role of regulatory focus and temporal distance. *Social Neuroscience*, 4, 412–425.

Philippi, C. L., Duff, M. C., Denburg, N. L., Tranel, D., & Rudrauf, D. (2012). Medial PFC damage abolishes the self-reference effect. *Journal of Cognitive Neuroscience*, 24, 475–81.

Piolino, P., Desgranges, B., & Eustache, F. (2000). *La mémoire autobiographique: Théorie et pratique*. Marseille: Solal.

Prebble, S. C., Addis, D. R., & Tippett, L. J. (2013). Autobiographical memory and sense of self. *Psychological Bulletin*, 139, 815.

Raffard, S., D'Argembeau, A., Lardi, C., Bayard, S., Boulenger, J. P., & Van der Linden, M. (2010). Narrative identity in schizophrenia. *Consciousness and Cognition*, 19, 328–340.

Raffard, S., D'Argembeau, A., Lardi, C., Bayard, S., Boulenger, J.-P., & Van Der Linden, M. (2009). Exploring self-defining memories in schizophrenia. *Memory*, 17, 26–38.

Rathbone, C. J., Conway, M. A., & Moulin, C. J. A. (2011). Remembering and imagining: The role of the self. *Consciousness and Cognition*, 20, 1175–1182.

Rathbone, C. J., Ellis, J. A., Baker, I., & Butler, C. R. (2015). Self, memory, and imagining the future in a case of psychogenic amnesia. *Neurocase*, 21, 727–737.

Rathbone, C. J. & Moulin, C. J. (2010). When's your birthday? The self-reference effect in retrieval of dates. *Applied Cognitive Psychology*, 24, 737–743.

Rathbone, C. J. & Moulin, C. J. A. (2014). Measuring autobiographical fluency in the self-memory system. *Quarterly Journal of Experimental Psychology, 67*, 1661–1667.

Rathbone, C. J., Moulin, C. J. A., & Conway, M. A. (2008). Self-centered memories: the reminiscence bump and the self. *Memory & Cognition, 36*, 1403–1414.

Rathbone, C. J., Moulin, C. J., & Conway, M. A. (2009). Autobiographical memory and amnesia: Using conceptual knowledge to ground the self. *Neurocase, 15*, 405–418.

Rathbone, C. J. & Steel, C. (2015). Autobiographical memory distributions for negative self-images: Memories are organised around negative as well as positive aspects of identity. *Memory, 23*, 473–486.

Rogers, T. B., Kuiper, N. A., & Kirker, W. S. (1977). Self-reference and the encoding of personal information. *Journal of Personality and Social Psychology, 35*, 677.

Rubin, D. C., Rahhal, T. A., & Poon, L. W. (1998). Things learned in early adulthood are remembered best. *Memory & Cognition, 26*, 3–19.

Ruby, P. & Legrand, D. (2007). Neuroimaging the self? In Y. Rossetti, P. Haggard, & M. Kawato (eds.), *Sensorimotor foundations of higher cognition* (22nd Attention & Performance Meeting, pp. 293–318). New York: Oxford University Press.

Schacter, D. L. & Addis, D. R. (2007). The cognitive neuroscience of constructive memory: remembering the past and imagining the future. *Philosophical Transactions of the Royal Society B: Biological Sciences, 362*, 773–786.

Schacter, D. L., Addis, D. R., Hassabis, D., Martin, V. C., Spreng, R. N., & Szpunar, K. K. (2012). The future of memory: remembering, imagining, and the brain. *Neuron, 76*, 677–694.

Singer, J. A. & Blagov, P. S. (2000). Classification system and scoring manual for self-defining autobiographical memories. Unpublished manuscript, Connecticut College.

Singer, J. A. & Blagov, P. S. (2004). The integrative function of narrative processing: Autobiographical memory, self-defining memories and the life story of identity. In D. R. Beike, J. M. Lampinen, & D. A. Behrend (eds.), *The self and memory* (pp. 117–138). New York: The Psychology Press.

Singer, J., Rexhaj, B., & Baddeley, J. (2007). Older, wiser, and happier? Comparing older adults' and college students' self-defining memories. *Memory, 15*, 886–898.

Singer, J. A. & Salovey, P. (1993). *The remembered self: Emotion and memory in personality.* New York: Free Press.

Staniloiu, A., Markowitsch, H. J., & Brand, M. (2010). Psychogenic amnesia—A malady of the constricted self. *Consciousness and Cognition, 19*, 778–801.

Stawarczyk, D. & D'Argembeau, A. (2015). Neural correlates of personal goal processing during episodic future thinking and mind-wandering: An ALE meta-analysis. *Human Brain Mapping, 36*, 2928–2947.

Suddendorf, T. & Busby, J. (2005). Making decisions with the future in mind: Developmental and comparative identification of mental time travel. *Learning and Motivation, 36*, 110–125.

Sutherland, K. & Bryant, R. A. (2005). Self-defining memories in post-traumatic stress disorder. *British Journal of Clinical Psychology, 44*, 591–598.

Symons, C. S. & Johnson, B. T. (1997). The self-reference effect in memory: A meta-analysis. *Psychological Bulletin, 121*, 371–394.

Tanweer, T., Rathbone, C. J., & Souchay, C. (2010). Autobiographical memory, autonoetic consciousness, and identity in Asperger syndrome. *Neuropsychologia, 48*, 900–908.

Thorne, A. & McLean, K. (2001). Manual for coding events in self-defining memories. Unpublished document. Department of Psychology, University of California—Santa Cruz.

Thorne, A., McLean, K. C., & Lawrence, A. M. (2004). When remembering is not enough: Reflecting on self-defining memories in late adolescence. *Journal of Personality, 72*, 513–542.

van der Meer, L., Costafreda, S., Aleman, A., & David, A. S. (2010). Self-reflection and the brain: A theoretical review and meta-analysis of neuroimaging studies with implications for schizophrenia. *Neuroscience and Biobehavioral Reviews, 34*, 935–946.

Vignoles, V. L. (2011). Identity motives. In S. J. Schwartz, K. Luyckx, & V. L. Vignoles (eds.), *Handbook of identity theory and research* (pp. 403–432). New York: Springer.

Voltzenlogel, V., Després, O., Vignal, J. P., Steinhoff, B. J., Kehrli, P., & Manning, L. (2006). Remote memory in temporal lobe epilepsy. *Epilepsia*, *47*, 1329–1336.

Williams, J. M. G., Ellis, N. C., Tyers, C., Healy, H., Rose, G., & MacLeod A. K. (1996). The specificity of autobiographical memory and imaginability of the future. *Memory and Cognition*, *24*, 116–125.

Zhu, L., Guo, X., Li, J., Zheng, L., Wang, Q., & Yang, Z. (2012). Hippocampal activity is associated with self-descriptiveness effect in memory, whereas self-reference effect in memory depends on medial prefrontal activity. *Hippocampus*, *22*, 1540–1552.

9

The Cue-dependency of the "Reminiscence Bumps" in Autobiographical Memory and Memory for Public Events

What They Reveal About Memory Organization

Jonathan Koppel and Dorthe Berntsen

Introduction

The *reminiscence bump* most commonly refers to the disproportionate number of auto-biographical memories, in adults aged ≥40 years, dating from youth and early adulthood (Rubin et al., 1986; for reviews, see Koppel and Berntsen, 2015b; Koppel & Rubin, 2016). It is an unusually robust effect; although we will describe several exceptions to the bump throughout this chapter, such exceptions are almost always explicable with reference to theoretical accounts of the bump.

Whereas the bump in autobiographical memory primarily has been studied by psychologists, it has been paralleled in the sociology literature in a spike in recall for public events that occurred at a similar period of the lifespan (Schuman & Scott, 1989; for reviews, see Corning & Schuman, 2015; Koppel, 2013). Though sociologists have adapted a different terminology, referring, for instance, to a *critical period* for memories of important public events (for discussion of this terminology, see Schuman & Corning, 2014), for the sake of convenience we will refer to this increase in memories for public events as the *reminiscence bump for public events*.

Besides the similarity of the individual reminiscence bumps in autobiographical memory and memory for public events on a descriptive level, another commonality between the two effects concerns the mechanisms that researchers have posited as underlying each bump. In both cases, researchers have tended to stress encoding processes as being primarily responsible for the bump, arguing that events of the bump period receive privileged encoding. Specific accounts vary, however, as to why events of the bump period receive this privileged encoding. For instance, in the case of the bump in autobiographical memory, an illustrative example is the *identity formation account*, which has also been termed the *self-narrative* account (Conway & Holmes, 2004; Conway & Pleydell-Pearce, 2000; Fitzgerald, 1988, 1996; Holmes & Conway, 1999; Rubin et al., 1998). Researchers who favor the identity formation account have drawn on theories of lifespan development, such as Erikson's (1950) theory of psychosocial development, in arguing that the importance of adolescence and early adulthood to identity formation means that this period of the lifespan is marked by a clustering of identity-salient events. Such events, in turn, receive increased encoding and retention, and have their availability maintained through increased rehearsal (for an extended discussion, see Koppel & Berntsen, 2015b).

This account does allow for a role of retrieval processes in producing the bump as well. For instance, in Conway and colleagues' recent iteration of the account, wherein the special relevance of events of the bump period to identity formation is framed in terms of their relevance to one's goals at the time of encoding, the eventual retrieval of these events is also contingent upon their relevance to one's goals at the time of retrieval (for discussion of this point, see especially Conway & Holmes, 2004). However, the core premise of the identity formation account is that the bump reflects and corresponds to a period of the lifespan that contains a peak of encoded autobiographical memories.

The premise that the bump corresponds to a period in which more autobiographical memories are encoded than at other periods of the lifespan is shared by other accounts of the bump in autobiographical memory. For instance, in the *cognitive account* (Pillemer, 2001; Robinson, 1992; Rubin et al., 1998), the bump is attributed to the bump period representing a time of rapid change, which therefore includes many novel events and first-time experiences (for discussion of the importance of first-time experiences in particular, see especially Robinson, 1992). The novelty of events of the bump period leads to their being preferentially encoded and retained, due to such factors as the increased effort after meaning they engender, the lack of proactive interference for such events, and their distinctiveness. Likewise, the *cognitive abilities account* holds that the bump is due to encoding efficiency being at its peak in the bump period, because this period represents the time of optimal cognitive and neural functioning (Janssen et al., 2015; Rubin et al., 1998).

In the case of the bump for public events, the dominant theoretical account is something of a combination of the identity formation and cognitive accounts of the bump in autobiographical memory. That is, following from Mannheim's (1928/1952) assertion that adolescence and early adulthood is uniquely important in the formation of a cohort's generational identity, researchers have argued that public events of adolescence and early adulthood are encoded especially well due to their importance to identity formation, which is derived in part because public events of this period are often the first event of their type which the individual both experiences first-hand and is old enough to follow and understand (Belli et al., 1997; Corning & Schuman, 2015; Schuman & Scott, 1989; see also Holmes & Conway, 1999, who offered an account of the bump for public events that represents a parallel of their identity formation account of the bump in autobiographical memory). Janssen et al. (2008) have also extended the cognitive abilities account of the bump in autobiographical memory to the bump for public events.

Notwithstanding this general emphasis on processes at encoding, recent findings and a reexamination of earlier work make it clear that the bumps in both autobiographical memory and memory for public events are sensitive to the cueing method used to elicit the memories. Specifically, in autobiographical memory, the temporal location of the bump varies according to the cueing method; relatedly, in memory for public events, the frequency with which the bump is found likewise varies across different cueing methods. These findings challenge encoding-based accounts of the bump, in that, as we will elaborate on below, the most important distinction between different cueing methods is that they trigger different retrieval strategies. Therefore, the differences in the bump across disparate cueing methods indicate, in effect, that the bump varies as participants' retrieval strategies are manipulated. This finding would not be predicted by encoding-based accounts, which would predict that, to the extent that the bump simply reflects a clustering of encoded memories at a certain stage of the lifespan, it should be expected to be relatively stable across different cueing methods.

To be sure, the sensitivity of the bump to cueing method does not suggest that encoding processes play no role in producing the effect. However, we would contend that these findings point to a larger role for retrieval processes than is currently allowed for in most existing theoretical accounts. Such findings therefore point to the need for existing accounts to accommodate retrieval-based processes as well, or to do so to a larger extent than is currently the case.

In this chapter, we review findings illustrating the sensitivity of the bump in both autobiographical memory and memory for public events to cueing method. We do so separately for the bump in each individual domain. In each case, we then go on to discuss the retrieval processes that we believe the reviewed findings implicate as partially underlying (or possibly partially underlying) the bump in each domain.

The reminiscence bump in autobiographical memory

Most researchers testing for the reminiscence bump in autobiographical memory have employed one of two dominant cueing methods. The first method, which we refer to as the *cue word method,* requires participants to retrieve autobiographical memories in association to cue words, most often nouns, such as *letter* (Crovitz & Schiffman, 1974; Galton, 1879; for subsequent studies employing this technique, see, e.g., Janssen et al., 2011; Rubin & Schulkind, 1997a, 1997b; Schuman & Corning, 2014; for a description of the type of cue words used in each individual study, see Table 1 in Koppel & Berntsen, 2015b); the second method, which we refer to as the *important memory method,* requires participants to retrieve important autobiographical memories of one form or another. The important memory method is an umbrella category, as we would include within it several different types of queries for important memories, such as requests to simply report important memories (Cuervo-Lombard et al., 2007; Glück & Bluck, 2007; Rubin & Schulkind, 1997a), or requests to list memories that the participant considers central to his or her life story or which he or she would include in a book about their life (Bohn, 2010; Fitzgerald, 1996; Thomsen & Berntsen, 2008).

As we noted above, these two cueing methods can be contrasted according to the retrieval strategy each method triggers, with the cue word method generally assumed to produce an associative search and the important memory method assumed to produce a narrative-based search (for further discussion of this point, see Koppel & Berntsen, 2015b). Relatedly, the cue word and important memory methods also differ in the putative representativeness of the retrieved memories with regard to the individual's total corpus of autobiographical memories, as the cue word method is intended to provide a neutral sampling of the contents of one's memory (Crovitz & Schiffman, 1974), whereas this is naturally not the case in the important memory method.

In the following, we first discuss the differences in the bump as attained for word-cued memories versus important memories. We then address shifts in the bump within word-cued memories and important memories, as well as when other cueing techniques are employed, before discussing the retrieval processes that are operative (or may be operative) in producing these individual bumps.

Word-cued memories versus important memories

The bump in autobiographical memory was first identified in relation to word-cued memories. Specifically, through a reanalysis of data presented in three earlier papers (Fitzgerald & Lawrence, 1984; McCormack, 1979; Zola-Morgan et al., 1983), combined with the presentation of new data, Rubin et al. (1986) demonstrated that the lifespan distribution of word-cued autobiographical memories features an exception to a typical retention function, whereby older memories would be less likely to be recalled than more recent memories (e.g., Ebbinghaus 1885/1964; Wickelgren, 1972). That is, Rubin et al. observed that middle-aged and older adults recall more word-cued memories from between the ages of 11 and 30 years of age than from the immediately following age interval.

Subsequent researchers, when specifying an age range for the bump, tended to characterize it as roughly corresponding to the age range over which Rubin et al. (1986) initially observed the bump. Therefore, they generally estimated the bump as spanning from approximately 10 or 15 to 30 years of age (e.g., Dickson et al., 2011; Koppel & Berntsen, 2014a; Morrison & Conway, 2010). However, a close examination of studies on the bump in word-cued memories reveals that researchers have often attained a markedly earlier bump, with the bump frequently extending back to soon after the full offset of childhood amnesia (e.g., age 5 or 6 years) and extending until around age 15 or 20 years. This is particularly true of more recent studies (see Table 1 in Koppel & Berntsen, 2015b, wherein we identified the beginning and endpoint of the bump in each individual study on the bump in word-cued memories).

One possible explanation for the tendency of more recent studies to yield an earlier bump in word-cued memories is that there has been a shift in the size of the age bins most often used in grouping memories together when plotting and analyzing the lifespan distributions of word-cued memories. Whereas researchers initially tended to use 10-year intervals when plotting the memories (e.g., 0–10 years, 11–20 years, etc; Fromholt et al., 2003; Rubin et al., 1986; Rubin & Schulkind, 1997a; Willander &

Larsson, 2006), the use of 5-year intervals has recently become more common (e.g., 0–5 years, 6–10 years, etc.; Alea et al., 2014; Janssen et al., 2011; Koppel & Berntsen, 2016b). Both Rubin & Schulkind (1997a) and Janssen et al. (2011) manipulated the type of age bin used in plotting their word-cued data, employing both 5- and 10-year bins. They each found that using 5-year bins produced an earlier bump, as, for instance, Janssen et al. found a peak from 11 to 20 years of age when employing 10-year bins, while the distribution peaked from 6 to 10 when employing 5-year bins. It may be the case, then, that in some instances the use of 10-year bins in many early studies on the bump in word-cued memories obscured an earlier beginning of the bump period.

In contrast to the markedly early bump that has often been attained for word-cued memories, researchers testing for the bump in important memories have generally found that, here, the bump's temporal location corresponds well to the common understanding of the location of the bump (see Table 2 in Koppel and Berntsen, 2015b, which reports the parallel information for studies on important memories that Table 1 does for word-cued memories). The differential locations of the bump in word-cued memories versus important memories was first demonstrated by Rubin & Schulkind (1997a), who compared the distributions of word-cued memories versus important memories in a within-subjects design. They found that the bump in word-cued memories was spread out over the ages 10–29 years, while the bump in important memories was concentrated in the 20–29 decade. We followed up on Rubin and Schulkind by likewise comparing the distributions of word-cued memories and important memories within-subjects, and attained similar results (Koppel & Berntsen, 2016b).

In an effort to provide a systematic demonstration of these contrasting temporal location of the bump, we have recently conducted a meta-analysis in which, as noted above, we identified the beginning and endpoints of the bump in each individual study we were aware of on the bump in either word-cued and/or important memories (Koppel and Berntsen, 2015b). We then averaged across all the relevant studies to calculate the mean beginning and endpoint of the bump. For word-cued memories, we found that the mean beginning and ending ages of the bump were 9 and 23 years of age, respectively; for important memories, the corresponding means were 15 and 28 years of age. Figure 9.1 illustrates the basic findings of this meta-analysis with reference to a single study; it also includes an estimate of the distribution of odor-cued memories, which we discuss below. Although these findings illustrate the differential bumps for word-cued and important memories, we would argue that, if anything, our calculations understate the true difference in the location of the bump across word-cued versus important memories, given the use of 10-year bins in some studies on the bump in word-cued memories.

Lastly, though in this chapter we focus on differences in the location of the bump across different cueing methods, it is worth noting that, in comparing word-cued memories and important memories, there are other differences in both the bump and the broader distribution of memories across the lifespan. First, the bump is less pronounced in the cue word method (Fitzgerald, 1988; Fromholt et al., 2003; Rubin & Schulkind, 1997a). Second, only word-cued memories exhibit, in addition to the bump,

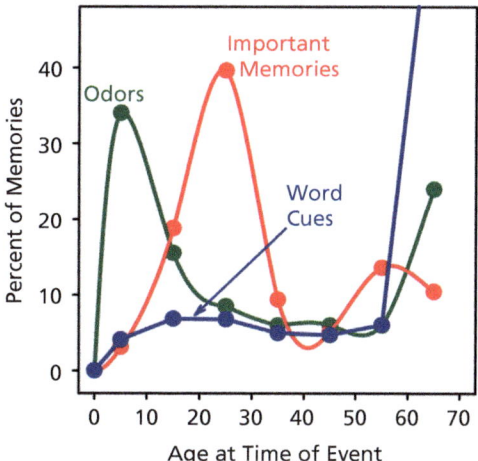

Figure 9.1 Illustration of the differential reminiscence bumps and broader lifespan distributions across word-cued, important, and odor-cued memories. The data for the last decade of the word-cued memories has a value of 57%.

Source: The data for the word-cued and important memories are from Rubin & Schulkind (1997a). The olfactory plot represents an estimate based on the figures presented in Chu & Downes (2000) and Willander & Larsson (2006, 2007), with the data for the 60–70-year bin estimated from the data presented in Chu & Downes.

an increase in memories recalled from the most recent years of one's life, as is a hall-mark of typical retention functions (Rubin & Schulkind, 1997a). Each of these other differences in the bump and the broader distributions of word-cued versus important memories are also illustrated in figure 9.1, and we would argue that they likewise speak to the importance of retrieval processes in the recall of autobiographical memories.

Shifts in the bump within word-cued memories and important memories

As we have seen, there is a clear difference in the location of the bump across word-cued versus important memories. At the same time, the bump also varies when examined *within* word-cued memories and important memories, respectively. In the case of word-cued memories, the memories yielded in response to less imageable cue words tend to be less remote than those yielded in response to more imageable cue words (Fitzgerald & Lawrence, 1984; Rubin, 1980; Rubin & Schulkind 1997b), suggesting that the bump would be earlier for more imageable cue words. Consistent with this prospect, in re-analyzing data from Fitzgerald and Lawrence (1984), Rubin et al. (1986) found that when 70-year-old participants were cued with affect words (e.g., *surprised*) there were relatively few memories until the 21–30 decade, whereas, when they were cued with nouns, the increase in memories began in the 11–20 decade (though this pattern was not evident for 50-year-old participants). Relatedly Maki et al. (2013) compared the bump for neutral words (which were comprised of object nouns), emotional words (which were similar to the affect words in Fitzgerald & Lawrence, 1984), and emotion-provoking words (e.g., *doctor*). As in Rubin et al.'s reanalysis of Fitzgerald and Lawrence, Maki et al. attained an earlier bump for neutral words than either emotional or emotion-provoking words.

The bump is likewise not entirely stable when examined within important memories. In our meta-analysis (Koppel & Berntsen, 2015b), one type of memory we classified within the important memory category was requests for particularly vivid or clear memories. However, of the four articles we included that reported on the bump in vivid or clear memories (Benson et al., 1992; Cohen & Faulkner, 1988; Fitzgerald, 1988; Robinson & Taylor, 1998), two of them reported an unusually early bump compared to other studies on important memories: Robinson and Taylor (1998) found a bump from 5 to 11 years of age, and Cohen and Faulkner (1988) found a bump from 0 to 10. This suggests that vivid or clear memories may represent a special class of important memories as far as the location of the bump is concerned.

Moreover, the bump in important memories is generally restricted to positive memories. This has been most frequently demonstrated in studies wherein participants have been asked to report important memories reflecting a specific positive or negative emotion, such as their memory of when they felt happiest, most in love, saddest, and/ or most afraid (Berntsen and Rubin, 2002; Berntsen et al., 2011; Dickson et al., 2011; Haque and Hasking, 2010; Rubin and Berntsen, 2003; Tekcan et al., 2017); researchers have generally found a bump for memories reflecting positive emotions, but not for memories reflecting negative emotions.

Other cueing techniques

Olfactory cues

Another technique that has been used to probe for the bump has been to ask participants to generate autobiographical memories in response to odor cues (e.g., tobacco; Chu & Downes, 2000; Willander & Larsson, 2006, 2007), or, relatedly, to ask participants to imagine an odor in association to the corresponding cue word (Willander & Larsson, 2008). In these studies, the resulting distributions have been compared to the distributions attained for word-cued memories. The findings from this literature on olfactory cues have been reviewed in Rubin (2015) and Koppel and Rubin (2016). To briefly relate the findings here, the olfactory literature has demonstrated that the bump in response to such cues draws even more heavily on the earliest part of the lifespan than the bump in word-cued memories, with the number of memories produced peaking in the first decade of the lifespan and falling rapidly thereafter (see figure 9.1).

Involuntary memories

Finally, there has also been limited research on the location of the bump in *involuntary memories*, referring to memories that come to mind spontaneously with no preceding attempt at retrieval (for a review, see Berntsen, 2010). For example, Berntsen & Rubin (2002) asked participants to think of the most recent instance in which they had had an involuntary memory, and to report their age at the time of the memory. Berntsen and Rubin found a bump that was like that in word-cued memories though skewed slightly earlier, peaking from 10 to 19 years of age, but also evident in the 0–9-year decade.

Similarly, Schlagman et al. (2009) conducted a diary study wherein older adults, with a mean age of 75 years, recorded and dated all their involuntary memories over a period of seven days. Schlagman et al. plotted the memories according to participants' reports of how long ago each memory had occurred (e.g., 10 years prior to the study), rather than according to participants' age at the time of the memory. They found a bump from 50 to 69 years prior to the study, which, by Schlagman et al.'s estimation, roughly spans the period over which the participants were 10–30 years of age.

Retrieval processes

At this point we have hopefully succeeded in establishing the premise that, rather than representing an inflexible or unitary phenomenon, the bump in autobiographical memory shifts in both its size and location depending on the cueing method used to elicit the memories. As already noted, the salient distinction between different cueing methods is that they trigger different retrieval strategies. Therefore, whereas the flexibility of the bump according to the cueing method employed should not be taken as indicating that the encoding processes posited in most accounts of the bump play no role in producing the bump, they do point to a significant role for retrieval processes as well.

We now martial two final pieces of evidence in support of this point. First, we have recently replicated the disparate locations of the bumps in word-cued and important memories, not in autobiographical memory per se, but when participants were asked to generate the word-cued and important memories that they imagined a prototypical 70-year-old would generate (Koppel and Berntsen, 2016c). Second, Bohn and Berntsen (2011) asked a sample of children and teenagers (ranging from Grade 3, with a mean age of 10.0 years, to Grade 8, with a mean age 14.6 years) to write their future life stories. The authors found that the distribution of events within these life stories demonstrated a bump that essentially mirrored the bump in important memories, peaking from ages 21 to 30 years.

Both the imagined memory task of Koppel and Berntsen (2016c) and the future life story procedure of Bohn and Berntsen (2011) strip away encoding-related factors and characteristics of memories themselves, leaving participants reliant on constructive, schematic factors, that would typically be operative at retrieval. The replication of the word-cued and important memory bumps in these studies therefor demonstrates that the schematic processes operative in these tasks are sufficient to produce these distributions, and that encoding-related processes are not necessary to do so.

However, these findings do not rule out the possibility that encoding-related processes nonetheless contribute towards the bump as attained in autobiographical memory. In light of the data currently at hand, one way to conceptualize the respective contributions of encoding and retrieval processes to the bump is to posit that the bump reflects an interaction between encoding and retrieval processes. That is, there may be a broad encoding advantage afforded to events taking place from around 7 to 30 years of age, for a combination of reasons potentially relating to the theoretical accounts of the bump we have already reviewed. At the same time, the retrieval strategy triggered by the cues provided at retrieval may focus on a narrower span within this broad range. In that case, the individual bumps found across the cueing methods we have discussed would reflect an interaction between (1) the encoding advantage broadly afforded to events from early in the lifespan, and (2) the more specific temporal focus of the retrieval strategy produced through each respective cueing method.

Proceeding from this conceptualization of the bump, a full account of the bump needs to include a description of the specific constructive, schematic processes that are operative, or may be operative, in producing autobiographical memories in relation to each type of cue. Here we make an initial effort to do just that. As the extent of relevant empirical data that we can bring to bear on this question varies across different cueing methods, we stipulate whether there is a firm empirical basis to posit that a given retrieval strategy is triggered through a given cueing method, or whether our arguments rely more on speculation. In the latter cases especially, we hope that our discussion here spurs further research.

Important memories

Of the existent accounts of the bump, the one account that primarily stipulates retrieval processes as underlying the bump is the *life script account*. This account starts with the premise that all cultures possess an individual cultural life script, referring to culturally shared representations of the order and timing of major transitional life events (Berntsen & Rubin, 2004). The standard method for collecting the life script of a given country follows Berntsen & Rubin's (2004) procedure of asking participants to imagine a prototypical infant of their own culture and gender, and then to list the seven most important events that would most likely take place in that infant's life (for subsequent studies using this procedure, see, e.g., Erdoğan et al., 2008; Ottsen & Berntsen, 2014; Rubin et al., 2009; Zaragoza Scherman et al., 2017; for a review of the life script literature, see Zaragoza Scherman, 2013). This life script is held to structure retrieval from autobiographical memory, though the importance of life script events can aid in their encoding and lead to greater rehearsal for these events as well (Berntsen & Rubin, 2004). In addition to the life script account's greater emphasis on processes at retrieval, it is distinguished from the other accounts by its stress on cultural semantic knowledge, rather than by episodic information or the personal significance of an event.

Importantly, Berntsen & Rubin's (2004) initial theoretical formulation of the life script account held that whereas the life script structures retrieval of important autobiographical memories, it is unlikely to structure the retrieval of word-cued memories, or of memories retrieved in response to other associative cueing techniques. This contention has been borne out in subsequent empirical work, as requests for important memories produce a much greater proportion of life script events than do requests for word-cued memories; correspondingly, life script events largely underlie the bump in important memories but not word-cued memories (Berntsen & Bohn, 2010; Koppel & Berntsen, 2016b).

The evidence in favor of the life script account takes several forms. At the most general level, the distribution of life script events features a bump that resembles the bump in important memories (see Zaragoza Scherman, 2013). Moreover, exceptions to the bump in important memories track with exceptions to the bump in life scripts; we noted above that researchers have generally found a bump for memories reflecting positive emotions, but not for memories reflecting negative emotions (e.g., Rubin & Berntsen, 2003). It is telling, then, that the age distributions of cultural *expectations* for when a hypothetical individual would have experienced the same events features a pattern similar to that of the recall data, with positive events typically demonstrating a bump, but not negative events (Dickson et al., 2011; Haque & Hasking, 2010; Rubin & Berntsen, 2003).

We have recently extended these autobiographical memory data by demonstrating that the life script likewise plays a role in structuring recall outside of autobiographical memory per se. First, we found that recall for a brief fictional life story was likewise structured by the life script, as for instance, participants were more likely to recall life script events that had occurred in the story than non-life-script events (Koppel & Berntsen, 2014a).

Second, in the study on imagined memories referred to above (Koppel & Berntsen, 2016c), when participants were asked to generate what they imagined the seven most important memories of a hypothetical person's life would be, 73% of the resulting "memories" were of life script events, and the bump for the imagined important memories was driven by life script events. For the imagined word-cued memories, conversely, only 25% of the resulting memories were of life script events, and life script events played little role in producing the bump.

Word-cued memories

As both we (Koppel & Berntsen, 2015b) and others (Janssen, 2015) have noted, there has been little research investigating the retrieval strategies employed in generating autobiographical memories in association to cue words. Our discussion of the retrieval processes in the generation of word-cued memories is therefore necessarily more speculative than in the case of important memories. While the important memory method restricts the memory search to a certain pool of memories, there is no such restriction built into the cue word method (Janssen, 2015). In light of the early bump in word-cued memories, one possible mechanism through which the memory search for word-cued memories may be restricted is that individuals may generally focus memory search strategies on the beginning and endpoints of the search space.

The evidence that memory search strategies are often focused on the beginning and endpoints of the search space comes from the broad range of types of memory which have exhibited serial-position-like functions (i.e., enhanced recall for the beginning and endpoints of the list of items or pool of memories to be recalled), outside of the verbal learning experiments on which the serial position curve was first demonstrated and with which it is most associated (e.g., Deese & Kaufman, 1957; Murdock, 1960; Rundus & Atkinson, 1970). Distributions resembling the serial position curve have been attained in autobiographical memory, such as memories for an academic year or semester (Pillemer et al. , 1986, 1988; Thomsen & Berntsen, 2005), a calendar year (Kurbat et al., 1998; Robinson, 1986), and memories for a romantic relationship (Thomsen & Berntsen, 2005). Additionally, there has recently been considerable research demonstrating serial position curves in semantic memory, such as in free recall and ordinal position recall of US presidents, the order of song lyrics, and the ordering of actors by age (Kelley et al., 2013, 2015; Overstreet et al., 2017; Roediger & DeSoto, 2014; see also Crowder, 1993; Roediger & Crowder, 1976).

Following this account, when individuals are asked to recall autobiographical memories in association to cue words, their search may be structured around the beginning and end points of their life to that point. A retrieval strategy along these lines would be expected to produce a bump extending back to soon after the offset of childhood amnesia, as is seen in word-cued memories.

An additional point in favor of this account is that it can explain one of the rare failures in the word-cued literature to attain a bump, namely, the lack of a bump in Howes & Katz (1992), wherein participants were instructed to recall an event from a particular time period for each cue word, rather than conduct an unrestricted search over their lifespan.[1] Lastly, such a retrieval strategy may also help contribute to the large number of recent memories seen in word-cued memories, though a special retrieval mechanism does not necessarily need to be invoked to explain this aspect of the distribution of word-cued memories, given that, as we noted above, a spike in the number of memories for the most recent period of one's life is more consistent with standard retention functions (Ebbinghaus 1885/1964; Rubin & Wenzel, 1996; Wickelgren, 1972).

Olfactory cues

Similar to the case of word-cued memories, there has not been empirical investigation of the retrieval processes involved in generating autobiographical memories in association to olfactory cues. Here as well, then, our discussion is somewhat speculative. However, within the distinction we laid out earlier between the cue word method as instigating an associative search and the important memory method as instigating a narrative-based search, odor cues may have more in common with word cues in that they also presumably trigger an associative search rather than a narrative search.

---

[1] In another cue word study, Rabbit and Winthorpe (1988) also asked participants to confine their search to a defined part of the lifespan. However, as they plotted the attained memories according to the given third of the participant's life in which the memory occurred, rather than specifying the precise age range, it is unclear whether Rabbit and Winthorpe attained a bump.

As Rubin (2015) noted, though, odor cues differ from word cues in that they can bypass the neural structures supporting language on which word cues rely, and possess a direct, preconscious link with one's emotions (see also Rubin, 2006). Rubin suggested that whereas word cues initiate a search that involves looking for a memory with a language-based context, the search process initiated through odor cues may have no such stipulation, and would therefore be more likely to invoke memories lacking a linguistic or narrative context. The same may also be true of the search process initiated when participants are asked to imagine an odor in association to a word cue (as in Willander & Larsson, 2008), though, unlike actual odor cues, this task does not bypass language-based neural structures.

Memories lacking a linguistic or narrative context may, in turn, tend to refer to especially early events, because they avoid interference by more verbally accessible memories (e.g., Lawless & Engen, 1977). This was supported by Miles and Berntsen (2011), who compared the distributions, in university students, of both memories and future thoughts generated in association to corresponding word, odor, and visual cues. Though Miles and Berntsen found that, in line with prior work, odor cues yielded more remote memories, this was not paralleled in the distribution of future thoughts; if anything, odor-cued future thoughts trended towards taking place closer to the present than the future thoughts generated in association to word and visual cues. Given that interference is a relevant concern for memories but not future thoughts, this suggests that lack of interference for odor-cued memories accounts for why such memories tend to be especially remote.

Involuntary memories

Although involuntary memories do not involve an intentional memory search, they are also more like word-cued memories than important memories, in that they reflect an associative rather than a narrative-based retrieval process. Specifically, involuntary recall is the product of an association triggered by situational cues, though, here, the remembering is unintentional and therefore takes place with little executive control (Berntsen, 2010). It nonetheless therefore makes sense that the location of the bump in involuntary memories corresponds more closely to the bump in word-cued memories than in important memories (Bernsten & Rubin, 2002: Schlagman et al., 2009).

Whether the retrieval process in involuntary remembering draws on memories with a language-based context, as in the retrieval process in word-cued memories, or whether it draws on memories lacking such a context, as in odor-cued memories, is likely a function of the specific cue that triggers the memory.

The reminiscence bump for public events

Although the reminiscence bump in autobiographical memory and the bump for public events each reflect a focus on youth and early adulthood, they are not precise parallels of one another in terms of how each effect is typically measured. Specifically, the bump in autobiographical memory is measured by asking participants to generate a given number of autobiographical memories, and then collapsing across all the generated memories in plotting and analyzing the data. Conversely, the bump for public events has most often been measured by contrasting recall for *individual* events across different cohorts (for exceptions, see Holmes & Conway, 1999, Howes & Katz, 1992; Koppel & Berntsen, 2016b; Tekcan et al., 2017). In the public event data, then, the unit of analysis is typically the individual event. This is important to keep in mind because later in the chapter we describe the percentages of individual events that evince a bump.

Relatedly, when we followed the typical autobiographical memory procedure and collapsed across all events in plotting open-ended recall for public events (see below for a discussion of the primary methods employed in testing recall for public events), we found no indication of a bump (Koppel & Berntsen, 2016b). Rather, we found spikes in recall corresponding to the occurrence of individual events (e.g., the fall of the Berlin Wall and the terrorist attacks of September 11th, 2001) rather than any consistent age pattern (Koppel & Berntsen, 2016b; see also Howes & Katz, 1992, for a suggestion of a similar effect, and Tekcan et al., 2017, who alternatively found either a relatively flat distribution or recency effects, depending on the specific cueing method; but see Holmes & Conway, 1999, who did find a bump when collapsing across all events). This suggests that event importance plays a stronger role than age effects, in that event importance obscured any age effects in our study (Koppel & Berntsen, 2016b). The influence of event importance on recall for public events is also evident in studies wherein the authors employed the more common practice of analyzing citations of individual events in open-ended recall, as these studies have likewise tended to yield considerable overlap across cohorts in the events that are recalled the best (e.g., Schuman & Rodgers, 2004; Schuman & Scott, 1989; Scott & Zac, 1993; see also Schuman & Corning, 2012, for a discussion of the role of event importance in recall for public events), in addition to any age effects.

This indicates that the bump for public events not only tends to be measured differently than the bump in autobiographical memory, but that, conceptually, it represents a different effect; whereas the bump represents the dominant pattern in the distribution of autobiographical memories over the lifespan—along with a more typical retention function in the case of word-cued memories—cohort effects in recall for public events compete with and can be obscured by event importance. We return to this large effect of event importance below, when discussing possible retrieval processes underlying the bump for public events.

Open-ended recall versus knowledge tests

Just as there have been two dominant cueing methods in testing for the bump in autobiographical memory, there have likewise been two dominant means of testing for the bump for public events. The first method has been to test open-ended recall for public events. The most frequent measure of open-ended recall has been what Schuman and colleagues refer to as the *standard events* question (see Corning & Schuman, 2015, for a discussion of the rationale for and development of the standard events question). Below we present Schuman and colleagues' first iteration of the standard events question from Schuman and Scott (1989), as quoted in Corning and Schuman (2015):

> "There have been a lot of national and world events and changes over the past 50 or so years – <u>say, from 1930 right up until today.</u> Would you mention one or two such events of changes that seem to you to have been <u>especially</u> important. [IF ONLY ONE MENTION, ASK: Is there any other national or world event or change over the past 50 years that you feel was especially important?]" (pp. 83)

In the initial use of the standard events question in Schuman and Scott (1989), it was employed on a US sample. Since then, Schuman and colleagues have used the question in numerous studies, testing samples of many different nationalities, including British, Chinese, German, Japanese, and Israeli samples, as well as testing US samples again in later years (e.g., Jennings & Zhang, 2005; Schuman & Corning, 2014; Schuman & Rodgers, 2004; Schuman et al., 2003; Scott & Zac, 1993; for overviews of this research program, see Corning & Schuman, 2015; Schuman & Corning, 2012). Although the question has conceptually remained the same, Schuman and colleagues have occasionally varied the number of events, asking, for instance, for "two or three" events rather than one or two events (Schuman et al., 2003). Over the decades, they have also gradually adjusted the time frame of the question from the 50-year span quoted above, so as to maintain 1930 as the beginning point in each of their studies. Ester et al. (2002) also used a version of the standard events question on a Dutch sample, Tekcan, et al. (2017) did so on a Turkish sample, and we have done so on both US and Danish samples (Koppel & Bernsten, 2016a, 2016b).

Finally, researchers have also used other measures of open-recall for public events. For instance, Holmes and Conway (1999) asked participants to list as many public events from their lifetime as they could think of over a 10-minute period; Howes & Katz (1992) employed a similar procedure, but gave participants five minutes to list public events that had occurred within specific 15-year intervals within their lifetime (e.g., from when they were between 0 and 15 years of age); and Tekcan et al. (2017) extended the practice in the autobiographical memory literature of querying important memories reflecting a specific positive or negative emotion, by similarly asking participants to cite public events of the last 70 years that reflected a specific emotion (e.g., the happiest public event and saddest public event).

The second dominant cueing method in testing recall for public events has been to test participants' knowledge of specific public events selected by the researchers. In one version of such knowledge tests, Schuman and colleagues have asked participants to briefly describe each of a number of public events or individuals (e.g., the Tet Offensive and Rosa Parks, among others, in Schuman et al., 1997). They have used this method on both US and Russian and samples (Schuman et al., 1997; Schuman & Corning, 2000; see also Belli et al., 1997, wherein the authors analyzed the errors made in response to the knowledge tests reported in Schuman et al., 1997). Rubin et al. (1998) and Jansen et al. (2008) also conducted different types of knowledge tests: Rubin et al. tested US participants' knowledge of Academy Awards, World Series, and current events of recent history, and Janssen and Murre tested Dutch participants' cued recall and recognition for a number of news items occurring over the 56 years preceding the study.

One possible way of conceptualizing the processes underlying the salient distinction between open-ended recall versus knowledge tests is that open-ended recall taps into accessibility in recall given the cues provided at retrieval, whereas knowledge tests tap into availability in recall (see Tulving & Pearlstone, 1966, for a discussion of this distinction). That is, open-ended recall taps into how readily an event is retrieved in response to a certain type of cue, whereas knowledge tests do not draw as heavily on retrieval processes, but primarily tap into whether an event is available to be recalled at all.

It is noteworthy, then, that the bump for public events appears to be stronger in open-ended recall than when recall is tested through knowledge tests. Koppel (2013) found some indication of this in comparing, across the two methods, the proportion of public events or public figures for which a bump had been attained to that point: In the most direct comparison possible he ascertained that 59% of events demonstrated a bump in open-ended recall, compared to 36% of events in knowledge tests.[2] However, given the limited amount of available data, Koppel concluded that this represented more of a suggestion of a difference across the two methods rather than dispositive evidence to that effect. Janssen et al. (2008) provided further indication that the bump is stronger when it is assessed through more open-ended cueing methods, finding that, in their individual study, the bump for public events was stronger in cued recall than in recognition.

Just as the shifting temporal location of the bump in autobiographical memory across different cueing methods suggests a prominent role for the retrieval strategy triggered by the cues provided at retrieval in underlying each individual bump, the varying frequency of the bump for public events across open-ended recall versus knowledge tests likewise indicates that the bump in this domain partially reflects retrieval processes; if the bump for public events were simply due to greater encoding for public events of the bump period, as is posited by the identity formation (Belli et al., 1997; Corning & Schuman, 2015; Holmes & Conway, 1999; Schuman & Scott, 1989) and cognitive abilities (Janssen et al., 2008) accounts of the bump for public events, then one would expect it to be stable across the two methods.

---

[2] This comparison excludes Belli et al. (1997) from the list of studies probing for the bump in knowledge tests. Koppel (2013) excluded this study because the authors reported the age effects found in participants' errors on a knowledge test. This means that the results of this study are not directly comparable to those of the studies included in Koppel's analysis, because the unit of analysis in Belli et al. was each type of error rather than each individual event (some events featured more than one type of error). Moreover, when compared to the studies employed in Koppel's comparison, Belli et al.'s method is biased towards more frequently finding a bump, in that they reported only those errors for which a meaningful and significant age pattern was evident.

Retrieval processes

Having established that, in our view, the greater frequency of the bump for public events in open-ended recall than in knowledge tests is likely due to the retrieval strategy triggered through measures of open-ended recall for public events, it is now incumbent upon us to put forth a proposal regarding the nature of that retrieval strategy. One possibility concerns a cognitive bias we have recently discovered, which we have termed the *youth bias*. The *youth bias* refers to the cultural expectation that important public events are most likely to occur in adolescence or early adulthood (Koppel & Berntsen, 2014b, 2016a). Our procedure in testing for the youth bias has been to ask participants to imagine a prototypical infant of their own culture and gender, just as in the instructions in the life script task (Berntsen & Rubin, 2004). Participants are then asked to indicate, from a number of response options representing 5-year intervals (e.g., ages 0–5, 6–10, etc., up to 86–90 years), the age this hypothetical person is most likely to be when the most important public event of their lifetime takes place, or, alternatively, when the most important exemplar of a given category of public event takes place, such as the most important death of a public figure. The youth bias has been demonstrated by the peaks we have attained in the number of responses for adolescence and early adulthood, which, broadly speaking, have been within the 11–30-year range. The youth bias represents a cognitive bias in that the actual timing of important public events is clearly not tied to the individual life course. The expectation that important public events are most likely to occur at a given part of the lifespan is therefore irrational.

In addition to our interest in the youth bias as representing a new type of cognitive bias, we have also been interested in whether the youth bias contributes towards structuring open-ended recall of important public events, similar to the role of the cultural life script in structuring retrieval of important autobiographical memories.[3] Towards that end, in one of our papers on the youth bias we tested for a relation between responses to the youth bias query and recall for public events (Koppel & Berntsen, 2016a). Here, in addition to responding to the youth bias question in relation to a specific category of public event (sporting events, deaths of public figures, or US presidential elections), participants (all of whom were aged ≥40 years) also responded to a measure of open-ended recall. On the recall question participants were asked (in a variation on Schuman and colleagues' standard events question described above) to cite what they considered to be the most important exemplar, from within their own lifetime, of the same category of public event (e.g., death of a public figure) that was the subject of the youth bias query.

---

[3] We note, however, that the youth bias should not be taken as a parallel of the cultural life script. Although we would suggest a role for each in structuring recall for either important autobiographical memories (in the case of the life script) or open-ended recall of public events (in the case of the youth bias), and both involve cultural expectations regarding the timing of certain events in the lifespan, the youth bias contains no information about either the specific public events that are expected to occur in a typical person's lifetime, or the order in which they are expected to occur. Unlike the cultural life script, then, the youth bias does not meet the necessary criteria of a script (see Koppel & Berntsen, 2015a).

We then tested for a relation between (1) the age each participant indicated the most important exemplar from the relevant event category would most likely occur in a typical person's life, and (2) the participant's age at the time of the event that he or she indicated as the most important exemplar from that category to occur in his or her own life. We found a relation for the category of sporting events, but not for either deaths of public figures or US presidential elections. We argued that we only attained a relation for sporting events because event importance played a relatively small role in driving recall for this category of events; whereas citations of the most important death of a public figure and US presidential election of one's lifetime were dominated by one or two events (i.e., the death of John F. Kennedy in the deaths of public figures condition, and the elections of Barack Obama in 2008 and Ronald Reagan in 1980 in the US presidential elections condition), there was no such event in the case of sporting events.

This finding suggests that, where event importance plays a relatively small role in open-ended recall for public events and thus leaves room for other factors, the youth bias helps structure recall by creating a focus on adolescence and early adulthood in participants' retrieval strategies. However, this conclusion should only be drawn tentatively, resting as it does on a relation obtained for only one event category in one study.

Final thoughts

We conclude by relating the implications of the findings we have discussed here, especially the findings concerning autobiographical memory, for models of the organization of autobiographical memory. In recent years the dominant model has been Conway and colleagues' hierarchical, goal-directed model, known as the *self-memory system* (SMS; Conway, 2005; Conway, Justice, & D'Argembeau, this volume, chapter 3; Conway & Pleydell-Pearce, 2000; Conway et al., 2004), through which they present their version of the identity formation account of the bump. In the SMS framework, autobiographical memories are the product of the interplay between the goals of the self at the time of retrieval and the autobiographical knowledge base, which is comprised of the events one has experienced over a lifetime.

The autobiographical knowledge base is organized hierarchically, with each level containing information at different degrees of specificity or abstraction. Although the exact structure of the autobiographical knowledge base has evolved over time, in the current iteration of the SMS, the autobiographical knowledge base contains four levels (Conway, 2005). In order from the most abstract to the most specific, these levels consist of: (1) the *life story*, referring to general factual and evaluative knowledge about the individual (see also Bluck & Habermas, 2000, for the initial elaboration of the life story schema); (2) *lifetime periods*, referring to knowledge of general periods in one's life, such as one's time at university; (3) *general events*, referring to knowledge of general, repeated events, such as lectures for a certain course while at university; and (4) *episodic memories*, such as one's memory of asking a particular question during a specific lecture. According to Conway and colleagues, autobiographical memories are most commonly reconstructed out of the raw material of this knowledge base, and the specific memories that are retrieved are a function of a match between the goals at encoding and goals at retrieval.

Brown (2016) has recently proposed an alternative to the self-memory system, in the form of *transition theory*. With transition theory, Brown endeavors to provide an account of the structure and content of autobiographical memory without reference to the "self" of the self-memory system, or the goal structures thereof. In Brown's framework, autobiographical memories from a given period of one's life are comprised of a set of interconnected networks of *event components*, referring to the aspects of a given event that are capable of being labeled (e.g. the individuals present). These associative networks are formed as, due to the repetitive nature of daily life, event components repeatedly co-occur with one another. Major transitions, however, such as a move, effectively terminate a large set of event components and replace it with another set of event components. In the parlance of the self-memory system, such transitions bring about new lifetime periods, which simply represent periods corresponding to a given set of event component networks. Transition theory predicts that, in addition to the bump, periods of transition should also be overrepresented in the distribution of autobiographical memories, due to the unusually high percentage of novel events experienced at such times. This prediction has been borne out in several empirical studies conducted by Brown and colleagues (e.g., Brown et al., 2016; Gu et al., 2017; Shi & Brown, 2016).

Though the SMS and transition theory are divergent in terms of whether they posit that autobiographical memory is structured by factors that are unique to autobiographical remembering (in the case of the self-memory system) or by more basic cognitive factors (in the case of transition theory), one commonality between these models is that each model posits that autobiographical memory is structured around factors relating to the individual's personal experience. However, the findings we have reviewed here pointing to the central contribution of schematic factors at retrieval to the bump in autobiographical memory indicate that autobiographical memory is only partly structured around personal experience. Rather, retrieval from autobiographical memory appears to be largely guided by schematic and constructive factors as well, such as the life script in the case of important memories, and, more speculatively, a search strategy focused on the beginning and endpoints of the search space in the case of the more neutral word cues.

Focusing on knowledge structures operating at the time of retrieval, rather than structures of organization laid down during encoding, implies that the organization of autobiographical memory is not fixed, but varies dynamically as a function of the current context and the task at hand. Going forward, we suggest that any model of autobiographical memory needs to incorporate schematic factors along these lines, as an accounting of the organization of autobiographical memory is incomplete without them.

Acknowledgments

This work was supported by the Danish National Research Foundation under Grant DNRF89.

References

Alea, N., Ali, S., & Marcano, B. (2014). The bumps in Trinidadian life: Reminiscence bumps for positive and negative life events. *Applied Cognitive Psychology, 28, 174*–184.

Belli, R. F., Schuman, H., & Jackson, F. (1997). Autobiographical misremembering: John Dean is not alone. *Applied Cognitive Psychology, 11,* 187–209.

Benson, K. A., Jarvi, S. D., Arai, Y., Thielbar, P. R. S., Frye, K. J., & McDonald, B. L. G. (1992). Sociohistorical context and autobiographical memories: Variations in the reminiscence phenomenon. In M. A. Conway, D. C. Rubin, H. Spinnler, & W. W. Wagenaar (eds.), *Theoretical perspectives on autobiographical memory* (pp. 313–322). Dordrecht, NL: Kluwer Academic.

Berntsen, D. (2010). The unbidden past: Involuntary autobiographical memories as a basic mode of remembering. *Current Directions in Psychological Science, 19,* 138–142.

Berntsen, D. & Bohn, A. (2010). Remembering and forecasting: The relation between autobiographical memory and episodic future thinking. *Memory & Cognition, 38,*

Berntsen, D. & Rubin, D. C. (2002). Emotionally charged autobiographical memories across the lifespan: The retention of happy, sad, traumatic, and involuntary memories. *Psychology and Aging, 17,* 636–652.

Berntsen, D. & Rubin, D. C. (2004). Cultural life scripts structure recall from autobiographical memory. *Memory & Cognition, 32,* 427–442.

Berntsen, D., Rubin, D. C., & Siegler, I. C. (2011). Two versions of life: Emotionally negative and positive life events have different roles in the organization of life story and identity. *Emotion, 11,* 1190–1201.

Bluck, S. & Habermas, T. (2000). The life story schema. *Motivation and Emotion, 24,* 121–147.

Bohn, A. (2010). Generational differences in cultural life scripts and life story memories of y younger and older adults. *Applied Cognitive Psychology, 24,* 1324–1345.

Bohn, A. & Berntsen, D. (2011). The reminiscence bump reconsidered: Children's prospective life stories show a bump in young adulthood. *Psychological Science, 22,* 197–202.

Brown, N. R. (2016). Transition theory: A minimalist perspective on the organization of autobiographical memory. *Journal of Applied Research in Memory and Cognition, 5,* 128–134.

Brown, N. R., Schweickert, O., & Svob, C. (2016). The effect of collective transitions on the organization and content of autobiographical memories: A transition theory perspective. *The American Journal of Psychology, 129,* 259–282.

Chu, S. & Downes, J. J. (2000). Long live Proust: The odour-cued autobiographical memory bump. *Cognition, 75,* B41–B50.

Cohen, G. & Faulkner, D. (1988). Life span changes in autobiographical memory. In M. M Gruenberg, P. E. Morris, & R. N. Sykes (eds.), *Practical aspects of memory: Current research and issues: Vol. 1. Memory in everyday life* (pp. 277–282). New York, NY: Wiley.

Conway, M. A. (2005). Memory and the self. *Journal of Memory and Language, 53,* 594–628.

Conway, M. A. & Holmes, A. (2004). Psychosocial stages and the accessibility of autobiographical memories across the life cycle. *Journal of Personality, 72,* 461–480.

Conway, M. A. & Pleydell-Pearce, C. W. (2000). The construction of autobiographical memories in the self-memory system. *Psychological Review, 107,* 261–288.

Conway, M. A., Singer, J. A., & Tagini, A. (2004). The self and autobiographical memory: Correspondence and coherence. *Social Cognition, 22,* 491–529.

Corning, A. & Schuman, H. (2015). *Generations and collective memories.* Chicago, IL: The University of Chicago Press.

Crovitz, H. F., & Schiffman, H. (1974). Frequency of episodic memories as a function of their age. *Bulletin of the Psychonomic Society, 4*, 517–518.

Crowder, R. G. (1993). Short-term memory: Where do we stand? *Memory & Cognition, 21*, 142–145.

Cuervo-Lombard, C., Jovenin, N., Hedelin, G., Rizzo-Peter, L., Conway, M. A., & Danion, J. M. (2007). Autobiographical memory of adolescence and early adulthood events: An investigation in schizophrenia. *Journal of the International Neuropsychology Society, 13*, 335–343.

Deese, J. & Kaufman, R. A. (1957). Serial effects in recall of unorganized and sequentially organized verbal material. *Journal of Experimental Psychology, 54*, 180–187.

Dickson, R. A., Pillemer, D. B., & Bruehl, E. C. (2011). The reminiscence bump for salient personal memories: Is a cultural life script required? *Memory & Cognition, 39*, 977–991.

Ebbinghaus, H. E. (1964). *Memory: A contribution to experimental psychology.* New York, NY: Dover. (Original work published 1885.)

Erdoğan, A., Baran, B., Avlar, B., Cağlar Taş, A., & Tekcan, A. İ. (2008). On the persistence of positive events in life scripts. *Applied Cognitive Psychology, 22*, 95–112.

Erikson, E. (1950). *Childhood and society.* New York: Norton.

Ester, P., Vinken, H., & Diepstraten, I. (2002). Reminiscences of an extreme century. Reminiscences of an extreme century. Intergenerational differences in time heuristics: Dutch people's collective memories of the 20th century. *Time & Society, 11*, 39–66.

Fitzgerald, J. M. (1988). Vivid memories and the reminiscence phenomenon: The role of a self narrative. *Human Development,* 31, 261–273.

Fitzgerald, J. M. (1996). The distribution of self-narrative memories in younger and older adults: Elaborating the self-narrative hypothesis. *Aging, Neuropsychology and Cognition, 3*, 229–236.

Fitzgerald, J. M. & Lawrence, R. (1984). Autobiographical memory across the life-span. *Journal of Gerontology, 39*, 692–698.

Fromholt, P., Mortensen, D. B., Torpdahl, P., Bender, L., Larsen, P., & Rubin, D. C. (2003). Life-narrative and word-cued autobiographical memories in centenarians: Comparisons with 80-year-old control, depressed, and dementia groups. *Memory, 11*, 81–88.

Galton, F. (1879). Psychometric experiments. *Brain, 2*, 149–162.

Glück, J. & Bluck, S. (2007). Looking back across the life span: A life story account of the reminiscence bump. *Memory & Cognition, 35*, 1928–1939.

Gu, X., Tse, C.-S., & Brown, N. R. (2017). The effects of collective and personal transitions on the organization and contents of autobiographical memory in older Chinese adults. *Memory & Cognition, 45*, 1335–1349.

Haque, S. & Hasking, P. A. (2010). Life scripts for emotionally charged autobiographical memories: A cultural explanation of the reminiscence bump. *Memory, 18*, 712–729.

Holmes, A. & Conway, M. A. (1999). Generation identity and the reminiscence bump: Memory for public and private events. *Journal of Adult Development, 6*, 21–34.

Howes, J. L. & Katz, A. N. (1992). Remote memory: Recalling autobiographical and public events from across the lifespan. *Canadian Journal of Psychology, 46*, 92–116.

Janssen, S. M. J. (2015). Commentary on Koppel and Berntsen: How many reminiscence bumps are there? *Journal of Applied Research in Memory and Cognition, 4*, 87–89.

Janssen, S. M. J., Kristo, G., Rouw, R., & Murre, J. M. J. (2015). The relation between verbal and visuo-spatial memory and autobiographical memory. *Consciousness and Cognition, 31*, 12–23.

Janssen, S. M. J., Murre, J, M. J., & Meeter, M. (2008). Reminiscence bump in memory for public events. *European Journal of Cognitive Psychology, 20*, 738–764,

Janssen, S. M. J., Rubin, D. C., & St. Jacques, P. L. (2011). The temporal distribution of autobiographical memory: Changes in reliving and vividness over the lifespan do not explain the reminiscence bump. *Memory & Cognition, 39*, 1–11.

Jennings, M. K. & Zhang, N. (2005). Generations, political status, and collective memories in the Chinese countryside. *The Journal of Politics, 67*, 1164–1189.

Kelley, M. R., Neath, I., & Surprenant, I. M. (2013). Three more semantic serial position functions and a SIMPLE explanation. *Memory & Cognition, 41*, 600–610.

Kelley, M. R., Neath, I., & Surprenant, I. M. (2015). Serial position functions in general knowledge. *Journal of Experimental Psychology: Learning Memory, and Cognition, 41*, 1715–1727.

Koppel, J. (2013). The reminiscence bump for public events: A review of its prevalence and taxonomy of alternative age distributions. *Applied Cognitive Psychology, 27*, 12–32.

Koppel, J. & Berntsen, D. (2014a). The cultural life script as cognitive schema: How the life script shapes memory for fictional life stories. *Memory, 22*, 949–971.

Koppel, J. & Berntsen, D. (2014b). Does everything happen when you are young? Introducing the youth bias. *Quarterly Journal of Experimental Psychology, 67*, 417–423.

Koppel, J. & Berntsen, D. (2015a). There may not be a cultural life script for public events, but there is a youth bias: Response to Janssen. *Applied Cognitive Psychology, 29*, 69–70.

Koppel, J. & Berntsen, D. (2015b). The peaks of life: The differential temporal locations of the reminiscence bump across disparate cueing methods. *Journal of Applied Research in Memory and Cognition, 4*, 66–80.

Koppel, J. & Berntsen, D. (2016a). The breadth and mnemonic consequences of the youth bias. *Quarterly Journal of Experimental Psychology, 69*, 1265–1277.

Koppel, J. & Berntsen, D. (2016b). The reminiscence bump in autobiographical memory and for public events: A comparison across different cueing methods. *Memory, 24*, 44–62

Koppel, J. & Berntsen, D. (2016c). The reminiscence bump without memories: The distribution of imagined word-cued and important autobiographical memories in a hypothetical 70-year-old. *Consciousness and Cognition, 44*, 89–102.

Koppel, J. & Rubin, D. C. (2016). Recent advances in understanding the reminiscence bump: The importance of cues in guiding recall from autobiographical memory. *Current Directions in Psychological Science, 25*, 135–140.

Kurbat, M. A., Shevell, S. K., & Rips, L. J. (1998). A year's memories: The calendar effect in autobiographical recall. *Memory & Cognition, 26*, 532–552.

Lawless, H. & Engen, T. (1977). Associations to odors: Interference, mnemonics, and verbal labeling. *Journal of Experimental Psychology: Human Learning and Memory 3*, 52–59.

Maki, Y., Janssen, S. M. J., Uemiya, A., & Naka, M. (2013). The phenomenology and temporal distributions of autobiographical memories elicited with emotional and neutral cue words. *Memory, 21*, 286–300.

Mannheim, K. (1928/1952). The problem of generations. In K. Mannheim (ed.), *Essays on the sociology of knowledge* (pp. 276–321). London: Routledge & Kegan Paul.

McCormack, P. D. (1979). Autobiographical memory in the aged. *Canadian Journal of Psychology, 33*, 118–124.

Miles, A. N. & Berntsen, D. (2011). Odour-induced mental time travel into the past and future: Do odour cues retain a unique link to our distant past? *Memory, 19*, 930–940.

Morrison, C. M. & Conway, M. A. (2010). First words and first memories. *Cognition, 116*, 23–32.

Murdock, B. B., Jr. (1960). The distinctiveness of stimuli. *Psychological Review, 67*, 16–31.

Ottsen, C. L. & Berntsen, D. (2014). The cultural life script of Qatar and across cultures: Effects of gender and religion. *Memory, 22*, 390–407.

Overstreet, M. F., Healy, A. F., & Neath, I. (2017). Further differentiating item and order information in semantic memory: Students' recall of words from the "CU Fight Song", Harry Potter book titles, and Scooby Doo theme song. *Memory, 25*, 69–83.

Pillemer, D. B. (2001). Momentous events and the life story. *Review of General Psychology, 5*, 123–134.

Pillemer, D. B., Goldsmith, C. R., Panter, A. T., & White, S. H. (1988). Very long-term memories of the first year in college. *Journal of Experimental Psychology: Learning, Memory and Cognition, 14*, 709–715.

Pillemer, D. B., Rhinehart, E. D., & White, S. H. (1986). Memories of life transitions: The first year in college. *Human Learning, 5*, 109–124.

Rabbitt, P. & Winthorpe, C. (1988). What do old people remember? The Galton paradigm reconsidered. In M. M. Gruenberg, P. E. Morris, & R. N. Sykes (eds.), *Practical aspects of memory: Current research and issues*, Vol. 1, *Memory in everyday life* (pp. 301–307). New York: Wiley.

Robinson, J. A. (1986). Temporal reference systems and autobiographical memory. In D. C. Rubin (ed.), *Autobiographical memory* (pp. 159–188). New York: Cambridge University Press.

Robinson, J. A. (1992). First experience memories: Contexts and functions in personal memories. In M. A. Conway, D. C. Rubin, H. Spinnler, & W. A. Wagenaar (eds.), *Theoretical perspectives on autobiographical memory* (pp. 223–239). Dordrecht: Kluwer.

Robinson, J. A. & Taylor, L. (1998). Autobiographical memory and self narratives: A tale of two stories. In C. P. Thompson, D. J. Herrmann, D. Bruce, J. D. Read, D. G. Payne, & M. P. Toglia (eds.), *Autobiographical memory: Theoretical and applied perspectives* (pp. 125–143). Mahwah, NJ: Erlbaum.

Roediger, H. L., III, & Crowder, R. G. (1976). A serial position effect in recall of United States presidents. *Bulletin of the Psychonomic Society, 8*, 275–278.

Roediger, H. L., III, & DeSoto, K. A. (2014). Cognitive psychology. Forgetting the presidents. *Science, 346*, 1106–1109.

Rubin, D. C. (1980). 51 properties of 125 words: A unit analysis of verbal behavior. *Journal of Verbal Learning and Verbal Behavior, 19*, 736–755.

Rubin, D. C. (2006). The basic-systems model of autobiographical memory. *Perspectives on Psychological Science, 1*, 277–311.

Rubin, D. C. (2015). One bump, two bumps, three bumps, four? Using retrieval cues to divide one autobiographical memory reminiscence bump into many. *Journal of Applied Research in Memory and Cognition, 4*, 87–89.

Rubin, D. C. & Berntsen, D. (2003). Life scripts help to maintain autobiographical memories of highly positive, but not highly negative, events. *Memory & Cognition, 31*, 1–14.

Rubin, D. C., Berntsen, D., & Hutson, M. (2009). The normative and the personal life: Individual differences in life scripts and life story events among USA and Danish undergraduates. *Memory, 17*, 54–68.

Rubin, D. C., Rahhal, T. A., & Poon, L. W. (1998). Things learned in early adulthood are remembered best. *Memory & Cognition, 26*, 3–19.

Rubin, D. C. & Schulkind, M. D. (1997a). Distribution of important and word-cued autobiographical memories in 20-, 35-, and 70-year-old adults. *Psychology and Aging, 12*, 524–535.

Rubin, D. C. & Schulkind, M. D. (1997b). Properties of word cues for autobiographical memory. *Psychological Reports, 81*, 47–50.

Rubin, D. C. & Wenzel, A. E. (1996). One hundred years of forgetting: A quantitative description of retention. *Psychological Review, 103*, 734–760.

Rubin, D. C., Wetzler, S. E., & Nebes, R. D. (1986). Autobiographical memory across the adult lifespan. In D. C. Rubin (ed.), *Autobiographical memory* (pp. 202–221). New York, NY: Cambridge University Press.

Rundus, N. & Atkinson, R. C. (1970). Rehearsal processes in free recall: A procedure for direct observation. *Journal of Verbal Learning and Verbal Behavior, 9*, 99–105.

Schlagman, S., Kliegel, M., Schulz, J., & Kvavilashvili, L. (2009). Differential effects of age on involuntary and voluntary autobiographical memory. *Psychology and Aging, 24*, 397–411

Schuman, H., Belli, R. F., & Bischoping, K. (1997). The generational basis of historical knowledge. In J. W. Pennebaker, D. Paez, & B. Rimé (eds.), *Collective memory of political events: Social psychological perspectives* (pp. 47–77). Hillsdale, NJ: Erlbaum.

Schuman, H. & Corning, A. (2012). Generational memory and the critical period: Evidence for national and world events. *Public Opinion Quarterly, 76*, 1–31.

Schuman, H. & Corning, A. (2014). Collective and autobiographical memory: Similar but not the same. *Memory Studies, 7*, 146–160.

Schuman, H. & Corning, A. D. (2000). Collective knowledge of public events: The Soviet Era from the great purge to glasnost. *American Journal of Sociology, 105*, 913–956.

Schuman, H. & Rodgers, W. L. (2004). Cohorts, chronology, and collective memories. *Public Opinion Quarterly, 68*, 217–254.

Schuman, H. & Scott, J. (1989). Generations and collective memories. *American Sociological Review, 54*, 359–381.

Schuman, H., Vinitzky-Seroussi, V., & Vinokur, A. D. (2003). Keeping the past alive: Memories of Israeli Jews at the turn of the millennium. *Sociological Forum, 18*, 103–136.

Scott, J. & Zac, L. (1993). Collective memories in Britain and the United States. *Public Opinion Quarterly, 57*, 315–331.

Shi, L. & Brown, N. R. (2016). The effect of immigration on the contents and structure of autobiographical memory: A transition-theory perspective. *Journal of Applied Research in Memory and Cognition, 5*, 135–142.

Tekcan, A. İ. Boduroglu, A., Mutlutürk, A., & Erciyes, A. I. (2017). Life-span retrieval of public events: Reminiscence bump for high-impact events, recency for others. *Memory & Cognition, 45*, 1095–112.

Thomsen, D. K. & Berntsen, D. (2005). The end point effect in autobiographical memory: More than a calendar is needed. *Memory, 13*, 846–861.

Thomsen, D. K. & Berntsen, D. (2008). The cultural life script and life story chapters contribute to the reminiscence bump. *Memory, 16*, 420–435.

Tulving, E. & Pearlstone, Z. (1966). Availability versus accessibility of information in memory for words. *Journal of Verbal Learning and Verbal Behavior, 5*, 381–391.

Wickelgren, W. A. (1972). Trace resistance and the decay of long-term memory. *Journal of Mathematical Psychology, 9*, 418–455.

Willander, J. & Larsson, M. (2006). Smell your way back to childhood: Autobiographical odor memory. *Psychonomic Bulletin & Review, 13*, 240–244.

Willander, J. & Larsson, M. (2007). Olfaction and emotion: The case of autobiographical memory. *Memory & Cognition, 35*, 1659–1663.

Willander, J. & Larsson, M. (2008). The mind's nose and autobiographical odor memory. *Chemosensory Perception, 1*, 210–215.

Zaragoza Scherman, A. (2013). Cultural life script theory and the reminiscence bump: A reanalysis of seven studies across cultures. *Nordic Psychology, 65*, 103–119.

Zaragoza Scherman, A., Salgado, S., Shao, Z., & Berntsen, D. (2017). Life script events and autobiographical memories of life story events in Mexico, Greenland, China, and Denmark. *Journal of Applied Research in Memory and Cognition, 6*, 60–73.

Zola-Morgan, S., Cohen, N. J., & Squire, L. R. (1983). Recall of remote episodic memory in amnesia. *Neuropsychologia, 21*, 487–500.

10

The Associative Nature of Episodic Memories

The Primacy of Conceptual Associations

John H. Mace and Amanda M. Clevinger

Introduction

Episodic memories are the most specific form of autobiographical memory. They serve as "records" of past experiences, allowing us to remember that we did return the milk to the refrigerator, took our morning dose of medicine, locked the door behind us when we left the house, how someone behaved at a party after too many drinks, passing our driver's test, and so on. When we experience these memories, we have a sense of re-living the events as they come to us in the form of mental images, often vivid, feeling like snapshots or brief video clips of our past. As a class of autobiographical memories, they are perhaps the most important and the most vulnerable memories. Given their sheer number, we forget more episodic memories than any other form of knowledge, and they are typically the most affected form of autobiographical memory in cases of neurological injury (e.g., in anterograde and retrograde amnesia). Functionally, as a whole they give us a sense of continuity in space and time, while individually they can guide in numerable ways (e.g., they may help us to remember how to change a flat tire, or find our way back on a mountain trail).

An important aspect of episodic memories is their ability to activate one another. For example, when one recalls a past episode (e.g., changing a flat tire), this memory may prompt the recall of an additional episodic memory (e.g., another instance of changing a flat tire). We believe this property of episodic memories increases their potential functional nature. We also believe that when one examines the relationships among episodic memories that prompt other episodic memories, their fundamental associative form is revealed.

This chapter concerns the associative nature of episodic memories. In it, we put forth a thesis on the associative form of episodic memories that contains several propositions. One, we argue that episodic memories always activate other episodic memories. Two, like semantic memory, these activations always follow orderly associative lines, rather than helter-skelter, non-associative lines. Three, whereas more than one type of association can be found among these lines, the fundamental form is conceptual (or thematic), where memories are associated (or activated) by their common content. Four, conceptual forms dominate, they are the fundamental (or default) form, they are the most enduring form, and they are perhaps largely of an endogenous nature. In addition to explicating these points, we further sketch out a theoretical view which attempts to explain how conceptually associated memories dominate the organizational structure of episodic memory.

Activations in autobiographical memory

It has long been established that autobiographical memories consist of many forms, ranging from the more general types (e.g., general memories, such as the knowledge that one played the violin as a child) to the more specific types (e.g., episodic memories, such as remembering the details of a solo violin performance given in the sixth grade) (see early views in Barsalou, 1988; Brewer, 1986; Conway & Rubin, 1993). Conway has argued that autobiographical knowledge structures are arranged hierarchically, where the more general (or abstract) forms (e.g., lifetime periods and general memories) occupy the top of the hierarchy and the more specific forms (i.e., episodic memories) occupy the bottom (e.g., see Conway, 2005; Conway, Justice, & D'Arembeau, this volume, chapter 3). In his view, activations can flow both between memory structures (e.g., from a general event memory to an episodic memory) and among memory structures (e.g., among episodic memories).

The first tenet of our view, memory activations, concerns and is limited to activations among episodic memories. At this level of autobiographical memory organization, we argue that activations are automatic, such that every time an episodic memory is activated, there is a spread of activation to other (related) episodic memories. These activations can occur both consciously and unconsciously. When activations occur unconsciously, the products of activations are neither visible to rememberers nor third parties (e.g., an experimenter) except on rare occasions (e.g., in cases where individuals notice that they are remembering events related to events they had recently recalled). In contrast, when activations occur consciously, their products are relatively transparent to both first and third parties. Conscious activations are instances where normal, automatic unconscious activations become conscious. Unlike unconscious activations, conscious activations do not occur all the time, but as the data reviewed below will make clear, they do occur on a fairly widespread and ubiquitous basis. Both conscious and unconscious activations serve as mechanisms that create, reinforce, and maintain associations among episodic memories.

Evidence that unconscious activations occur among episodic memories can be found in several episodic memory priming studies (Barzykowski & Niedzwienska, 2017; Mace, 2005; Mace & Clevinger, 2013; Mace & Unlu, 2018). In these studies, researchers primed episodic memories by having participants recall memories in one (or more) laboratory sessions and then observe how they activated conceptually or temporally related memories on subsequent voluntary (Mace & Clevinger, 2013; Mace & Unlu, 2018) or involuntary memory measures (Barzykowski & Niedzwienska, 2017;

Mace, 2005; see reviews of involuntary autobiographical memories in Berntsen, 2009; Mace, 2007b, 2018). For example, Mace (2005) had participants attend a number of sessions in which they were required to recall memories from different lifetime periods (e.g., when they were in high school). These same participants were also simultaneously engaged in a diary study where they recorded their everyday involuntary memories for a period of two weeks. Examinations of the content of the involuntary memories recorded in the diaries revealed that significant proportions of them were related to memories from the primed lifetime periods.

Evidence of conscious activations among episodic memories can be found in a memory phenomenon (involuntary memory chains) that has only recently appeared in the literature (e.g., Mace, 2005, 2006, 2007a). Involuntary memory chains are an involuntary retrieval phenomenon that occurs when one is deliberately recalling past episodes (Mace, 2006) and when memories of past come to mind unintentionally (e.g., Mace, 2005; Mace et al., 2015). For example, participants engaged in voluntary recall on an autobiographical memory task report that retrieved memories sometimes lead to the immediate and involuntary retrieval of one or more additional memories (e.g., Mace, 2006), and participants in diary studies of everyday involuntary memories also report that spontaneously retrieved memories sometimes result in one or more additional involuntary memories (see reviews in Mace, 2007a; 2010a, b). Rates of this type of spontaneous memory generation are substantial in the case of voluntary recall (i.e., some 40% of deliberately recalled memories result in additional involuntary memories: Mace, 2006; Mace & Unlu, 2018), moderate in the case of everyday involuntary memories (some 15% of involuntary memories result in additional involuntary memories, e.g., Mace et al., 2013, though we believe that they are underreported in diary studies: see Mace et al., 2015).

Whether activations in episodic memory occur consciously or unconsciously, we have argued that they represent spreading activation among episodic memories (Mace, 2007a, 2014; Mace et al., 2010, 2013). There are reasons for taking this position. One, these activations appear to be automatic, or involuntary. Two, they consistently show orderly patterns where activated memories are always related to one another (Barzykowski & Niedzwienska, 2017; Mace, 2005, 2006, 2007a; Mace & Clevinger, 2013; Mace et al., 2010; 2013; Mace & Hall, 2018), and the same patterns of associations have occurred repeatedly across numerous observations (Mace, 2006, 2007; Mace et al., 2010, 2013; Mace & Hall, 2018). Three, in the case of involuntary memory chains, one can observe the patterns of activation across multiple, successively produced memories, and here they have consistently revealed patterns of activations that conform well with notions of spreading activation (Mace, 2007a). For example, the second memory in a chain is always related to the first memory, but not necessarily to the cue that produced the first memory. Similarly, the third memory in the chain is always related to the second memory, but not necessarily to the first memory, and so forth. Such patterns show that memories in a chain are not merely instances where a precipitating cue had produced different and multiple instances of memories related to the cue (see further details in Mace, 2007a). Instead, what one sees in memory chains is how the content in one memory led to the content in another, which in turn led to the content in another, or in other words, how memories produce other related memories.

Because there is good reason to believe that involuntary memory chains are conscious and observable patterns of spreading activations among episodic memories, we have argued that the patterns of associations apparent in them reflect the underlying associative structure of episodic memory (Mace, 2005, 2014; Mace et al., 2010, 2013; Mace & Hall, 2018). Our logic here is the same as the logic that has been applied in the study of semantic memory, and, as the method of studying automatic memory activations (priming) has proved informative in that case, so too should it prove informative in the case of autobiographical memory.

The associative structure of episodic memories

Our view on the associative structure of episodic memories has its primary roots in priming and involuntary memory chaining studies. As argued above, given the automatic nature of these unconscious and conscious activations, it is reasonable to assume that the associative forms produced by them represent the preexisting associative structures of episodic memories. Studies conducted in our laboratory with priming approaches (Mace, 2005; Mace & Clevinger, 2013; Mace & Unlu, 2018) or involuntary memory chains (Mace, 2006; Mace et al., 2013, 2010) have demonstrated remarkably consistent patterns of activations across a wide degree of circumstances (e.g., formal laboratory designs, quasi-naturalistic designs, and relatively pure naturalistic observations). From these observations, we have concluded that three associative forms exist among episodic memories, general-event associations, conceptual associations, and lifetime period associations. We believe that general-event and conceptual associations represent primary organizational structures, where the conceptual class is the dominant, overarching form, whereas lifetime period associations represent a sub-level of organization (i.e., found to be secondary to general-event or conceptual associations). We are confident in these assertions because they were derived from observations of naturally occurring, automatic retrieval mechanisms or phenomena (i.e., priming and involuntary memory chains). Laboratory tasks designed specifically to study episodic memory associations may be unreliable because they introduce variables that are difficult to control (e.g., how a participant may interpret instructions to recall related memories, etc.: see, for example, critiques of the event-cuing procedure, Brown & Schopflocher, 1998, in Mace et al., 2010, and related discussions in Mace & Hall, 2018).

In this section, we fully describe the three types of episodic memory associations (general-event, conceptual, and lifetime periods), we begin to make our case for the conceptual association dominance, and we discuss the role of temporal associations in episodic memories.

Table 10.1 Examples of general-event-related memory pairs

Memory pair
   When I first got my driver's license (aged 16)
   Having a party that evening to celebrate (aged 16)
Memory pair
   Taking a trip to St. Louis to watch a baseball game (aged 18)
   Visiting the Arch on my trip to St. Louis (aged 18)
Memory pair
   Going to Magic Kingdom at Disney World with family (aged 20)
   Watching fireworks at Magic Kingdom on that trip (aged 20)

Three types of episodic memory associations

General-event associations

In general-event associations, associated episodic memories (e.g., two or more adjacent memories in a chain) belong to the same extended event (e.g., a wedding, a two-week vacation in London, such as seeing the mummies in the British Museum, attending the mummy lecture there that evening), to the same repeated event (e.g., Sunday walks in the park, etc.), or to the same causal sequence of events (i.e., where one event leads to another, such as breaking one's tooth on hard candy, visiting a dentist later that day—see examples in Table 10.1).[1] General-event associations can range from mundane events (e.g., remembering two separate incidents from a long, routine car trip) to special and unique events (e.g., high school graduation, a medical procedure). Whereas these memories share content (e.g., visiting a museum), their connection appears to be the extended event, summary event, or causal events to which they belong. Given this common temporal link, these memories are typically temporally proximate (e.g., spanning the same day, evening, week, month, etc.). Given such temporal relatedness, we have frequently referred to general-event associated memories as temporally associated memories (e.g., Mace et al. 2013; Mace & Hall, 2018). General-event associations are one of two primary associative forms. They appear in involuntary memory chains and various laboratory measures (Mace, 2006; Mace et al., 2010, 2013; Mace & Hall, 2018; Mace & Unlu, 2018). These associations appear to be important initially (i.e., when events are less than a year old), where they equal conceptual associations, but their importance appears to wane with time as data show that many of them are forgotten after this initial period (e.g., Mace et al. 2013, discussed below).

---

[1] General-event associations overlap with Brown & Schopflocher's (1998) notion of event clusters, except that the latter emphasizes the story-like nature of associated memories. Although some general-event associations may be perceived as having a narrative structure, we do not regard them as such, nor do we believe that they form from narrative processes.

Table 10.2 Examples of conceptually related memory pairs

Memory pair
    Having a car accident in high school (aged 17)
    Having a car accident in college (aged 21)
Memory pair
    At a tennis match with my friend Sam (aged 26)
    Watching a tennis match on TV with my sister when we were
    young (aged 13)
Memory pair
    Visiting an art gallery in New York City (aged 25)
    Looking at spaces to rent for my art show in Boston (aged 24)

Conceptual associations

Unlike general-event associations, conceptually associated episodic memories lack temporal connections or connections to the same larger event (e.g., high school graduation or a wedding). Instead, these memories have overlapping content (i.e., about the same people, objects, activities, or other common themes, such as work or school) without connections to an extended or repeated event, or a causal sequence of events. Relatedness (or uniformity) of content or themes is what appears to be associating these memories. For example, they could be two different concert memories (e.g., seeing an opera in New York City, seeing an opera in Italy), museum memories (e.g., a recent visit to the British Museum in London, visiting the American Museum of Natural History in New York on a school field trip), or different memories about the same friend (visiting my friend Jack in Chicago, the time that Jack visited me in New York City—see examples in Table 10.2). Conceptually related memories may belong to the same lifetime period (e.g., spanning months or a couple of years), or they may be separated by years or decades. We use the label conceptual for these associations, instead of themes or personal concepts, because often they have a generic nature or can be thought of in generic terms (e.g., two memories about a common concept), and they also may be activated by semantic memories (explained in "Theoretical perspectives on the associative structure of episodic memories," below). It is important to note that the conceptual category is not conceived as (nor observed to be) schemas or scripts (e.g., Schank, 1982, see critique in Lancaster & Barsalou, 1997), but more simply cases where memories have overlapping thematic content. Conceptual associations are the other primary type of associative form, appearing in involuntary memory chains and other laboratory measures of association, including priming paradigms (Mace, 2005, 2006; Mace et al. 2010, 2013; Mace & Hall, 2018; Mace & Unlu, 2018). With the exception of recent events, conceptual associations greatly outnumber general-events associations, and this is one of the reasons why we regard them as the dominant associative form in episodic memory.

Lifetime period associations

Lifetime period associations are cases where episodic memories come from the same extended temporal period (e.g., episodic memories from one's high school days). Unlike general-event associations, lifetime period associations cover relatively long temporal periods (e.g., episodic memories from one's teenage years). Although having the same label, lifetime period associations do not directly correspond to Conway's notion of lifetime period knowledge, which is a more general (abstract) and idiosyncratic (e.g., when I worked at university X) form of autobiographical knowledge (see Conway, 2005). Lifetime period associated memories are not conceptual associations (e.g., associated by the concept of high school or elementary school), but instead appear to be "pure" temporal associations (we explain this in more detail in "The role of temporal knowledge in associated episodic memories," below). These associations have been primed repeatedly with different types of memory measures (i.e., voluntary and involuntary measures) and a wide variety of different temporal periods (e.g., one's high school or elementary school years) (Barzykowski & Niedzwienska, 2017; Mace, 2005; Mace & Clevinger, 2013; Mace & Unlu, 2018). We do not regard them as primary associative forms because they do not appear in involuntary memory chains (or other laboratory measures of association) as standalone associations (i.e., where the only link between memories is a lifetime period). Instead, they appear as secondary to general-event associations (a trivial observation) or conceptual associations (e.g., J. H. Mace & M. Unlu, unpublished study).

The case for conceptual association dominance

Numerous observations of involuntary memory chains have shown that the memories contained within them are always related, and the same two types of relationships are witnessed to occur—general-event and conceptual associations (Mace, 2006, 2007a; Mace et al., 2010, 2013; Mace & Unlu, 2018). The most striking feature of these observations is the finding that conceptual associations have repeatedly and consistently outnumbered general-event associations by very wide margins (see Table 10.3). Such conceptual association dominance is found when involuntary memory chains occur in laboratory settings where involuntary memories result from intentionally retrieved episodic memories on standard autobiographical memory tasks (Mace, 2006), and when involuntary memory chains occur naturally in diary studies of everyday-occurring involuntary memories (e.g., Mace et al. 2010, 2013). An interesting additional feature of

Table 10.3 Examples of episodic memory associations reported in various studies

	General Event Associations	Conceptual Associations
Mace (2004)*	0.17	0.83
Mace (2005)*	0.14	0.86
Mace (2006)	0.11	0.89
Mace et al. (2010)	0.19	0.81
Mace & Hall (2018)	0.08	0.92

*Reported in Mace (2007a).

involuntary memory chains is that they sometimes contain multiple memories (i.e., three or more memories, sometimes as many as eight in a chain—see Mace et al. 2013). Here, conceptual association dominance manifests itself in another way, in that chains that begin as general-event associations (i.e., seen in the first two memories in the chain) are more likely to turn into conceptual associations (e.g., starting with the association between the second and third memories in the chain) than continue as chains of general-event associations, whereas chains that begin as conceptual associations are more likely to continue as chains of conceptual associations instead of turning into general-event associations.

In addition to their appearance in involuntary memory chains, conceptual associations have also been primed in naturalistic and laboratory settings (Mace, 2005; Mace & Unlu, 2018), and they have also appeared in laboratory tasks that were designed to gauge episodic memory associations (Mace et al., 2010; Mace & Hall, 2018; J. H. Mace & M. Unlu, unpublished study), where they could also be compared to general-event associations. The most compelling evidence from these studies comes from tasks where participants freely generated memories or free-associated to memories that had been generated (e.g., Mace & Hall, 2018). For example, in a free recall design, participants generate streams of episodic memories without cues or any direction or restriction on how memories are generated. In a free association design, participants generate an episodic memory and then they are required to free associate to that memory and to all subsequently retrieved memories, producing a string of memories where each is a free associate of the last. Not surprisingly, the free association task produced more pairs of associated memories than the free recall task (94%, free association, 78%, free recall), mimicking involuntary memory chains, whereas examinations of the associated pairs showed extraordinarily high conceptual associations relative to general-event associations (e.g., 92%, conceptual, 8%, general event) in both tasks.

In addition to being the dominant associative form, conceptual associations are also the most enduring associative form. The data shown in figure 10.1 are involuntary memory chains partitioned in three retention intervals (originally reported in Mace et al., 2013). When associated memories are events that occurred within the most recent 12-month period, conceptually associated memories are just slightly more numerous than general-event associations. However, conceptual associations gain significantly in number in retention intervals beyond one year. These data suggest that general-event associations are temporary, as many are forgotten after one year, whereas this same fate does not await conceptual associations, which endure with time, increasing as time progresses.

There may be reasons why conceptual associations increase with time. One reason is the simple numerical gain that occurs as recent general-event memories, perhaps mostly mundane events, are forgotten quickly with the passage of time. Another explanation involves a more long-term, gradual temporal process where some general-event clusters lose most of their memories in time, leaving the surviving members more likely to activate conceptually related memories than members in their general-event

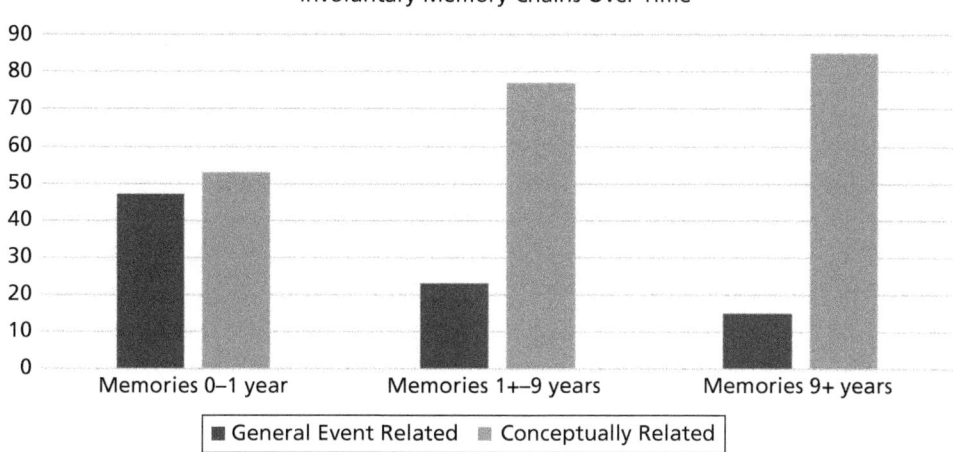

Figure 10.1 General-event associations and conceptual associations in involuntary memory chains across three retention intervals.

cluster, a competition which probably always exists (see "Theoretical perspectives on the associative structure of episodic memories", below). An extreme example of this occurs when only one memory remains in a general-event cluster. For example, imagine that a general-event cluster for a wedding only contains one memory (e.g., attending the reception). Given that this remaining memory can no longer activate other members in the cluster, it will now activate other related events (e.g., memories from other weddings), thereby forming conceptual associations.

The role of temporal knowledge in associated episodic memories

Temporal information plays a primary role in recent episodic memories (i.e., events that occurred within minutes or hours—see Conway, 2005; also Anderson & Conway, 1993; Burt et al., 1998), whereas its role in more remote episodic memories appears to be of a secondary nature. Whereas temporal relatedness is a key factor in general-events associations, allowing us to distinguish one event from another (e.g., discriminate one wedding from another), conceptual coherence is also a key factor, allowing us to know that these memories belong to the same type of event (e.g., discriminating wedding memories from concert memories). Lifetime period associations, though temporal in that event memories are from the same lifetime period, are only secondary to general-event and conceptual associations. One way to conceptualize this relationship is to think of lifetime period associations as being embedded in general-event and conceptual associations. Thus, the primary organizing factor among lifetime period-associated memories is general-event or conceptual knowledge. Because this is a trivial point in the case of general-event associations, we focus our attention here on conceptual associations.

As noted earlier, we do not believe that lifetime periods are primary forms of organization because they do not appear in involuntary memory chains as memories that are connected solely on the basis of their lifetime period membership. They do, however, appear as secondary to conceptual associations, where nearly three-quarters of the memories cluster within the same lifetime period (Mace & Unlu, 2018). Whereas lifetime period priming studies have not presented a clear picture on this question (e.g., Mace, 2005; Mace & Clevinger, 2013), additional support comes from a method—lifetime period free recall—developed in our laboratory (Mace & Hall, 2018). In lifetime period free recall, participants freely generate memories from specific lifetime periods (e.g., when one was in elementary school or high school). In these protocols, participants show a very strong tendency to recall memories in conceptual or thematic clusters (i.e., school), or general-event clusters, accounting for 76% of all generated memory sequences.

Thus, we believe that lifetime period associations form around conceptual or thematic structures. We also believe that involuntary (i.e., unconscious and conscious activations) and voluntary (i.e., rehearsal) processes are responsible for their formation within these cognitive structures. For example, when individuals reminisce about the past, they are likely to recall events surrounding people, places, themes, and so forth. Whether done contemporaneously or about the near or distant past, this process will have the effect of setting up conceptual associations in lifetime periods. Regarding involuntary processes, unconscious and conscious activations, as these processes occur contemporaneously, on perhaps a daily and consistent basis, they too will have the effect of creating conceptual associations within lifetime periods, most likely very strong associations, given the potential repetitiveness of such processes. We discuss these processes in greater detail in the next section.

Theoretical perspectives on the associative structure of episodic memories: Why conceptual associations dominate

In the preceding section we reviewed the associative forms of episodic memories, emphasizing how the conceptual form dominates the associative framework of episodic memories. In this section we attempt to explain why conceptual organization is dominant among episodic memories. Here, we return to our basic premise, automatic memory activations, and argue that the activation process inherently favors conceptual information, and that this default process (or predisposition) makes the activation of conceptually related memories most likely when memories are activated (either consciously or unconsciously); further, that each time this occurs, associations among conceptual classes of memories are formed, maintained, and strengthened, thereby making various conscious and unconscious activational processes rehearsal mechanisms. In this view, we regard the default process as *activational affinity*, and the rehearsal processes as *involuntary rehearsal*. We explain each process below in greater detail.

Regarding activational affinity, we believe that when memories are activated, the patterns of activation inherent in them capture (or activate) like or overlapping patterns of activations in other memories (cf. lexical neighborhood models, e.g., Harley & Bown, 1998; Vitevitch, 2002). Cognitively, "like patterns of activation" refers to memories within the same conceptual class (i.e., memories about the same general topic, e.g., a person, summer, work, school, music, etc.), whereas overlapping patterns of activation refers to central and non-central information contained within the memories. For example, a memory of visiting a natural history museum and seeing the mummy collection will activate other museum memories (i.e., same conceptual class, e.g., the same museum on different occasions, other natural history museums, and other types of museum), memories about mummies (i.e., central information, e.g., attending a lecture on mummies at school), as well as non-central information (e.g., learning about ancient Egypt in a high school history class). Many of these types of activation can be seen in consciously activated memories (e.g., involuntary memory chains), where memories spread among their general conceptual class (e.g., museum memories) to central and non-central information (Mace et al., 2013). Such "sympathetic" activation is at the heart of conceptual association dominance, as activated memories have a basic affinity to spread among memories with like or overlapping information. Given this propensity, and the potentially large number of different conceptual classes, and the number of memories that may exist within them (e.g., number of memories that one might have involving a theme like school or close relative), there are many more opportunities for memories to spread along conceptually linked lines than non-conceptually related (or unlike) general-event-associated lines. For example, consider a conscious activation involving the abovementioned museum memory when it is a part of a general-event memory (visiting the British Museum on a trip to London). The activational affinity for like conceptual information sets up a competition between massive amounts of conceptually related memories and non-conceptually related general-event memories such that the conceptually related memories (e.g., visiting the British Museum on other trips or other museum memories) have a higher probability of being consciously activated than non-overlapping (or unlike) general-event memories associated with the precipitating memory (e.g., renting a car while in London). Even if, in this example, non-conceptually related general-event memories are activated (renting a car in London), they now will have the potential of activating conceptual memories in their class (i.e., other car rental memories, activations which should occur at least unconsciously). Indeed, this competition probably explains why general-event memory chains are more likely to turn into conceptually related memory chains than remain as general-event chains (Mace et al., 2013). Regardless of how these activations may manifest in consciousness, the point that we our emphasizing here is that when memories are activated, there are potentially massive amounts of conceptually related memories that are activated, and that, even when memories in general-event clusters are activated, there is still a set of conceptually related memories that are activated in the process of activating them, an asymmetric process favoring conceptual activations.

These basic activational affinities not only make it more likely that when memories are activated that conceptually related memories have the highest probability of retrieval, but that each time this occurs conceptual associations among and between memories are formed, maintained, and reinforced. Thus, both conscious and unconscious memory activations serve as involuntary rehearsal mechanisms for conceptual associations, and the continuous and repeated nature of these processes sets up multiple, enduring conceptual associations. Whereas conscious activations (e.g., every time one experiences an involuntary memory chain) offer many opportunities for such rehearsal, the opportunities in unconscious activations are massive by comparison.

There are ways in which unconscious activations can serve as rehearsal mechanisms. As discussed throughout this chapter, reminiscing is a process that is likely to result in multiple unconscious memory activations, potentially many more than from conscious activations like involuntary memory chaining. Thus, daily reminiscing, for example, can result in a considerable amount of covert conceptual association rehearsals. Though this process is likely to outstrip the rehearsal frequency of conscious activations, the potential for reminiscing to serve as a rehearsal mechanism is probably dwarfed by another process, activations of autobiographical memory by generic processing, otherwise known as semantic-to-autobiographical memory priming (Mace, 2010). Based on ideas originally proposed by Conway (e.g., see Conway, 2001; Conway & Pleydell-Pearce, 2000), Mace and colleagues (Mace, 2010; Mace et al., 2019) argued that daily generic processing (e.g., reading a newspaper or a book, watching television, engaging in conversation, etc.) continuously activates sets of autobiographical memories. The fundamental premise of this idea is that in addition to accessing semantic information, every time one encounters the words *car, music, gardening,* and so forth while reading a novel or newspaper, for example, that sets of episodic memories associated with these words are unconsciously activated (e.g., remembering helping your grandmother in her garden, working in a garden at school, etc.). Evidence for such semantic-to-autobiographical memory priming can be found in Conway (1990) and in a more recent study by Mace et al. (2019), where it was shown that word primes (e.g., *summer*) presented in a lexical decision task had led to episodic memories about their contents in subsequent measures of voluntary and involuntary autobiographical memory. If, as this evidence strongly suggests, sets of personal memories are activated as a result of generic processing, then massive amounts of episodic memories are likely to be activated daily, resulting in untold amounts of covert conceptual association rehearsals.

Unconscious activations of this sort probably produce more uniform memory activations than conscious activations. For example, in semantic-autobiographical memory priming, concept cues (e.g., the word museum) are likely to strongly activate large sets of episodic memories within this class (e.g., museum memories), and only weakly activate overlapping central and non-central information. By contrast, in conscious activations the propensity for like activations is also strong, but the focus of attention on different aspects of memories (e.g., non-central information) can send the activations in different directions, a process that on its face cannot happen in the case of unconscious activations.

Thus, we believe that associations of conceptually linked memories are formed by numerous and continuous involuntary rehearsal mechanisms that tend to favor conceptual activations (or rehearsals) over general-event activations (or rehearsals). But what about the voluntary rehearsal processes that are connected with selectively reminiscing and recounting of the past? There is no reason to believe that conceptual rehearsal is more likely to be favored over general-event rehearsal here, except possibly in the case of lifetime period reminiscing (see end of "The role of temporal knowledge in associated episodic memories") where it may have a slight advantage. Indeed, voluntary rehearsal processes may not confer an advantage on conceptual or general-event association rehearsals, or they may favor general-event association rehearsals. Regardless, it is important to bear in mind that associations formed by selective voluntary rehearsals in autobiographical memory are likely to be weaker and less enduring than those formed by involuntary rehearsal processes, given the volume and continuous nature of the latter. Thus, in order for associations formed through voluntary rehearsals to have the same strength and endurance as associations formed through involuntary rehearsals, they would have to occur with the same degree of regularity as involuntary rehearsals. This is highly unlikely, and just the opposite is likely to occur with voluntary rehearsals—they are likely to be considerably less frequent, typically diminishing with the passing of time. For example, events are more likely to be selectively rehearsed when they occur, but as time goes by, one is likely to stop rehearsing them. This could be a factor in the diminishing endurance of general-event associations (see figure 10.1), but the greater point here is that voluntary rehearsals cannot compete with involuntary rehearsals, and the associations connected with the latter form, as per our view, quite naturally then will make up the bulk of associations in episodic memory.

Finally, we have suggested here that the corpus of memories in conceptual classes is greater than the corpus of memories in general-event classes. To illustrate this point, we re-analyzed the association data from Mace & Hall's (2018) first experiment according to event topic (recall that in this experiment participants freely generated episodic memories or free-associated to them, producing clusters of conceptual or general-event-related memories). The results of this analysis showed that conceptually associated memory clusters (sequences of memories with two or more memories in a class) pertained to 149 different topics (ranging from animals to work—see examples in Table 10.4), whereas general-event associated memory clusters pertained to only seven different event topics (e.g., a sporting event, a trip, etc.). This analysis, therefore, highlights the notion that there are more memories belonging to different conceptual classes than there are memories belonging to different general-event classes. In addition to this general frequency advantage, it is reasonable to imagine that there are typically more conceptually associated memories in a given conceptual class than there are general-event associated memories in the same class (e.g., in the concert memory class, one may have more memories of attending different concerts than memories from one or more particular concerts). Our general point with this illustration is that experience sets up more memories in conceptual classes than in general-event classes, and that once individual events are permanently retained in the autobiographical memory

Table 10.4 Examples of topics associating memory pairs*

Animals	Driving	Hunting
Animals	Driving	Hunting
Anxiety/stress	Education	Husband
Art	Exams	Marching band
Aunt	Family	Marriage
Backyard	Fear	Men
Bad weather	Fishing	Moving
Band	Food	Music
Baseball	Football	Pain
Bike	Friend	Parents
Bird	Friends	Party
Birth	Getting in trouble	Person
Birthday	Grades	Police
Boyfriend	Graduation	Pool
Brother	Grandparents	Redecorating
Camping	Gymnastics	Relationship
Car	Hair	Sad Things
Cheerleading	Halloween	School
Children	High school	Sewer
Christmas	Friends	Shopping
Cleaning	Getting in trouble	Sister
Clothing	Grades	Sports
Coach	Graduation	Study
College	Grandparents	Tattoo
Cousin	Gymnastics	Teachers
Crying	Hair	Travel
Dad	Halloween	Vacation
Daughter	High school	Volleyball
Dinner with family	Hiking	Water
Dog	Hospital	Wedding
Dressing up	House	Work

*Drawn from data reported in Mace & Hall (2018).

system, the activational and involuntary rehearsal mechanisms described above work to create, maintain, and enhance them.

Concluding comments

We have reviewed evidence that makes a strong case for the primacy of conceptual associations in episodic memories. We have argued for the existence of involuntary rehearsal mechanisms that create and maintain conceptual associations. Although one might take issue with our activational affinity hypothesis, there is, however, strong empirical evidence that priming (semantic and autobiographical) and involuntary memory chaining serve as rehearsal mechanisms, and that these mechanisms favor the activation of conceptual associations (e.g., Mace, 2005, 2006; Mace et al., 2013, 2019). We believe that the possibility that these mechanisms function on a daily basis as rehearsal vehicles is not only plausible, but highly probable. The view that episodic memories are embedded in narrative-like structures has not been supported by our data (e.g., Mace et al., 2010; Mace & Hall, 2018). Furthermore, the proposition that narrative forms dominate in episodic memory rests on the assumption that they are created and maintained by planning and intentional rehearsal. We do not believe that individuals continuously plan, reflect on, and actively rehearse events. To be clear, we are not saying that narrative processing does not occur. What we are saying is that such selective rehearsal is very likely to vary considerably in the population, and that it is unlikely that it occurs on a consistent and widespread basis. The three distinct rehearsal mechanisms (semantic-autobiographical priming, autobiographical priming, and involuntary memory chaining) that we have discussed here are automatic processes, and therefore can be predicted to occur on a consistent and widespread basis, particularly semantic-autobiographical priming (Conway, 1990; Mace et al., 2018). Even if it could be unequivocally established that narrative rehearsal of episodic memories occurs on a widespread and continuous basis, proponents of such views would have to account for the involuntary/automatic rehearsal mechanisms that produce conceptual associations, which almost certainly would occur concomitantly and independently with both equal and greater frequency, and explain how narratively organized episodic memory associations could come to supersede conceptual associations.

Our conceptual organization framework is consistent with abundant findings from traditional laboratory studies on memory organization (e.g., see classic studies such as Bousefield, 1953; Deese, 1959; Tulving & Pearlstone, 1966, see reviews in Baddeley, 1997). Whereas some may prefer not to compare studies of autobiographical memory to verbal learning studies, these studies have long suggested that there are endogenous processes governing the organization of knowledge and experience along conceptual lines. There have been other principles and findings emanating from verbal learning studies that have been shown to apply to autobiographical memories (e.g., Moreton & Ward, 2010). For example, the retrieval of involuntary autobiographical memories appears to conform to the principles of encoding specificity (Tulving & Thomson, 1973; see Ball et al., 2007; Berntsen, 1998, 2007, 2009; Mace, 2004; Mace et al., 2015). On the flipside, word-list approaches to the study of memory have also well emulated autobiographical memory phenomena. For example, implicit memory studies using verbal stimuli have demonstrated that spontaneous word recollection (i.e., involuntary conscious memory) can occur on measures of implicit memory (e.g., Bowers & Schacter, 1990; Kinoshita, 2001; Mace, 2003a,b; Richardson-Klavehn et al., 1994) much like it does in naturalistic and laboratory measures of involuntary autobiographical memory (e.g., Berntsen, 1996; Schlagman & Kvavilashvili, 2008; Mace, 2006). Implicit memory studies have also shown that involuntary memory chaining will occur with words (Mace, 2009), much like it does with involuntary autobiographical memories (e.g., Mace, 2005, 2006; Mace et al., 2013). Whereas it seems clear that autobiographical memories are more complex than memories for verbal material, we should not dismiss or ignore the findings from word-list studies, as many of the principles discovered using that approach appear to apply to autobiographical memory, especially in the case of episodic memory. The data reviewed in this chapter appear to represent one such case.

Finally, our semantic-like view of episodic memory associations is certainly not new to traditional memory studies (e.g., Mandler, 1972), nor is it necessarily new to views of autobiographical memory (e.g., Conway, 2005). We agree with Tulving (1972, 1984, 2002) that episodic memory "shares many features with semantic memory." It makes good theoretical sense that declarative memory systems would have overlapping functions, processes, and organizational principles.

References

Anderson, S. J. & Conway, M. A. (1993). Investigating the structure of autobiographical memories. *Journal of Experimental Psychology: Learning, Memory, and Cognition, 19*, 1178–1196.

Baddeley, A. (1997). *Human memory: Theory and practice.* Hove, UK: Psychology Press.

Ball, C. T., Mace, J. H., & Corona, H. (2007). Cues to the gusts of memory. In J. H. Mace (ed.), *Involuntary memory* (pp. 113–126). Malden, MA: Blackwell.

Barsalou, L. W. (1988). The content and organization of autobiographical memories. In U. Neisser, & E. Winograd (eds.), *Remembering reconsidered: Ecological and traditional approaches to the study of memory* (pp. 193–243). New York: Cambridge University Press.

Barzykowski, K. & Niedzwienska, A. (2018). Priming involuntary autobiographical memories in the lab. *Memory, 26*, 277–289.

Berntsen, D. (1996). Involuntary autobiographical memory. *Applied Cognitive Psychology, 10*, 435–454.

Berntsen, D. (1998). Voluntary and involuntary access to autobiographical memory. *Memory, 6*, 113–141.

Berntsen, D. (2007). Involuntary autobiographical memories: Speculations, findings and an attempt to integrate them. In J. H. Mace (ed.), *Involuntary memory* (pp. 20–49). Malden, MA: Blackwell.

Berntsen, D. (2009). *Involuntary autobiographical memories: An introduction to the unbidden past.* Cambridge: Cambridge University Press.

Bousefield, W. A. (1953). The occurrence of clustering in the recall of randomly arranged associates. *Journal of General Psychology, 49*, 229–240.

Bowers, J. S. & Schacter, D. L. (1990). Implicit memory and test awareness. *Journal of Experimental Psychology: Learning, Memory, and Cognition, 16*, 404–416.

Brewer, W. F. (1986). What is autobiographical memory? In D. C. Rubin (ed.), *Autobiographical memory* (pp. 25–49). Cambridge: Cambridge University Press.

Brown, N. R. & Schopflocher, D. (1998). Event clusters: An organization of personal events in autobiographical memory. *Psychological Science, 9*, 470–489.

Burt, C. D. B., Watt, S. C., Mitchell, D. A., & Conway, M. A. (1998). Retrieving the sequence of autobiographical event components. *Applied Cognitive Psychology, 12*, 321–338.

Deese, J. (1959). Influence of inter-item associative strength upon immediate free recall. *Psychological Reports, 5*, 305–312.

Conway, M. A. (1990). Associations between autobiographical memories and concepts. *Journal of Experimental Psychology: Learning, Memory, and Cognition, 16*, 799–812.

Conway, M. A. (2001). Sensory-perceptual episodic memory and its context: Autobiographical memory. In A. Baddeley, J. P. Aggleton, & M. A. Conway (eds.), *Episodic memory: New directions in research* (pp. 53–70). New York: Oxford University Press.

Conway, M. A. (2005). Memory and the self. *Journal of Memory and Language*, 53, 594–628.

Conway, M. A. & Rubin, D. C. (1993). The structure of autobiographical memory. In A. F. Collins, S. E. Gathercole, M. A. Conway, & P. E. Morris (eds.), *Theories of Memory* (pp. 103–138). Hove, UK: Erlbaum.

Conway, M.A. & Pleydell-Pearce, C.W. (2000). The construction of autobiographical memories in the self memory system. *Psychological Review*, 107, 261–288.

Harley, T. A., & Bown, H. E. (1998). What causes a tip-of-the-tongue state? Evidence for lexical neighbourhood effects in speech production. *British Journal of Psychology*, 89, 151–174.

Kinoshita, S. (2001). The role of involuntary aware memory in the implicit stem and fragment completion tasks: A selective review. *Psychonomic Bulletin & Review*, 8, 58–69.

Lancaster, J.S. & Barsalou, L.W. (1997). Multiple organizations of events in memory. *Memory*, 5, 569–599.

Mace, J. H. (2003a). Involuntary aware memory enhances priming on a conceptual implicit memory task. *American Journal of Psychology*, 116, 281–290.

Mace, J. H. (2003b). Study-test awareness can enhance priming on an implicit memory task: Evidence from a word completion task. *American Journal of Psychology*, 116, 257–279.

Mace, J. H. (2004). Involuntary autobiographical memories are highly dependent on abstract cuing: The Proustian view is incorrect. *Applied Cognitive Psychology*, 18, 893–899.

Mace, J. H. (2005). Priming involuntary autobiographical memories. *Memory*, 13, 874–884.

Mace, J. H. (2006). Episodic remembering creates access to involuntary conscious memory: Demonstrating involuntary recall on a voluntary recall task. *Memory*, 14, 917–924.

Mace, J. H. (2007a). Does involuntary remembering occur during voluntary remembering? In J. H. Mace (ed.), *Involuntary memory* (pp. 50–67). Malden, MA: Blackwell.

Mace, J. H. (ed.) (2007b). *Involuntary memory*. Malden, MA: Blackwell.

Mace, J. H. (2009). Involuntary conscious facilitates cued recall performance: Further evidence that chaining occurs during voluntary recall. *American Journal of Psychology*, 122, 371–381.

Mace, J. H. (2010a). Involuntary remembering and voluntary remembering: How different are they? In J. H. Mace (ed.), *The act of remembering: Toward an understanding of how we recall the past* (pp. 43–55). Malden, MA: Wiley–Blackwell.

Mace, J. H. (2010b). Understanding autobiographical remembering from a spreading activation perspective. In J. H. Mace (ed.), *The act of remembering: Toward an understanding of how we recall the past* (pp. 183–201). Malden, MA: Wiley–Blackwell.

Mace, J. H. (2014). Involuntary memory chains: Implications for autobiographical memory organization. *Frontiers in Psychiatry*, 5, 183.

Mace, J. H. (2018). Involuntary autobiographical memories: Spontaneous recollections of the past. In K. C. R. Fox & K. Christoff (eds.), *The Oxford Handbook of spontaneous thought: Mind-wandering, dreaming, creativity, and clinical disorders* (pp. 469–476). New York: Oxford University Press.

Mace, J. H., Bernas, R. S., & Clevinger, A. M. (2015). Individual differences in recognizing involuntary autobiographical memories: Impact on the reporting of abstract cues. *Memory*, 23, 445–452.

Mace, J. H. & Clevinger, A. M. (2013). Priming voluntary autobiographical memories: Implications for the organization of autobiographical memory and voluntary recall processes. *Memory*, 21, 524–536.

Mace, J. H., Clevinger, A. M., & Martin, C. (2010). Involuntary memory chaining versus event cuing: Which is a better indicator of autobiographical memory organization? *Memory*, 18, 845–854.

Mace, J. H., Clevinger, A. M., & Bernas, R. S. (2013). Involuntary memory chains: What do they tell us about autobiographical memory organization? *Memory*, 21, 324–335.

Mace, J. H. & Hall, A. J. (2018). Demonstrating conceptual clustering in autobiographical memory with voluntary recall tasks: More evidence for the conceptual organization view. *American Journal of Psychology*, 131, 283–293.

Mace, J. H., McQueen, M. L., Hayslett, K. E., Staley, B. A., & Welch, T. J. (2019). Semantic memories prime autobiographical memories: General implications and implications for everyday autobiographical remembering. *Memory & Cognition*, 47, 299–312.

Mace, J.H., & Unlu, M. (2018). The role of lifetime periods in the organization of episodic memories. *Memory, in press*.

Mandler, G. (1972). Organization and recognition. In E. Tulving & W. Donaldson (eds.), *Organization of memory* (pp. 146–167). New York: Academic Press.

Moreton, B. J. & Ward, G. (2010). Time scale similarity and long-term memory for autobiographical events. *Psychonomic Bulletin & Review, 17*, 510–515.

Richardson-Klavehn, A., Gardiner, J. M., & Java, R. I. (1994). Involuntary conscious memory and the method of opposition. *Memory, 2*, 1–29.

Schank, R. C. (1982). *Dynamic memory: A theory of reminding and learning in computers and people.* New York: Cambridge University Press.

Schlagman, S. & Kvavilashvili, L. (2008). Involuntary autobiographical memories in and outside the laboratory: How different are they from voluntary autobiographical memories? *Memory & Cognition, 36*, 920–932.

Tulving E. (1972). Episodic and semantic memory. In E. Tulving & W. Donaldson (eds.), *Organization of memory* (pp. 381–403). New York: Academic Press.

Tulving E. (1984). Relations among components and processes of memory. *Behavioral and Brain Sciences, 7*, 257–68.

Tulving E. (2002). Episodic memory: From mind to brain. *Annual Review of Psychology, 53*, 1–25.

Tulving, E. & Pearlstone, Z. (1966). Availability versus accessibility of information in memory for words. *Journal of Verbal Learning and Verbal Behavior, 5*, 381–391.

Tulving, E. & Thomson, D. M. (1973). Encoding specificity and retrieval processes in episodic memory. *Psychological Review, 80*, 353–373.

Vitevitch, M. S. (2002). The influence of phonological similarity neighborhoods on speech production. *Journal of Experimental Psychology: Learning, Memory, and Cognition, 28*, 735–747.

Index

Note: Tables and figures are indicated by *t* and *f* following the page number